MERRY CHRISTIANS

HOW TO BE A HAPPY CHRISTIAN
AND
CO-CREATE HEAVEN ON EARTH

ARNE KLINGENBERG

Copyright © 2016 Arne Klingenberg

All rights reserved. This book, or any parts thereof, may not be reproduced, stored or transmitted in any form or by any means (mechanical, optical, electronic and otherwise), without the prior permission of the publisher, in writing.

No permission is required for short quotations used for book reviews, articles and discussions.

First Edition

First Published: July 29, 2016

Paperback
ISBN-10: 1-876538-03-1
ISBN-13: 978-1-876538-03-3

National Library of Australia Cataloguing-in-Publication entry
Creator: Klingenberg, Arne, author.
Title: Merry Christians: how to be a happy Christian and co-create heaven on earth / Arne Klingenberg.
ISBN: 9781876538033 (paperback)
Subjects: Christian life. Happiness. Self-actualization (Psychology)
Dewey Number: 248.8
Published by:
Beam Publishing Pty. Ltd.
P.O. Box 405
Port Douglas QLD 4871
Australia
Phone: +61-7- 40 993 888
Email: editor@beampublishing.com
Web: www.beampublishing.com

Cover Art by: Erelis Design, Nada Orlic (www.nadaorlic.info)
Book Design by: Ebook Launch (www.ebooklaunch.com)

Disclaimer:

All information contained in this book are the personal opinions, insights and practices of the author, and are presented purely for educational purposes. This book is not intended to be a substitute for professional medical or financial advice of any kind. There are no representations or warranties, express or implied, about the completeness, accuracy, reliability, or suitability with respect to the information contained in this book for any purpose. Any use of this information is at the reader's own risk.

Dedicated to:

All the merry Christians who'd like to feel even more joy and bliss!
All the not yet merry Christians who really should be happy too!
Anyone who feels attracted by Christian thoughts and traditions!

In Honor of:

My Godfather, Peter Klingenberg

My Godmother, Ursula Dillitzer

With Special Thanks to:

My darling wife, Miyuki Klingenberg - Yamaguchi

In Memoriam:

Ninja Klingenberg

Table of Contents

The Big Picture 1
Happy is Good 4
Happy Fruits 7
Merrily United 12
The Merry Way 16
Love God 19
Feel God's Love 21
Love your Self 26
Love All 29
Appreciate 40
Smile 47
Surrender 52
Hope 62
Breathe 68
Stay Kind 73
Mind your Mind 81
Love your Body 90
Be your Self 113
Follow Love 135
Respect 141
Admire 150
Wish well 165
Help 171
Do it with Love 180
Relax 185
In Summary 197
In His Words 200
Obstacles to Love 206
The Divine Deal 214
Merry Money 230
Love in Separation 242
Merry Realizations 247
Post Scriptum 254
About the Author 255
Notes Merry Christians 256

The Big Picture

The contents of this book were dear to my heart for a long time. And although the thoughts that follow kept bubbling up on my mind, I continued to hesitate writing them down, thinking that there is perhaps no further need for it. After all, my first book on happiness, published in 1999, aimed to cover the subject from all the many angles, to the best of my abilities.

Yes I Am Happy Now! [1] was intended for a general public, and yet, its spiritual principles are thoroughly based on the essence of Christianity, without actually saying so in an explicit manner.

The events of the last seventeen years and the 'writing on the wall' we can see while contemplating the state of our world of today, have spurned my bickering and wavering into renewed action, and made me put the proverbial pen to paper once again.

We aim to cover a lot of ground together. We will strive to achieve the following three distinctive goals, all separate yet one at the same time:

1. How to be a Merry Christian in today's world.
2. How to co-create Heaven on Earth by being a Merry Christian.
3. How to update and unite Christianity by going back to its essential core.

Lofty goals? Perhaps. Achievable? For sure. But now let's dive in and start to turn these goals into reality. We will discover that Christianity really is a most beautiful way of life when it is felt and lived in all its sublime deep simplicity, and true to the very essence of what God and

Jesus and all the Saints desire for us and life on Planet Earth - unity in love, peace and happiness!

"But the fruit of the Spirit is love, joy, peace, patience, kindness, goodness, faithfulness." (Galatians 5:22)

How should we define happiness? Early Christian writers have often separated 'joy' and 'happiness', with the first meaning the joy derived from living our faith while the latter was reserved for the fleeting joys of worldly pleasures. Material things or mundane pursuits were somewhat looked down upon as unholy, ungodly or outright immoral.

Here is how I defined it many years ago:

"Happiness. You know how it feels. Being joyful. Playful. Laughing and smiling. Feeling relaxed and confident. Totally at ease with yourself. Completely satisfied."

The way to feel happy in the above ways is not possible by simply or exclusively pursuing worldly pleasures and things. Yet one who feels spiritually connected with God will certainly and easily experience and exhibit these characteristics.

Do you think buying a new luxury car will make us feel like this? Nope, it won't. The pleasure of a new car quickly fades off, within a week or two, a few months at best. After all, we can see lots of people driving around in fancy cars yet looking all grumpy and sour, or sad and mad.

Similarly, a good meal with a great bottle of wine will not truly make us feel as defined above. It helps for a short little while, yet many of the gourmets of the world suffer from anxieties and depression.

Life is full of examples of the rich, powerful and famous who have turned into alcoholics or drug addicts, have committed suicide, were seriously sick or went through nasty divorces, power struggles and so on. They seemingly had it all, yet obviously the most essential ingredients were missing.

There is certainly nothing wrong with a good and healthy meal or a nice bottle of wine in great company, and neither is driving a beautifully crafted motor car. These and other things can surely add a bit to our joy and happiness - once it is present already in the first place. When we are feeling united with God, grateful to the ultimate source of it all.

Let's have a quick look at some definitions of the word 'Merry':

Cheerful, happy, joyous, joyful, upbeat, light-hearted, carefree, glad, jolly, festive, genial, fun-loving, chirpy, vivacious, rollicking, convivial, gleeful, mirthful, sportive.

Many of us feel like that during the month of December. We start to wind down from another busy or even hectic year, go to jolly corporate functions and other festive events, buy gifts and otherwise prepare for the big days, wishing each other a "Merry Christmas", or at least a politically correct "Happy Holidays". Imagine how nice it would be to feel merry all year round… We really can and should always be merry Christians. Let's see how we can achieve that easily and happily!

In the coming pages, we will use the words happy, joyful and merry interchangeably but always in a holistic way, one that incorporates it all yet is always founded on the solid and strong foundations of our spiritual heritage. Here, the meaning of happy, joyful and merry encompass and embrace the culmination of the best of the spiritual worlds with the current realities of the 'Here and Now'.

Happy is Good

Christians deserve to be happy. They can be happy and they really *should* be happy!

But many are not. Or not quite.

We will talk a little bit about the reasons why, yet our main focus is to identify the easy and joyful paths leading to the blessed and blissful life of a merry Christian. Surely, one impediment is that quite a few 'good' Christians disagree with the very basic premise that they should be happy. Some think so consciously, and others without being fully aware of this underlying obstacle.

"May God protect me from gloomy saints." St. Teresa of Avila [2]

Being serious and a bit stern or solemn are often seen as the attributes of a pious and good Christian. The welcome acceptance of suffering, making sacrifices in life, or perhaps even doing some penance are quite often considered to be Christian values. And unfortunately, being merry is rarely seen as a prominent characteristic of Christians. By Christians and non-Christians alike... For now, let's just say that some people cause happiness *wherever* they go - and others *whenever* they go!

Indeed, as we will see, we can quite easily come to the conclusion that *Every happy Christian is a good Christian*. Or put differently, in a perhaps more thought-provoking way: *All good Christians are merry Christians*.

During over three decades of studies, work and travel around the world I have met Christians of many kinds and denominations. Sadly, the one thing that almost all seemed to have in common is the lack of joy and happiness in their lives. The wrinkles in their faces were all too often a testimony to a life full of hardships, disappointments, sorrows and yes, even anger.

One could object here and say that the joys of being a Christian are only felt within and therefore one can't really make superficial conclusions. Yes, real joy and happiness one feels deep within. It is not something one wears on the outside to masquerade or compete, to fake or brag about. And yet, true happiness cannot help but radiate from within to the outside world - just like the sun is shining so bright that it can't help but illuminate the universe.

A beautiful flower cannot hide its beauty, even if it wanted to... Real *"love, joy, peace, patience, kindness, goodness, and faithfulness"* always manifests in a myriad of pleasant, pleasing and positive ways. It is built in, it is automatic.

"It is not fitting, when one is in God's service, to have a gloomy face or a chilling look." St. Francis of Assisi [3]

Our facial expressions do not lie. And neither do the small mountains of antidepressant or anti-anxiety pills taken daily by Christians the world over. Quite a few resort to abusing alcohol and drugs of many kinds. And others indulge in comfort foods to the point of becoming obese or suffering from disease. This and more is sad to witness and especially so since it is entirely uncalled-for, and wasteful to the full promise and potential of Christian philosophy.

Of course, it is not easy to be a Christian in today's modern world - or so it may seem sometimes: Believe in God when there is widespread disbelief to the point of getting ridiculed in the 'official world' of government, academia and media. Feel compassion and trust in goodness when we witness cruel and heartless acts of many kinds. Know abundance when there is still hunger and starvation in the world. Have faith in our eternal life while being confronted with daily pictures of death. Trust in fairness and justice while watching or reading the news...

Furthermore, history is filled with examples of the persecution of Christians for no other reason than trying to follow the path of Jesus Christ. And unfortunately, in today's 'modern' world we have to once again witness a large increase in such appalling murder and mayhem in all too many parts of the world. [4]

Yet despite the plentiful challenges, it is possible, desirable and rightful to be joyful and happy in the here and now. It is the birth right and destiny of all of us. Indeed, it is very much our natural state in the same way as water in its liquid state is wet.

We all want to be happy - regardless of our actual creed, culture or country of origin. At least deep down we all do, even if we have managed to bury this natural God-given desire under an avalanche of conflicting or harmful beliefs and behavior. We all do what we do because we believe it will make us happier, or turn our life around for the better. This happens either more or less consciously.

People do all kinds of silly, crazy and even evil things in the pursuit of happiness. A suicide bomber believes that a better and happier world will await, where his every whim is taken care of by beautiful virgin girls, or something like that. Whatever the individual expectations may be, the evil deed is done because it holds the promise of a happier personal future, an escape from a current unpleasant reality or state of mind.

"All men seek happiness. This is without exception. Whatever different means they employ, they all tend to this end. The cause of some going to war, and of others avoiding it, is the same desire in both, attended with different views. The will never takes the least step but to this object. This is the motive of every action of every man, even of those who hang themselves." Blaise Pascal [5]

Happy Fruits

Some Christians say that the pursuit of happiness is a very selfish goal and totally unbecoming of a good Christian…

Yet when we are totally honest with ourselves, we find that we pray and worship and seek spiritual growth for the simple reason that we desire to be happy. We ask for health and wealth, redemption and salvation, freedom from suffering and pain, the protection from evil, and so on. Why would we pray like this unless we'd hope that it will improve our life once our wishes were granted? How many of us simply and honestly pray only to get to (once again) know and love God - without having any ulterior motives whatsoever?

Reality is that we pray for things or circumstances and events because we expect their fulfilment to make us happier. Otherwise we would not ask.

Is that selfish? Well, this is simply so by divine design and therefore it's not something to be ashamed of. Or to feel guilty about. By default we all have needs that need to be taken care of. *"Ask and you shall receive."* Besides, isn't this a really smart way to make sure that we're going to stay in touch with 'The Big Boss', the creator and sustainer of it all? By God, it is simply in our best self-interest to remember God!

"Ask, and it will be given to you; seek, and you will find; knock, and it will be opened to you." (Matthew 7:7)

God wants us to be happy; he tells us clearly to simply ask for what we want and need - whatever makes us fulfilled and happy! After all, nobody really asks for things or circumstances that bring about misery, sorrow and pain… The divine desire to see us happy and well will be confirmed in many other ways and places, as we shall see as we move on.

And all things, whatever you shall ask in prayer, believing, you shall receive. (Matthew 21:22)

There are Christians who say that we need to be more or solely concerned with spreading the 'Good News' and doing charitable work rather than being selfish, wanting and striving to be happy…

And yet, only merry Christians are truly in a position to offer the solutions to the world and its people, while the unhappy can very easily become part of the problem - even despite them having only noble motives and the best of intentions.

One reason why this is so is that we simply cannot pass on something that we do not have. Or talk about something that we do not personally experience.

If we had never tasted chocolate ice cream, how would it be possible to explain its taste to someone else who has never eaten it either? In the same way, if we do not truly feel the love, peace and joy of God within our hearts, how could we possibly pass it on to anyone else?

"Blessed are the peacemakers, for they will be called children of God." (Matthew 5-9)

This teaching by Jesus is part of the *Beatitudes*, the anglicized word from the Matthean Vulgate Latin section title: *Beatitudines*. It is derived from the Latin adjective *beatus* which means *happy, fortunate, or blissful*. [6]

Yes, joy and happiness are inherent parts of being a child of God. And so is being light-hearted and playful, laughing and smiling, feeling secure and confident, fully trusting - knowing even - that *All is Well*.

"The best argument for Christianity is Christians: their joy, their certainty, their completeness. But the strongest argument against Christianity is also Christians - when they are somber and joyless, when they are self-righteous and smug in complacent consecration, when they are narrow and repressive, then Christianity dies a thousand deaths." Joe Aldrich [7]

Nominally, Christianity is the world's largest religion with about 2.2 billion adherents.[8] Of course, not everybody is 'really into it' in their daily lives. It is up to each one of us to decide how serious or determined we are with our spiritual life and practice. And that often depends on our current stage in life. Usually, the older we get the more we are inclined to find out what happens next. Or the more we feel the urge to make peace with our maker. Sometimes it's not our physical age, but other trying circumstances in life that makes us want to be closer to God once again.

That is how it is meant to be. We all move ahead at our own leisure. There is no fixed time table in life. And just like with a delicate flower, we can't force someone to grow (up) faster, without uprooting and hurting that person. We people only really change when we are ready and willing to change. (Of course we can always pretend or act like it, but that won't make it real in the eyes of God.)

While individually it is all up to each one of us, in the big picture view of things, it matters a great deal whether the majority of 2.2 billion Christians is happy or not. Because happy people are also peaceful people. And because happiness is contagious in the same way as anger, discontent and hatred can easily spread in any given society. I have elaborated more on this, including the mechanisms of how this works in *Yes I Am Happy Now!*[1]

Merry Christians help to bring about Heaven on Earth because they are truly alive and live life to the fullest. Anytime we actually feel and experience the presence of Holy Spirit, we are full of energy, enthused with love, filled with peace, and brimming with joy and happiness. Attuned to the flow of life to the point of over-flowing, of being able to freely give and share...

"O Holy Spirit, descend plentifully into my heart. Enlighten the dark corners of this neglected dwelling and scatter there Thy cheerful beams." Saint Augustine [9]

This is the way we can help to uplift (in the truest sense of the word) our friends and families, our local community and the immediate environment we live in. And ultimately, just like waves are spreading all over the endless yet connected oceans of the world, these positive and powerful contributions will spread to benefit mankind as a whole.

The world needs more loving, joyful, generous, compassionate, and happy people who will inspire others to be more loving, joyful, generous, compassionate, and happy!

Merry Christians lead by example; they practice what they preach by living according to the path so clearly outlined and prescribed by Jesus. They actually and effortlessly preach simply by being their fulfilled and merry selves.

Happiness is not only contagious, it is also most attractive and enchanting!

"Why are you so happy?", people may start to wonder upon meeting a merry Christian.

"What is the secret to his/her inner peace and joy?", some will quietly ask themselves. Or they will ask you directly. And if they do, tell them.

"Preach the Gospel at all times, and when necessary, use words." St. Francis of Assisi

Here are a few quotes that illustrate the flip side of the coin:

"I would have met Jesus sooner if not for Christians who led double lives." Keith Green [10]

"I might believe in the Redeemer if His followers looked more redeemed." Friedrich Nietzsche [11]

"Men never do evil so completely and cheerfully as when they do it with religious conviction." Blaise Pascal

In our modern world with its many possibilities, amusements and distractions, not too many people are attracted by a stern, critical, judgmental, self-righteous, sour, sad or miserable person who extols the virtues of 'suffer now and be happy later'… even if that comes gift wrapped and labeled 'Christian'. Besides, external labels or clothes and badges of status and honor won't help or count one little bit once we have left this worldly stage. Only what is real will make a difference.

"A man reaps what he sows." (Galatians 6:7)

The fruits are either sweet or sour, bitter or juicy, alive and fresh, or stale and rotten.

"Even so every good tree bringeth forth good fruit; but the corrupt tree bringeth forth evil fruit." (Matthew 7:17)

Love, peace, joy and happiness are the good fruits of Christianity. Grow and pick them. Then taste and enjoy them. And finally, pass them around!

Merrily United

Over time, Christians have become separated by so many squabbles and disagreements. Catholics, Orthodox Christians, Protestants, Anglicans, Methodists and countless other denominations and organizations differ in their teachings, methodologies and beliefs - and thereby needlessly make a simple yet most profound message much more complicated, and much less appealing…

Arguing over doctrinal issues and such brings about ever more division and separation. It only adds to the myriad of conflicts in the world, instead of reducing and perhaps even eliminating them.

"I have given them the glory that you gave me, that they may be one as we are one." (John 17:22)

Maybe you have already heard or read the following joke that illustrates quite nicely the divisive state of mankind in general, and Christianity in particular. This divisiveness and disharmony is likely to be a key reason why some otherwise interested people reject its messages.

I was walking across a bridge one day and I saw a man standing on the edge, about to jump off. I immediately ran over and said, "Stop! Don't do it!"

"Why shouldn't I?" he asked.

I said, "Well, there's so much to live for."

"Like what?" he asked.

"Well… are you religious or atheist?"

"Religious."

"Me too! Are you Christian or Jewish?"

"Christian."

"Me too! Are you Catholic or Protestant?"

"Protestant."

"Me too! Are you Episcopalian or Baptist?"

"Baptist."

"Wow! Me too! Are you Baptist Church of God or Baptist Church of the Lord?"

"Baptist Church of God."

"Me too! Are you Original Baptist Church of God, or are you Reformed Baptist Church of God?"

"Reformed Baptist Church of God."

"Me too! Are you Reformed Baptist Church of God reformation of 1879, or Reformed Baptist Church of God, reformation of 1915?"

"Reformed Baptist Church of God, reformation of 1915."

To which I said, "Die, heretic scum!" and pushed him off.

Here we will not look into the particular reasons why Christianity has become so splintered as it is not really relevant in the task to be(come) a merry Christian. I have covered the general subject of organized religion and its inherent weaknesses like fierce competition, a fixation on dogmatic or absolute beliefs and behavior in *Yes I Am Happy Now!*, including the need to overcome such weaknesses and instead find the uniting common grounds.

We will also not discuss the many bigger or smaller differences between denominations since we are solely interested in identifying the core essence of it all, the practical and real-life task of sowing and reaping the happy fruits Christianity provides. And the good news is that Jesus has actually made that task very simple and easy as we shall see shortly in chapter *The Merry Way*.

It can be applied by anyone. Maybe you are part of one particular tradition. Maybe you have become disillusioned with organized religion and practice your faith quietly by yourself 'only', among family or like-minded friends. Maybe you have changed your denomination along your way. And maybe you wouldn't even call yourself a Christian, or practice another faith altogether.

Regardless, as with everything, "the proof of the pudding is in the eating". Is our practice truly making us happy every day - filled to the brim or even over-flowing with God's love, peace and happiness? This result alone will be the relevant yardstick we will apply and follow in the coming pages.

"The truly wise talk little about religion and are not given to taking sides on doctrinal issues. When they hear people advocating or opposing the claims of this or that party in the church, they turn away with a smile such as men yield to the talk of children. They have no time, they would say, for that kind of thing. They have enough to do in trying to faithfully practice what is beyond dispute." George MacDonald [12]

It is my hope that you will read, contemplate and apply the *The Merry Way* with an open heart and mind. No matter which tradition or faith you may presently follow and adhere to, for now simply overlook any perceived differences or theoretical objections that may arise. Focus instead solely on actually experiencing the wonderful reality of being a merry Christian.

And very quickly you will get to notice that your growing and glowing happiness has an ever expanding ripple effect that gently spreads to your friends, family, colleagues and… beyond. The people in your life will suddenly become happier too! And this is so without them even knowing the reasons why.

Original Christianity in all its simplicity and beauty has the potential to become the foremost philosophy on Planet Earth. Once it is fully lived and thereby recognized by its happy fruits, it can very easily be integrated by other creeds and cultures. Because the very essence of what makes a merry Christian is universally valid and applicable, even inherent, to every soul.

'On an institutional level', it is my hope that the very practical steps outlined in the following pages will help to bring about much-needed unity and harmony amongst all Christian denominations. Indeed it is my conviction that the focus on these core messages by Jesus will reward its adherent churches with renewed vigor, faith and life.

Divine love is by its very nature uniting, inclusive and healing rather than dividing, exclusive and hurting. Understanding, teaching and living 'the very basics' first and foremost still allows to keep one's particular traditions, paraphernalia and so on. So nothing is lost but much can be gained:

We will be getting closer and closer to the age-old dream of Co-creating Heaven on Earth where we all live united as merry children of God on this beautiful planet we call home away from home.

The Merry Way

The merry way consist of the twenty key insights and applications of a merry Christian; all are practical and perennial while easy and effective. The first four are the primary and essential ones; the must-do's. The sixteen secondary parts will start to increasingly and automatically happen as we apply the primary ones on a daily basis.

All of the principles fully complement and enhance each other. So sometimes, when perhaps challenging events of our daily lives make it a bit difficult to remember and apply one of the insights, any of the other ones will help us to stay connected and happy. Or to quickly regain our inner peace and joy. And of course, the more of the realizations we are able to apply at the very same time, the merrier we will feel!

One amazing fact about joy and happiness is that there are actually no limits to it. It's not like eating ice cream where we simply had enough after a certain number of scoops. Or if we overindulge we start to feel sick or get a stomach ache. Happiness expands first in time, or 'quantity'. In the beginning we may only be happy once or twice a day, depending on the condition we were in when we've started out. But with a little bit of practice, our happiness will soon start to expand further and further to finally include most of the day.

Occasionally we may still get upset or depressed for a moment or two, but as soon as we apply one of the twenty ingredients we will be able to quickly recover and go on our merry ways.

Happiness also expands in 'quality' or put differently, in intensity. It's a bit like adding extra syrup to water so that it tastes sweeter, with the only difference that there is no end to it! We can come to feel joy and happiness to the point of feeling absolute ecstasy and total bliss. The loving union with God can make this happen as saints and sages throughout the ages have experienced and attested.

Happiness also transcends time and space: "As you sow, so shall you reap."

In other words, if you feel happy now, you will also feel happy later. By being happy in the here and now you are sowing the seeds of happiness that you will reap in the future. Ultimately this is so throughout all dimensions, transcending the physical death of our bodies. So there is no need to ever worry about what might happen. If we constantly worry about the bad things that might happen, we are only sowing that kind of seeds, and that is obviously not a good idea.

To worry is essentially a lack of trust in God. It shows that we are currently not feeling our eternal connection. Applying the twenty principles outlined below will quickly reconnect us once again.

Another amazing fact that the merry ways have in common is that they are totally free. That's right: Nobody will ever (be able to) charge you a dime for it! It's all yours for the taking, now and forever. Furthermore, nobody can ever stop you from applying these insights into your life. It simply can't be prevented in any way whatsoever. The only person that could do so would be you yourself.

There's one more amazing fact to the joy and happiness we talk about here: No matter how often or how much you feel it, there is always plenty left for everybody else. Nobody will have to starve or suffer in any way because of you 'helping yourself' to very generous quantities of happiness. Quite to the contrary. The more you go for it the more there will be for everyone else to taste and experience too!

In the following chapters we will go through each of the twenty applications, starting with the four primary ones - the four essential pillars of strength and happiness:

Love God
Feel God's Love
Love your Self
Love All
Appreciate
Smile
Surrender
Hope
Breathe
Stay Kind
Mind your Mind
Love your Body
Be your Self
Follow Love
Respect
Admire
Wish Well
Be a Friend
Do it with Love
Relax

Love God

When Jesus was asked: "Master, which is the greatest commandment in the Law?", he replied: *"Love the Lord your God with all your heart, soul, and mind."* (Matthew 22:36, 37)

In Matthew 22:38, he added: *"This is the greatest and the first commandment."*

His wording in both verses is most powerful and clear. It doesn't really leave any room for ambiguity or interpretations of any kind. There is simply no need to discuss what it might mean.

Once we do *love the Lord our God with all our heart, soul, and mind*, we will feel happy. All else will follow, as we shall see in our discussions to follow.

But still, how can we love God when we don't really know him? When we are not exactly sure who or what God is?

Furthermore, the commandment to love God may sound like a particularly challenging proposition for the many Christians who have been taught that God is the supreme judge and avenger to be feared. *How could we possibly love someone when we are actually afraid of that very same someone?* That sounds like a most difficult if not impossible thing to do!

Or how could we come to love God when we are disappointed in him, feel neglected or outright abandoned? When we are consciously or subconsciously angry about our prayers that went seemingly unanswered? When our loved ones have passed away? Or when we witness injustice and suffering in the world and cannot explain or understand the reasons why? Plenty of people have given up on God, became skeptics or atheists for just those reasons.

These are all fair questions that many of our minds are or have been asking. We will discuss many of the answers a bit later in chapter *The Divine Deal*, but first things need to come first: Satisfying the needs of our hearts is simply more important than discussing matters of the mind.

In his first and greatest commandment Jesus told us what the priorities are. He knew all about the doubting nature of our critical minds when he asked us to first and foremost love God. But he also knew that the answers will automatically start to come forth from within once we do what he asks us to do!

And more so, Jesus knew that once we do love God, a great many of our worldly problems will get solved more easily too - sometimes to the point of them not even happening anymore at all.

"If you love me, you will keep my commandments." (John 14:15)

Jesus didn't command or expect something that would be too difficult or even impossible to do for most. Of course not, as he is the embodiment of love. So how do we easily come to (once again) love God? The quick and easy way is to simply feel God's love for us first!

"We love because He first loved us." (1 John 4:19)

"And so we know and rely on the love God has for us. God is love. Whoever lives in love lives in God, and God in them." (1 John 4:16)

REALIZATION:

I love to love God

Feel God's Love

When we once again desire to feel Gods love for us, we will feel it. *All that is needed is our strong and heartfelt desire.* There is no need to do anything else beforehand. Like purifying yourself first, or do, respectively don't do certain things. All we need to do is to *sincerely* want to feel his love once again.

You surely noticed that I repeatedly mentioned the term 'once again': The loving connection with God exists already and as such, it does not need to be established. It was always there and will always be there. No matter what. It is an eternal bond that binds us together. We don't even need to believe in it. It is not a matter of having faith in this love. It is only a matter of experiencing it, or not.

Simply express your *heartfelt desire* to feel this loving bond in a silent prayer or during a quiet moment of meditation:

"Dear God, please let me feel your love for me!"

Of course, you can choose your own words, the way you feel most comfortable expressing yourself. After all *it is the sincerity and strength of our desire that really counts*, and not some precise or formal way of wording. And don't worry about any doubting, restricting or objecting thoughts your mind may want to come up with. Disregard them all. And instead *focus only on stating your strong desire to feel God's love in every prayer and during every meditation.*

Then simply feel within and experience this love. It will accept you the way you are, without imposing any conditions. It will embrace you, hug you and cherish you. It will strengthen you and fill your heart with peace and joy.

At times we may also experience some physical sensations in our mind and body. A pleasant tingling or pulsating of energy within. A letting go of tensions, stress and anxieties. A lessening or disappearing of pain. Sensations of light that illuminate and (literally) brighten our mind. Feelings of intense warmth. Shades of white and/or various other colors whirling around. And so on.

Feel God's love for you first thing in the morning when you wake up, midday during your lunch break, or any time throughout the day when you start to feel uneasy about something or someone giving you a hard time; whenever you're stressed out or afraid and anxious in any way. Then ask for and feel it again at night before you start to drift off into a deep and relaxing sleep (see also chapter *Surrender*).

By feeling his love every day we will be able to easily return this love - thereby fulfilling the first and greatest commandment Jesus wants us to keep and follow! It is easy simply because it is inherent in every soul. It's a built-in characteristic. A natural ability of all of us. Once we truly feel this deep spiritual love for us we will naturally want to love this love (back). It is something that we have always known and done. But sometimes we unlearn or forget about it for a variety of reasons.

"God loves each of us as if there were only one of us." Saint Augustine

Love always comes in two forms. One is active where we love someone, the other one is passive where we feel loved by somebody. Both feel good and make us happier. Feel God's love for you and return this love. Feel secure and comforted being united in this love and enjoy this bliss. It's a happy way of life.

And The Happy Rabbit Says…

"A loving person is always enjoying happiness - love to feel loved!" [13]

Whenever we feel his love, we will also get to know the answers to some of the mind's questions mentioned above. Gradually and increasingly we will simply feel the truth and have a deep inner knowing that will calm our nagging or doubting minds.

As we increasingly feel his love we will also know for sure that God wants us to be happy! Because we can feel that pure love doesn't desire to see suffering (see also chapter *The Divine Deal*). Even though our love may not be perfect yet, just think about one person you dearly love from the bottom of your heart. Did you ever wish that person to suffer in any way? Of course not! And no, not even for 'educational purposes'…

When we truly love someone we only want to see that person happy, healthy and well. God's love for us is completely pure, unwavering and strong. It is ever-present as he is omniscient. Connect and feel it. Enjoy it and be merry!

In our current world we also get occasional glimpses of unconditional and selfless love. Like the father who jumps into the raging surf to rescue his sons, even at a serious risk to his own life. Or the hero who sacrifices his own life to save hundreds. [14] Or the sweet mother who loves her child - no matter what. Regardless of some perceived or actual shortcomings, respectively the odd misbehavior here and there.

We don't have to first do this or that in order to win or deserve divine love. Or don't do this or that before becoming worthy of it. At first, this is perhaps a tough one to understand for our conditioned and limited minds, and yet it's how it is as we can quite easily come to feel and experience this reality. Fact is that we really are 'good enough'. By God's grace and design.

God's love is impartial just like the rain is falling on wheat and weeds alike:

"that you may be sons of your Father in heaven. He causes his sun to rise on the evil and the good, and sends rain on the righteous and the unrighteous." (Matthew 5:44-45)

"Rain does not fall on one roof alone" (Proverb)

"As freely as the firmament embraces the world, or the sun pours forth impartially his beams, so mercy must encircle both friend and foe." Friedrich Schiller [15]

It is us alone, individually, who decide to accept his endless love and blessings, or not. We all have the ability to accept it graciously and happily. It is not strenuous or difficult in any way since it is an inherent inborn feature of us all. It's like knowing how to swallow or smile.

Even when we refuse or ignore this love and all its associated blessings, it is nevertheless still available to us.

All we need to do is to decide to let it in (again). To just welcome the natural course of things to simply happen and be. God is always loving, patient and available - even during the sometimes long years we may have 'relegated him to the waiting room'!

"Prayer is an act of love; words are not needed. Even if sickness distracts from thoughts, all that is needed is the will to love." Saint Teresa of Avila

God loves all his children, all that he created, 'All That Is', as extensions or parts and parcels of his divine Self. To feel this nourishing love, unwavering support and wise guidance within is indeed the easiest and quickest way we can perceive God in our daily lives.

"If any of you lacks wisdom, let him ask God, who gives generously to all without reproach, and it will be given him." (James 1:5)

Many Christians describe themselves openly (and often rather proudly...) as 'God-fearing' - as if that would be a good thing that we should all aspire to as well. While this may be their (current) reality (which is fine as we all learn and move ahead at our own pace and leisure), we can find far wiser council that reflects a much happier reality:

"There is no fear in love, but perfect love casts out fear. For fear has to do with punishment, and whoever fears has not been perfected in love." (1 John 4:18)

Should we listen and follow the advice and example of someone who loves God or the ones who fear God? Jesus and all the prophets clearly and dearly want us to love God, and forcefully say so!

"For God hath not given us the spirit of fear; but of power, and of love, and of a sound mind." (2 Timothy 1:7)

They don't ask us to be afraid of him, and to be too scared to experience and enjoy our life to its fullest potential... Perfect unconditional love is the prescribed way of life as it contains the solutions to all of our problems. And incidentally, it is also the way that makes and keeps us happy!

"May the grace of the Lord Jesus Christ, and the love of God, and the fellowship of the Holy Spirit be with you all." (2 Corinthians 13:14)

REALIZATIONS:

I love to feel God's love

I love to feel Your love

Love your Self

Many contemporary social critics feel that society as a whole has become increasingly narcissistic, for all kinds of psychological or other reasons like the usage of social media and so on. Whether this general observation is true or not, when we talk here about loving our Self, we don't mean to advocate ego love in a narrow and selfish way.

Ego is both a Latin and Greek word for 'I'. Psychologist Sigmund Freud considered it to be a

theoretic construct that explains the functioning of our mind, rather than a neurological structure of the brain. For many it is their sense of 'self', self-concept' or 'self-identification'. We commonly refer to some people as having a 'big ego' to mean that they have a totally inflated sense of their own importance.

Ego love is by default a bit of a narcissistic type of love, to various degrees, ranging from mild versions to the totally obsessed. It is basically a 'love of labels' where we primarily identify ourselves as being our physical body only and the associated descriptions we attach to it to compare and describe ourselves.

So we define and love ourselves as being say a young, slim and white American woman with a beautiful face, a well-earning lawyer who is married, a good Christian and mother of a lovely boy. One problem with label love is that circumstances in life can and do change - along with the labels and the importance we have attached to them.

Maybe over time the above person will have turned into an elderly, obese and white American woman with a wrinkly saggy face, an unemployed alcoholic lawyer who is divorced, a now cynical atheist whose boy is sitting in jail for assorted petty crimes and drug offenses…

What would happen to her sense of self-worth and self-esteem, or ego love, when it was all just based on previously true but temporary and fleeting labels that no longer apply?

A simple yet undeniable fact of life is that we were all born free of any and all man-made concepts such as race or religion, country or culture. Imagine a baby or very young child that could already talk; would it ever say: "Hey, I'm a wealthy Caucasian male and currently still a little person, I am a devout Christian, and a proud American Republican to top it off. Oh, and I'm a Vegan too and later in life I'm gonna be a famous movie star." Quite clearly that is most unlikely!

While that may all be or become true one day, we simply are not our labels that describe certain external facts about us but don't reveal anything about the real person we eternally are. To love ourselves as labels is simply not real and bound to lead us in the wrong direction. With rather unhappy results.

Love your self as God loves you! Feel his love first, then love your self in the very same way.

His love is for our true and eternal Self, the spiritual Soul he created, not for our external and ever-changing labels, projections and delusions. By feeling his love for us, and by returning this divine love - being immersed in a loving union - we can then extend and feel this same divine love for ourselves.

This is gracious and compassionate, pure and unconditional self love that is natural, healthy and normal, thereby making us happy. Instead of the narcissistic and uncaring 'love' that will only bind us to an unreal world of ever-insecure and permanently hurt egos. The love of our real self is based on reality, instead of the fictional stories and imaginations of ego.

Self love is steady and permanent love instead of fickle and temporary sentiment that continually needs to be artificially nurtured and pampered. True self love is always empowering and strengthening us while ego love is only weakening, degrading and hurting. By default illusions will never be able to claim to be real.

"Pride makes us artificial and humility makes us real." Thomas Merton [16]

An ego or illusion is inherently unstable or put differently, insecure. And as such big and small egos alike constantly need to mask over their insecurities. The built-in insecurity that comes from not knowing who it really is. It is us when we deny ourselves our true spiritual heritage. (We will talk a lot more about our eternal identity a bit later in chapter *Be your Self*.)

And The Happy Rabbit Says…

"A loving person is always enjoying happiness - love your Self as you are!"

Loving our real self is important, not only for our own happiness, but the happiness of our friends and family, and ultimately the happiness of the entire world. We simply cannot pass on what we don't really feel within ourselves, and thereby directly and personally know to be true.

Jesus confirmed the importance of self-love in the following verse:

"And the second is like it: 'Love your neighbor as yourself." (Matthew 22:38)

In order to be able to love our neighbors we have to *first* feel true love for ourselves. And once we do that we are also in the position to love one another in just the same way. Not more, not less, but simply equally so!

Love All

The first and second commandments are repeated many times in the Holy Bible. Other verses also stress their supreme importance:

"All the Law and the Prophets hang on these two commandments." (Matthew 22:40)

"There is no commandment greater than these." (Mark 12:31)

But how can we love all?

"Dear friends, since God so loved us, we also ought to love one another." (1 John 4:11)

How can we love some of the people we know, read or hear about? The uncaring and selfish ones? The ones that are such 'brutes' or even 'low life scum of the Earth', or something like that...

Well, much could be said about the people we don't agree with. We may not like, strongly dislike, even hate, how others think, talk and act, and yet we are asked to love them anyway. Sounds like a tough proposition, but with a few insights plus a bit of practice it can actually become both possible and easy.

We can come to understand that variety and diversity is part of the design of God's creation. It is there to help us learn and love, in other words, for good reasons. We all have a reason and the right to be here. And we all have to play our part in the unfolding expansion of the Universe. The sheer fact that we were born and presently 'occupy some space' in this dimension is somewhat evidence in itself.

We also have been given the freedom to choose and thereby make mistakes in life, even grave ones. And yes, we will need to face the consequences sooner or later too (see also chapter *The Divine Deal*). The universe is set up in a 'self-policing' or self-correcting way, and as such it is totally 'fair and square' for everyone. That too may be a tough thing to realize at first, and yet we can come to understand that this is so.

Everybody makes progress in life, some sooner and others later. Some quicker and easier, while others - for their own reasons - take a more long-winded, tough or difficult approach. Sometimes we fall off the right track for a while, even for many years. And yet we will eventually find back our ways. Perhaps after we have reached a really low point in life and gained some necessary and valuable insights.

It is never too late to make some positive changes and turn around our life. And there is always divine love and guidance available to all of us. Sometimes we feel and listen, and at other times we choose to ignore it, consciously or not.

"The love that you withhold is the pain that you carry." Ralph Waldo Emerson

None of us truly knows how life is for anyone else (even if we could walk the proverbial mile in their shoes). Yes, we can listen, feel and emphathize. But we can't really know the full picture or all the reasons why someone has come to make their particular choices in life. Only they do, and so does the 'Big Boss', the supreme creator and knower of it all.

"Why do you look at the speck of sawdust in your brother's eye and pay no attention to the plank in your own eye?" (Matthew 7:3)

"If you judge people, you have no time to love them." Mother Teresa [17]

We can learn both from good and bad examples in life. The good ones show us how to do things while the bad examples show us how *not* to do things. We should be grateful to both. Because in the end the only thing that counts is that we have learnt something and made progress in life, becoming more loving, merry and wise, thereby helping to make the world an even better place.

And The Happy Rabbit Says…

"There is something we can learn from everyone we meet - listen carefully and find out what it is!"

An interesting part of life is the insight that some of the people that are getting on our nerves are annoying only because there is a part in their personality that we actually dislike in ourselves. They feel irritating simply because the very same thing unconsciously irks us within ourselves. Otherwise that aspect would not vibrate so strongly in our mind and we could easily overlook it.

"What you dislike in another take care to correct in yourself." Thomas Sprat [18]

Best is to always be tolerant and keep smiling. After all we know that we do have a bit of that character trait or behavior as well. Or we could potentially have it, respectively we did have in the past at some time.

According to Wikipedia: "There is only one verb 'to tolerate' and one adjective 'tolerant', but the two nouns 'tolerance' and 'toleration' have evolved slightly different meanings. Tolerance is an attitude of mind that implies non-judgmental acceptance of different lifestyles or beliefs, whereas toleration implies putting up with something that one disapproves of." [19]

"I have learned silence from the talkative, toleration from the intolerant, and kindness from the unkind; yet, strange, I am ungrateful to those teachers." Khalil Gibran [20]

" When you are offended at any man's fault, turn to yourself and study your own failings. Then you will forget your anger. " Epictetus [21]

So why should I love X, Y or Z? The very people I don't quite like or can't stand at all?

Besides doing what Jesus asks us to do and follow in his footsteps, which is the enlightened point of view, we can also answer the question in a more self-centered way:

We should love X, Y and Z simply because loving them feels good and makes us happy!

Love is self-satisfying in two senses of the word. For one it satisfies us - the eternal self we really are. And, the act of loving is the reward in itself. There is absolutely no need for reciprocity. We can love anyone anyway - whether they love us back or not. And if someone chooses to dislike us or even 'hate our guts', well that is their personal choice and matter to contend with in their own life.

Hating doesn't make for a happy life, not in the here and now, nor anytime in the future.

When you love you feel joy in your heart and peace in your mind. Love doesn't even need any (external) acknowledgment as it is self-evident. Both within and without.

There is also no need to put this or that condition in place before we allow ourselves to love a particular person. Just love him or her anyway - and feel great while doing so - and chances are that things will turn out for the very best, for both of you.

"True love begins when nothing is looked for in return."

Antoine De Saint-Exupery [22]

There is no reason to be stingy with our love either. After all, we don't lose anything but only gain. By loving more we add love to our life and there will be ever more to manifest itself in the various ways love expresses itself.

"Lovin' is easy with both eyes closed

You know that's the best way to feel it

Lovin' is easy with both eyes closed

Just get a hold and watch how it grows"

John Lees, Barclay James Harvest [23]

Love is a word, like God, that gets easily used and abused. We use it to express a fondness for a particular brand of ice cream or chocolate or whatever. We use it to express a physical attraction to someone's body even though we may not really care that much for the actual person within that body.

Love is often tainted by our fleeting emotions, and sometimes it is used as a form of emotional blackmail to get us the things we want.

Love is a lot like water. Imagine a source of pristine pure water somewhere up in the mountains. As the water of the little stream flows further and further towards the ocean, joining other streams to become an ever wider river, it becomes more and more polluted. In the end it is still water but it doesn't taste the same any longer, or worse, it could be toxic and detrimental to our health.

God is the source of love, so it is always totally pure, supremely fresh and absolutely refreshing. It is unconditional and flows freely and in abundance. Forever. The smart way is to get our water from the very source. Jesus asks us to be smart and go directly to the source.

"God is love, and whoever abides in love abides in God, and God abides in him." (1 John 4:13)

When we feel (once again) love for God and our (true eternal) self, we will truly be able to extend this pure love to both our immediate and extended family. It will be healing, uplifting, and gently nurturing. It will smooth out difficulties to the point of non-existence, or at least, reduce them to a bare minimum.

And when this love is overflowing from our hearts, it will 'travel' further and further afield. To our friends and our neighbors. Ultimately, with a bit of practice, we can't help but include all fellow travelers with whom we come in contact with. At work, at play, at random (or so it seems). It will become so, automatically.

"But I tell you: Love your enemies and pray for those who persecute you, that you may be sons of your Father in heaven. He causes his sun to rise on the evil and the good, and sends rain on the righteous and the unrighteous." (Matthew 5:44-45)

We simply cannot feel a) God's unconditional love for us, b) our love for him, c) love for our self, and then go out into the world and deny it to our brothers and sisters. Or worse, treat them with disrespect, lie, cheat and steal. And so on.

True love always nourishes and heals. It always flows and expands. It knows no obstacles or barriers of any kind.

But when we deliberately hold back love - for whatever reasons our limited minds can come up with - we cut *ourselves* off the flow too and won't be able to feel or taste it… And the longer we live in this 'self-imposed exile' or isolation, the more we 'dry up and out' - all the way to the point of anxiety, desperation and depression.

"The love that you withhold is the pain that you carry." Ralph Waldo Emerson[24]

"If anyone says, 'I love God,' and hates his brother, he is a liar." (1 John 4:20)

By following Jesus' first and second most important commandments we are also taking care of all the other commandments. That just happens naturally in the same way as snow melts in the warming sun. As our love grows it literally melts the cold and frozen hearts of the world, starting with our own, and expanding in ever wider circles.

When we feel true love within we wish nobody harm. We will stand for peace and justice. We desire to make progress in life. And we like to help making the world a better place for all of us. In other words, we enjoy co-creating heaven on Earth!

"Let no debt remain outstanding, except the continuing debt to love one another, for whoever loves others has fulfilled the law. The commandments, "You shall not commit adultery," "You shall not murder," "You shall not steal," "You shall not covet," and whatever other command there may be, are summed up in this one command: "Love your neighbor as yourself." Love does no harm to a neighbor. Therefore love is the fulfillment of the law." (Romans 13:8-10)

"God Is Love." (1 John 4:5)

When we feel divine love we do have peace of mind. And the value of having true peace of mind is simply but totally priceless. Because no matter how much wealth a person has accumulated in life, one cannot buy it.

I have met very wealthy men who have achieved it all in terms of worldly success. And yet they simply could not sleep without their daily heavy sedation of whiskey and sleeping pills. Somewhere along their way they have simply lost their innocence and peace of mind, knowing deep down that there were victims along their ascent to riches and fame.

When we feel supreme love in our hearts we automatically focus on the lovable sides in people. We all have them. Simply take the best (in people) and overlook the rest. After all, we all have very much in common. Much more so than not.

We all share the same spiritual father as there is only one God - no matter the names we assign, and no matter our in any case limited group-think, respectively personal understanding. We share the same planet in an infinite and incomprehensible universe. We (ultimately) breathe the same air and drink the same water - as it gets all recycled and dispersed globally.

We all want a safe, warm and dry place we can call home. We all want to be healthy. Eat and drink well. Be respected. Appreciated. Loved. Recognized. Have a family. And good friends. We want to be entertained and happy. Learn and grow. Create and achieve. Live a long life. And be remembered once our time here has come to an end.

Our individual desires and specific preferences surely differ in endless shades and nuances and yet, in the big picture we all want to experience the above very same things!

The things that seemingly divide us are mostly external in nature. We use descriptive labels like our country of birth to define and distinguish ourselves. Yet nationality is a very shifting concept as borders have changed thousands of times over the course of human history. [25]

The color of our skin too is still being used to separate ourselves from 'the others', yet all blood beneath our skin is equally pink. Our culture and 'official' creed is also a reason for much fear (of the unknown...) and fighting. But that may also change over time as we move to another country, respectively adapt our thoughts and feelings over the course of a lifetime.

We define and label ourselves as 'what we do' and yet our professions, qualifications and jobs rarely stay the same. And neither do our ever-changing clothes and individual style, no matter how hard we may identify ourselves with it at the time. And so on and so forth. The world is a myriad of labels. And none of them mean all that much in the eyes of the eternal reality.

'Love All' will ultimately come to include all our fellow brothers and sisters on planet Earth. After all we are all friends and family - even the ones who are not yet aware of this fact or those who would vigorously deny it. Nevertheless each person's current state of understanding, we can still share our love by sending it out to the world as a whole and everybody 'out there', to the proverbial strangers that are just friends we haven't met yet.

It's a bit like the sun that is beaming out its rays of light from its core, seemingly unaware of where it may travel to or which corners of the universe it may 'enlighten'.

The more we feel pure love the easier we will understand the sorrows and needs, the problems and pains of our fellow brothers and sisters. That doesn't mean that we have to agree with unkind deeds and other mistakes. But we can better understand their particular situation in life, and are thus able to keep our peace of heart and mind. We may even feel inspired to offer some assistance and help to bring about more peace and harmony.

"Our souls may lose their peace and even disturb other people's, if we are always criticizing trivial actions - which often are not real defects at all, but we construe them wrongly through our ignorance of their motives." Saint Teresa of Avila

All of us have our own individual set of psychological issues, twists and quirks, and most of them are actually quite lovable and endearing - once seen through the eyes of love.

Love comes in many different flavors. And just like with ice cream, all flavors (or most of them anyway) are delicious and enjoyable. Some are more prominent or important than others, and that often depends on our stage or age in life. At birth our mothers are usually the very nearest and dearest while later in life it may be that very special sweetheart we came to meet.

In any case there really is no need for jealousy or competition in matters of love; we can and should cultivate and enjoy all forms of love in our life, or at least as many as we possibly can. The more the merrier!

The love between brothers and sisters. Love between friends (including friendly or fatherly teachers and preachers, respectively mentors and spiritual guides). Love as a mother, father or as a child. The love between a couple. Love between grandparents and grandchildren. Uncles and aunties, their nephews and nieces. Or cousins and other bonds of love within our extended families.

Love really has no boundaries: Every pet and animal lover knows how lovable and loving they are, always craving our love and attention (besides food, care and plenty of play time!). We can witness the love that flows between animals too, even totally different species, or very unlikely ones. [119] Plants too respond very much to feelings of love and appreciation as many a farmer or hobby gardener knows very well.

None of our loving relationships need to have a negative effect on any other relationship or kind of love. My love for my wife does not alter or diminish the love I feel for my mother in any way. It's just a different flavor of love and both are most pleasant in their own ways.

We don't have to choose a preferred love or take sides even if some of our loved ones don't seem to get along all that well. We can and should ignore their 'internal' squabbles and love them all anyway. After all we know that there is an endless supply of love, so let it show! And all will be well.

Most of us experience at least some of these loving relationships. At best we can express our love openly, at other times quietly only, or from a distance. Sometimes loving is easy, yet at times there are various obstacles that can obscure or cover up our mutual love, perhaps even to the point of non-existence, or so it may seem.

What should we do when someone dislikes or even hates us? The best way is to stay relaxed and loving. Just let them be, knowing full well that their negative emotions have absolutely nothing to do with you. It is simply a cry for love.

Haters in the real or online world basically hate themselves, even though that may be hidden in their subconscious mind and disguised as arrogance or other attempts to feel superior. People who hate others in essence hate themselves first, hence the need to project it to the external world (we have discussed the distinction between ego-love and self-love in the previous chapter).

Here's a little insight (learned the hard way) that keeps serving me well: Best is to never take or make things personal. Most people act and react purely based on their own inner world of dreams and fears. Things are very rarely personal. After all, we all just try to be happy (or happier)! And the journey through the strange and wonderful adventure of life on planet Earth is not always smooth sailing. So we might as well give each other a bit of a break and the benefit of the doubt.

"Blessed is the man who remains steadfast under trial, for when he has stood the test he will receive the crown of life, which God has promised to those who love him." (James 1:12)

We all know that relationships are not always easy. But we have to acknowledge the fact that when there are bands of love between people, they cannot just disappear. They are there for good. Even if it is presently covered up with anger. Real love is not something we can just fall into and then out again. Love just is. Always. Once we truly love somebody we cannot just stop it simply because that person doesn't behave the way we want. That of course is not love. It is a desire to control, or attraction respectively attachment at best, and it is based on conditions.

So what to do in a difficult relationship? Jesus made it easy for us. He is asking us to first focus on our loving exchange with God. And once we do that (again), we can inject this same pure divine love into our troublesome relationships. At first perhaps we can only do so quietly within our hearts. Expand it to our minds. Then show our love and care in small little bits and pieces here and there.

Speak with love and kindness only - or not at all. And take it from there. There is magic in God's love and it will (start to) show!

And The Happy Rabbit Says…

"Close your eyes and send out positive, warm and loving thoughts to all your loved ones!"

Happiness is what we want for ourselves when we feel love for ourselves. And it is what we want for all the people we love. Let's love all and be happy.

"Anyone who does not love does not know God, because God is love." (1 John 4:8)

"Beloved, let us love one another, for love is from God, and whoever loves has been born of God and knows God." (1 John 4:7)

REALIZATIONS:

I love to love

I love to feel loved

Appreciate

Always appreciate - never complain.

We cannot be in an appreciative spirit and at the same time complain about something or someone. It is simply not possible. It is always either or... We have to chose sides as they are total opposites of each other. One mindset makes you happy, the other doesn't.

Some may argue here and say that complaining actually makes them happy, and that may well be true for them. Yes, it may feel good to have someone who truly listens to our problems, offers a sympathetic ear and perhaps a solution too. But frequent or constant 'whinging and whining' is a different story; nobody really appreciates it in the long run.

People have a natural tendency to avoid negative or sick people. Just look around the faces in a room full of people when someone starts to have a sneezing or coughing fit...

We can easily experience the difference that results from complaining often versus being grateful most of the time. But of course, to each their own or 'different strokes for different folks'. In the same way as there are different shades of darkness and light, there are also different shades of depression, or happiness. It is our choice, once we are fully aware of it.

When we complain we are basically saying that we are not happy with someone or something. And immediately as we do so we are acknowledging our unhappiness. Our mood will have soured right away and we start to feel like a victim - instead of being a merry Christian.

At every such moment we need to turn around the situation by looking for the solutions, while at the same time appreciate whatever comes to mind, whatever is visible or possible to appreciate.

No matter the problem, there are always solutions to be found. And no matter the circumstances, there will always be something pleasant to appreciate. That may sound unlikely at first, but with a little bit of practice that can soon become a way of life.

Of course we are not talking about only seeing what's good and nice 'out there'. Going through life with rose-colored glasses and ignoring the things that can or need to be improved. Or worse, fool ourselves by saying that black is as actually white, that war is peace, or other such Orwellian doublethink. Not at all.

We should be aware of what's happening around us, be mindful and awake. But nevertheless the mean and ugly sides we can choose to see the beautiful and positive aspects - even in an unfortunate situation - and focus on those.

We don't need to appreciate what is not good or right. What feels bad or wrong. However, we can appreciate and highlight what is good within or around the unpleasant… See and appreciate the wisdom that a problem contains and exposes. And maybe help to bring about a great solution. In other words, concentrate on the good that is already present everywhere and the improvements that can be made. Rather than feeling depressed about the seemingly hopeless…

And The Happy Rabbit Says…

"Be truly grateful for all the good people and things in your life - and you're happy right away!"

When we complain we essentially don't love. Instead we are angry about the perceived lack of standards in someone or something. We look at the imperfections and dwell on them, while we really could move on right away - to greener pastures where the sun is shining and the weather is sweet. Either literally, or within our hearts and minds only, or both.

When we mostly focus on what is wrong we cannot see what is already right or could be better. Let's see all the already good or the improvements that will be helpful and uplifting to us all.

Whenever we complain we are sowing seeds. Seeds of complaints that will results in future harvests of new reasons to complain. Tiny seeds of anger that will produce returns of *d*anger.

And likewise, when we feel appreciation and gratitude, we are sowing the seeds that will bring about ever more reasons to be grateful and happy.

The way of the merry Christian is to always appreciate. Find, see and recognize all the good things around you. From the small ones to the bigger ones - simply all of them! Soon you will find so many things to appreciate that you will feel most bountiful and blessed. It can be(come) almost confusing and overwhelming at times. So many of 'God's goodies' are right here, over there, and everywhere. Moreover, we can discover them *within* our heart, our mind, and our body.

No matter whether we are rich or poor or somewhere in between, we can all find plenty of reasons to appreciate. People, things, events and circumstances. Yet quite often the well-to-do seem to have forgotten to truly enjoy the good things in life (despite being surrounded by lots of treasures and luxuries) while the ones 'traveling light' are still able to 'see the light and smell the roses'.

To feel content is not difficult, but it needs some practice anyway. At least initially in a phase of transition, while moving away from the mindset of a 'pure consumer-robot' who is told what to do or buy. All the things we see in both subtle and flashy ads or promotions that promise to produce happy smiles (or at least a superior grin) if only we bought it too… perhaps with money we don't have and need to borrow at a steep price… maybe to impress people we don't even know.

One easy and fun way to re-learn the art of appreciation is to go camping, perhaps on an extended hiking or biking tour into a beautiful remote area.

Bring along only the things you really need and can easily carry, a sleeping bag, a small tent, some food and supplies. It is amazing how happy we can be without all of the assorted contents of our home. And more so, how much we can come to appreciate the luxuries of our modern world, the things we so easily take for granted.

Amenities like a washing machine, a comfortable warm and dry bed, a stove that warms up at the flick of a switch, or an AC that cools us down whenever we want. Electricity, gas, lights, a hot shower, and *hurray hurray*, a dishwasher! All the things that make our basic tasks in life so much easier than it ever was before in the history of mankind.

Even a king or queen living in an opulent castle and surrounded by servants of all kinds didn't have a big flat TV or much of the goodies most of us would consider to be normal. We take these blessings so much for granted that we mostly don't even think or talk about them. But we should notice it all.

To live a life of appreciation, gratitude, and contentment becomes very easy once we have well and truly made up our mind to do so - to already and always be pleased with what is good and nice and available in the here and now. Even though we may have as of yet unfulfilled desires too.

This mindset still leaves room to expand and improve one's life further and further, and indeed it makes it easier to actually do so. It certainly beats leading a life full of complaints, malcontent and misery while postponing joy and happiness to a distant future - once a range of predetermined conditions or desires have somehow or another been fulfilled. Or perhaps be bitter or mad at the supreme creator of it all for not being a good or quick enough supplier of one's wants and needs.

To always be appreciative and grateful is a smart decision to make. Indeed it is a most happy decision, and it will bring God even closer into our lives. We simply can't admire and appreciate God's bounty and beauty and feel very far away at the same time.

And of course, you know the saying that the best things in life are free. They truly are! This fact alone is another thing to be grateful for.

To love God and feel his love is free. To love our friends and family and everybody else is free. To enjoy their love and affection is free too. To smile and laugh is free. And so is to joke and feel good. Treasuring the beauty of nature is free. Real friendship is free. To think is free. And so is to pray and meditate. To day-dream costs nothing. Neither does sleeping. To exercise is free. To enjoy the senses and sensations of our bodies is free. Being creative is free. To be positive, appreciative and grateful is free. To feel happy is free too!

It is not even necessary to own something first before we can appreciate it. While on the road I much enjoy looking at a beautifully designed and constructed car driving by, even though it belongs to someone else. That little fact does nothing at all to detract from my enjoyment. A beautiful flower in my neighbors garden is still a marvelous sight, even though it's on the other side of the fence.

And likewise, an architectural beauty of a house can be appreciated just like that, without owning it. Ultimately all things belong to God as it's all made out of elements created by God. And none of us get to take any of it with us, once our time is up.

We can appreciate all kinds of other things as well, like seeing a happy couple laughing in a coffee shop, the loving smile of a passing father with his daughter, and the supportive embrace of a son walking with his elderly mother. Simply as a witness there are so many opportunities out there to appreciate and be grateful for. The magnificent beauty of a sunrise over the ocean or a sunset over the mountain range. The delicate beauty of a freshly opened flower sprinkled with drops of dew. The innocent beauty of a smiling baby, or the happy laughter of children playing.

"Gratitude is not only the greatest of virtues, but the parent of all others." Cicero, 106 BC-43 BC

But what should we do when we hear others complain? Chances are that this happens quite a lot. No matter how much or how little money one has, there will always be plenty of potential causes to feel bad about - if we wanted to. Material wealth and comfort is not really a factor at all. One can be happy with very little, and one can be unhappy with very much. Whether we complain a lot or not only depends on our mindset, our attitude, and our consciousness.

Anybody can easily come up with a plethora of bad things happening in their lives or 'out there'. Within a short period of time. Even billionaires can and do it. Society at large shows us this way, from our parents to friends, teachers, and so on. Even the clergy (of all stripes) is not immune. And of course the media lives off writing or broadcasting complaints, all that is bad and ugly in the world. Rarely do they - or indeed do we all - praise and give thanks or outline the many positive developments and happenings.

What shall we do when we hear the latest tirades or know it's about to start? It all depends how you feel at this point in time, or your life… If you currently feel a bit tired or otherwise down you need to first energize yourself and connect within to the flow of eternal love.

And if you feel already joyful and strong plus you have the time to listen, well, just love and listen. Feel divine love within your heart, let it illuminate your mind, and listen. Be understanding and, if it's called for, offer a solution, perhaps formulated as a question to make it easier to absorb or otherwise more palatable.

Or point out something positive and uplifting that is happening right now. Like, it's so nice, the sun is shining and the weather is sweet. Or how the clouds drifting by look totally awesome. "Yay, it's gonna be a long weekend!" And so on.

Often though, solutions or cheers are not what is really wanted or truly needed. Understanding and love is. Every soul needs and wants to be loved. Accepted and respected. Appreciated and praised.

It is an easy and universal solution because these are natural desires of all of us. When people complain (and ultimately, when they become sick) they are looking for love. So give them directly what is indirectly asked for, what is so greatly needed: Love and understanding. And then keep going on your own merry ways. You know where and how to get and feel infinite divine love. It is easy to pass around and share, then go back within for ever more!

And remember to apply this insight in your own life as well in times of trouble or upheavals. Anytime you suddenly find yourself 'on the complaining side', you too need some more love and understanding. Appreciate the fact that you already know how to get love, then go within and feel it!

We can focus on seeing the holes in Swiss cheese or be busy with eating and enjoying it. There are always going to be endless reasons to complain, and there will always be endless reasons to feel appreciation, gratitude and joy! It is our choice.

"Content makes poor men rich; discontentment makes rich men poor." Benjamin Franklin [26]

Every moment of every day, count and enjoy your blessings. Appreciate all that is (already) good and nice, magnificent and beautiful, helpful and inspiring, nourishing and tasty, pleasing and pleasant, loving and caring, and so on. Always give Thanks and enjoy your life with an attitude of gratitude.

A loving heart is naturally a grateful heart. And a grateful heart is instantly a happy heart. Greet all that is good and beautiful in life with a thankful happy smile. And it will bring about ever more opportunities to be grateful for!

REALIZATIONS:

I love to appreciate

I love to feel appreciated

I love to be grateful

I love to feel blessed

Smile

Smile a lot. Even if you don't feel like smiling. Anytime you really don't feel like smiling is actually the very same time you need to smile the most!

That may initially sound like a tough proposition but it is much easier than it sounds simply because to express joy and smile is also a natural part of our eternal identity. Of course, the idea is not that you smile when you see something dreadful or very sad in front of your eyes. But even in a tough situation we can find the solution within.

Close your eyes and go within. Connect with God and feel his love. Your mind will become filled with light and peace. Thoughts calm down. You may suddenly get inspirations (inspired - 'in-spirit-ed') on how to solve a situation that seemed like a big problem only moments earlier. And as you feel comforted, strengthened and happier, your inner smile will naturally want to show itself on your face as well.

"Peace begins with a smile." Mother Teresa

When you feel peace within because you are at peace with yourself, God, the world and All There Is, you will naturally have an almost imperceptible smile on your lips.

Make it a habit to walk through life with just such a smile. Your problems will be easier to bear and easier to solve.

"Life is too important to take seriously." Corky Siegel [27]

Over time the corners of your mouth will be slightly turned upwards all the time - literally 'turning that frown upside down'. Doing so -

even if we sometimes have to force it for a few moments, perhaps in front of a mirror - will help us to see things clearer. We will see the 'big picture' once again, become more cheerful again, and can take things easier, thereby helping to truly solve a problem with a smile. It works, try it!

"A smile is a curve that sets everything straight." Phyllis Diller [28]

Taoists practicing Traditional Chinese Medicine have consciously used the technique of 'The Inner Smile' for over two thousand years to help heal themselves and their patients.

Again, go within and connect with God in love. Feel your inner peace and smile. Then send this loving and happy smile to all areas in your body that feel sore or painful. Send it to your heart, lungs and liver. Feel it in your toes and knees. Let it caress your spine from the bottom to the top. Anywhere it is needed. Send this divine love and smile. It will help you feel better and recover quicker, respectively preserve your health and vigor.

Western medicine has shown that a smile releases positive, mood-enhancing chemicals in our brains that help to relax the nervous system and thus our entire body. Neuroscience has shown that a smile even helps with improving the retrieval of memories.

It is said that it takes fewer facial muscles to smile than to frown, hence it makes more sense to smile. Although strictly speaking that is not quite true (it takes 12 muscles for an authentic 'zygomatic' smile versus a total of 11 for frowning), surly a smiling face looks much more beautiful and attractive!

And The Happy Rabbit Says…

"Smile a lot today and enjoy seeing your face look so much more beautiful and bright!"

Research has shown that smiling:
- increases our likeability
- implies greater trust
- increases cooperation
- conveys respect and patience

- signals self-confidence and inner satisfaction
- shows empathy and compassion
- shows our hospitality [29]

All around the world, everyone understands a genuine smile, regardless of our color, culture or creed. No matter our foreign language skills, we can all communicate via smiles and laughter. It is easy and it literally transcends the Tower of Babel. [30]

People who smile also receive more help, as evidence shows that it produces the 'Good Samaritan' effect even by total strangers. [31] And last but not least, smiling results in greater financial earnings as well.

"Let us always meet each other with smile, for the smile is the beginning of love."
Mother Teresa

A great smile really does produce great results. Of course, for a smile to be great it has to be genuine as we can all instinctively spot a fake smile. But for a sincere Christian, being gentle and to love and smile is really quite an easy task: Anytime you feel God's love in your heart, the peace and strength you feel within will make your smile radiate and your eyes shine with joy and happiness.

Smile like this even when you're all by yourself, and no one is watching. From the small and almost unnoticeable smile to the really broad and happy one. Gentle and loving and kind. *Anytime you look into a mirror, always end up with a smile!*

For some that may sound a bit silly, for others it actually is a very hard thing to do. And nevertheless it is very much worth the effort. The reasons why we may feel a bit awkward about it is rooted in insecurity and a lack of proper self-esteem. Once we are able to feel real self love (as discussed in chapters *Feel God's Love* and *Love your Self*), we will also be able to express it with smiling at ourselves in the mirror.

It is said that 'The eyes are the windows to the soul'. When we are truly at peace with ourselves we can easily look into our eyes and smile. At first it may be a bit of a shy or hesitating smile... Yet over time our smile will grow ever more radiant, loving and... happy!

Smile to your self. And then, extend it and smile to the world as well. Smile to the stars and the moon at night. To the birds that are singing in the trees and the butterflies playing in the wind. Smile to your boss or employees when you think about them. Smile while thinking about your kids or other loved ones in your life. Smile even to the people you had an argument with, or the ones that seemingly don't like you very much.

You will find that your smile will start to literally melt away your problems. Sometimes that happens gradually and at other times quite instantly. Your life will certainly become much more pleasing. To you, to God, and to all the people in your life.

Always be generous with the smiles you are offering to the world. And the world in turn will increasingly smile back at you!

"Whoever sows sparingly will also reap sparingly, and whoever sows generously will also reap generously." (2 Corinthians 9:6)

Sometimes of course there are times, places or circumstances where a smile is not appropriate or called for. And yet we can still smile quietly within our hearts and minds and offer the right expression for the moment. An inner smile sometimes just shows itself as a positive expression, pleasant to see while not overtly revealing our inner happiness in situations when it is uncalled for.

Sadly but true, in an all too often serious, materialistic and unhappy world, sometimes one has to somewhat hide one's happiness. After all, there are certain kind of people who do get jealous when they come across someone who is truly happy - instead of enjoying to see a smiling face, or take it as living proof that it is actually possible to be happy in this world, and thus feel inspired to smile more and become happy too.

"Who is the happiest of men? He who values the merits of others, and in their pleasure takes joy, even as though they were his own." Johann Wolfgang von Goethe [32]

Believe it or not, but in my experience, such envy and jealousy often comes from the very wealthy who have it all in terms of worldly comfort and luxury. And yet they have failed to discover the source of real joy. Or they just don't know anymore how to find peace within their hearts and minds.

Making the pursuit of money, power, and fame one's primary goal in life is like running in the wrong direction to an elusive goal that only keeps getting further and further away. At some point it would simply be wise to reconsider and change course: Seek love, peace and happiness first and foremost. Everything else will follow at the right time.

The ability to smile, joke and laugh 'from the bottom of our hearts' is simply a natural by-product of doing things the right way; living life the loving way!

"Smile at each other, smile at your wife, smile at your husband, smile at your children, smile at each other - it doesn't matter who it is - and that will help you to grow up in greater love for each other." Mother Teresa

REALIZATIONS:

I love to smile

I love to be joyful

I love to laugh

Surrender

Some Christians have a bit the tendency to 'carry the weight of the world' on their shoulders. Sometimes they almost desperately want to solve its myriad of problems, or at least they feel strongly obliged to 'do something'. Quickly.

While their motives may be totally pure in heart there is no need to be anxious, sad or depressed about the state of the world because it is not broken - even if some people or organizations say so. Ultimately there are only two kind of situations in life. The ones where we can actually do something about it. And those where we can't, even if we really really wanted to. This is true both on an individual as well as collective level.

We are simply not all-powerful, even though we'd like to think so at times. Even those people who have somehow or another convinced themselves that *they* are God, the Supreme Lord and Creator, can't just change a red traffic light to green at will, while approaching an intersection. They too will have to wait!

What we can and should do is live in the flow of life, in harmony with God and his creation. And yes, that can occasionally result in being able to ride the green wave of a few traffic lights in a row. It's very nice when that happens, but we simply can't control it at our whim… no matter what we want or believe.

Perhaps without being aware of the reasons why we really need to make a stop at a particular red light and take a bit of a break. To think an inspiring and uplifting thought. To re-focus and become centered once again. To breathe and let go of a stressful event. Or to simply look at the merry birds flying into that dazzling sunset.

There are always things that we don't know or can't control - and that is actually a good thing. Just imagine the utter chaos and trouble in the world if all of our 'little' whims and wishes just happened, as in *instantly*... It would obviously result in total mayhem, lots of regrets and a great deal of sorrows.

"There are more tears shed over answered prayers than over unanswered prayers."

Saint Teresa of Avila

We have been given free will and choice, yet much if not most of what is actually happening is beyond our direct influence. For example, no matter how hard we'd tried we simply can't control what happens while we're asleep. Lots and lots is happening within our bodies and minds, and all is beyond our thoughts and determination. And while asleep, all kind of things could be happening 'out there' in the 'real world' as we are completely oblivious of our surroundings...

So to fall asleep is an act of surrendering as we never really know if we are ever going to wake up in this dimension! To travel in a car, bus or train, or to fly across the oceans in an airplane, is also an act of surrendering. We simply don't know what is going to happen. We may do everything alright but perhaps someone else is making a mistake and careens his truck into our lane. Or the pilot is doing it all right but a mechanic forgot to properly tighten some screws. Whatever it may be...

During several decades of almost constantly flying around the world I surely had my share of scary moments. In really turbulent situations I quickly learned the art of surrendering, and perhaps strangely, in a way I started to actually appreciate and enjoy these special moments. They serve as reminders of the deeper truth that we are very fragile beings and that we don't have all that much to say after all.

In business life too we never know whether we will succeed or not. No matter how hard we plan or work. Maybe our products or services were simply not as great as we thought so nobody is buying them. Or the company we targeted will buy from a competitor instead, despite our really great sales presentation. Ultimately, being in business is an act of surrendering to the customers and clients.

And in the big picture, being alive is an act of surrendering to God, the presence and flow of life. We can do it consciously while awake or only sub-consciously while asleep. Partially or fully, it's our choice.

Our physical health is influenced by many factors. We can influence a great deal by choosing a healthy and sane lifestyle. Yet even that is not a guarantee for good health. Many factors are simply beyond our control, no matter how hard we try or believe otherwise.

"Too many cooks will spoil the broth" - too many people trying to be the boss will only spoil it all. In other words, the universe simply works better without our constant (or desperate) fine-tuning and micro-management. This is again very true in the corporate world. Any Chief Executive Officer worth his or her salt is very much aware of this: Micro-management does not work well at all. Quite the opposite because people will rightly perceive it as a lack of trust in their abilities.

When we try to micromanage it all because we believe the world is lost we only show our lack of trust in God, his creation and plan. Just because we don't know it all doesn't mean that God doesn't know it too…

We need to trust in the Goodness of It All. Have faith and know that all is good, all is well. What is not perfect today is simply not yet completed. It's work in progress.

There are two big philosophical mistakes we can make in life and both will have far-reaching repercussions to the quality of our life. We can live the illusion that there is no God, respectively come to believe the delusion that "I am God the Supreme Master of the Universe".

Both mistakes have the same origin; they are made for the very same reason: It is the desire to play God. To rule over the world, or at least a big chunk of it, the bigger the better. To rule or dominate other people, and be in charge. Control things, situations, all eventualities.

To force our will and way. Make it happen. At the time we want it to happen.

Essentially, the desire to play God is the primary cause of all trouble in the world - whether we do it for totally selfish or mostly altruistic reasons doesn't really matter all that much. Plenty of initially benevolent or pious rulers ended up making a huge mess even though they originally may have had good intentions. At least in their own mind and assessment…

"Power tends to corrupt, and absolute power corrupts absolutely. Great men are almost always bad men." Lord Acton [33]

The quest (or lust) for power, domination and supremacy over people and things, circumstances and time, comes in many shapes and forms. From the very subtle to the very obvious. We all have the tendency wanting to be in charge - to various degrees, which often depends on our age and stage in life. Some of us get to do it in more prominent positions of power and prestige while most try to exert control over their immediate circumstances and circles only.

We learn from an early age that we need to become a winner in order to lead a successful and happy life. Nobody wants to be a loser so we have started to also jostle and fight, to compete and dominate, rather than trying to cooperate or 'live and let live' in peace and harmony.

We also learn that to surrender means to give up in defeat. So it's the worst thing we could possibly do, according to the materialistic and mechanical point of looking at life. It's for the meek and weak only. Winner types never surrender. At worst they will battle to a draw, both sides all bloody but unbowed. The status quo has prevailed, but at least nobody got to have an advantage over the other. But of course, to 'achieve' that nothing has changed, many people still had to die 'the hard way' or got to live on permanently bruised and battered.

Of all the various battles I have witnessed, read or heard about, there was rarely a truly happy outcome for either side. And that includes our modern day battles in court where even eventual winners ended up doing so only at huge costs, including to their health and happiness.

Effectively, they were not really winners either. They were just 'lesser losers'!

Trying to always be in charge of every aspect of one's life is a most tiring affair. Trying to micro-manage it all takes a lot of our mind space, time and energy and usually ends up in disappointment and burn-outs anyway. Sooner or later. It's neither a happy nor a particularly smart way to go through life.

To surrender doesn't mean to be weak (or to not say what we want, or to not speak up), but to yield oneself to the influence, power and wisdom of God, the ultimate source of it all. We really don't need to always be 'in charge of it', desperately trying to force our will and way. The universe works entirely in a self-organizing and self-correcting way. There is order even if some people only perceive chaos and disorder.

When we fully surrender to God we either completely trust him already, or we learn it once again because we are so desperate that we have simply no place else to turn to. Say in a life and death situation when absolutely nobody else could possibly help us. Or in otherwise very dire circumstances that force us to go 'back to our roots'.

Originally, while awaiting birth in our mother's womb, we fully trusted God, while being immersed in his divine love. Some may question that, yet no one can deny that at the latest as new-born babies we already (automatically) know how to trust. We simply do so as it is inborn in all of us. Nobody has ever refused their mother's milk. Or first asked where the milk actually came from and whether it is organic or not.

These are things we only learn later in life. To become distrusting, skeptical, or worse, cynical. We learn it from our parents, teachers, friends and colleagues, or simply as a result of our own lifestyle while feeling disconnected in heart and mind. Indeed, that's also how we learn to distrust God. We take our 'educated' adult mind and project our growing distrust in people onto God, the very source of it all.

Suddenly in life we have started to look for reasons or events to confirm this distrust rather than wanting to experience the daily proof of his ever-loving and supporting presence.

Focus on divine love, say what you want, do your best and forget the rest. Surrender the situation to God once you have done what you could do. We only need to do the best we can at any given moment or situation. And sometimes it means to do nothing at all and to simply let things be in God's able hands.

Love, let it be, and see.

To really be letting go of the urge to control and dominate also includes subtle ways like 'magical' stuff. Using our mental powers to get what we want. Like visualizing things day in and day out. That is all work and unnecessary because what we desire is known to the All-knowing and All-powerful anyway. If we can let things go and surrender in love, things have the chance to actually turn out even better than *we* have imagined. Because God knows it all and best.

"Trust in the Lord with all your heart, and do not lean on your own understanding. In all your ways submit to him, and he will make straight your paths." (Proverbs 3:5-6)

To surrender and be fully trusting is a rather relaxed way to go through life and yes, it's the happy way too! It's the art of letting go and being merry in the flow.

Of course, at times we try to force things. Particularly in my younger years I have often run against brick walls to get my way. Again and again. In a "It's my way or the highway" kind of approach to life. And often it did actually work, but it always came at a rather steep price. It could literally mean to pay a lot more than I would have had to pay otherwise. Or it ended up causing all kinds of other trouble, friction or exhaustion. In short, it was the opposite of smooth 'sailing'...

"It was pride that changed angels into devils; it is humility that makes men as angels." Saint Augustine

Dying is the ultimate form of surrendering, letting go of our body and earthly life, all the people and things we hold dear while here. We don't know when, where and how it will be happening, but we do know that it *will* happen one day, sooner or later.

Letting go of aches and pain and disease, becoming again at ease, is also a form of surrendering, to the all knowing and all loving healing energies that pervade everything everywhere. Including every atom and molecule within our bodies.

We can also surrender our past regrets, sorrows and pain to God, knowing that it somehow served a purpose, even though we may initially not know the reasons why. But we can come to understand them if we really wanted to… Because living in love means to be able to understand. When we love God and ourselves while looking back in time we will surely gain a much deeper perspective of things.

That will help us to let go of any anger we may direct at both known and unknown people. And to surrender our dislike, disgust or disapproval of their mistakes, shortcomings or transgressions. With love in our hearts and peace on our minds we will come to realize that all that has happened was necessary for us to grow and become the person we are now.

Surrendering also means to (be able to) hand over our current problems to God, to submit them to his intelligence and grace. We may still have to do some work, but we will know exactly *what* to do, where and how. Somehow or another it will be revealed to us. That may happen as an internal 'spark of genius' that suddenly arises on our mind. Or via external events or sources of news, information and knowledge that will clearly illuminate the way to go forward.

When we truly surrender a problem or situation to God we will also know *when* to do it. Much about success and happiness in life depends on perfect timing. Some people are so good at letting go and going with the flow of the universe that all seems to miraculously happen at the right time, seemingly effortlessly.

That indeed is an art and the act of surrendering will allow it to happen. Some of us are already naturally good at this while others may need to practice it. Because they are very much inclined or accustomed to wanting to always be in charge, and thus they resist the natural order and flow of energy and time.

But even if we have missed one particular opportunity as it approached and passed us by without us seizing it, there will always be new chances and opportunities to come along. Not the exact same ones but something that will nevertheless be for our best. Life is very forgiving and good because God is.

There is never the need for hurry or haste, worry or fear when we surrender the will to control the timing of everything. Yes, we can make plans to the best of our abilities, but thereafter it is simply best to let it go and happen at the right time. And be open-minded, even welcoming, about the sweet surprises awaiting next. Knowing that all really does happen at the right time.

When we surrender we can feel the perfect timing of every moment unfolding exactly as it should. It will help us to enjoy the perfection of every single moment. One at a time. Savor the ever-present *Now*, as it is always now. Time is relative and one moment eternally flows to the next. And as discussed in chapter *Appreciate*, there is always something good, sweet and happy going on, even though that may not be obvious to the skeptic, a cynic, or seen with untrained or overly critical eyes.

The antonym or opposite of the word 'struggle' is surrender… A lot of people struggle through life, and while that is understandable when we consider the various pressures of a generally fast-paced, even hectic, modern life, it is not really necessary to (agree to) live like that. Struggle is not prescribed by God, or worse, ordered. We can choose. Even if it doesn't look like it at first, say in the heat of a particularly tough moment.

We don't need to participate in a life of struggle when we realize that we can opt out of the stressful parts. At least to a large degree. When we learn to turn over and relinquish our will to control it all to the all-knowing and loving, we also part with much of the sorrows and pain. When we entrust the finding of the solutions to our problems to God we will come to know them too. And often our problems seem to somehow simply fade away. They disappear as they serve no further purpose.

"We can only learn to know ourselves and do what we can - namely, surrender our will and fulfill God's will in us." Saint Teresa of Avila

To surrender also means to waive and discard the urge to control or manipulate people. We all have been given free will (see also chapter *Respect*) and we need to respect each other's right to choose. For our own sake. Even God does it. Besides, we cannot really change people. No matter how hard we try. People are simply unpredictable. We often do the unexpected. Even powerful corporate or political leaders experience this fact of life, perhaps (or probably) to their utter frustration.

"The north wind and the sun were disputing which was the stronger, and agreed to acknowledge as the victor whichever of them could strip a traveler of his clothing. The wind tried first. But its violent gusts only made the man hold his clothes tightly around him, and when it blew harder still the cold made him so uncomfortable that he put on an extra wrap. Eventually the wind got tired of it and handed him over to the sun.

The sun shone first with moderate warmth, which made the man take off his topcoat. Then it blazed fiercely, till, unable to stand the heat, he stripped and went off to a bathe in a nearby river. Persuasion is more effective than force." Aesop [34]

We people only really change when we are ready and willing to change. Once we are fully convinced and have thus changed our beliefs. But that often only happens when we really *have* to change, out of pure necessity. Or when we really want to.

We can't change people's thoughts, feelings or behavior by force. Sometimes it may work for a little while by way of manipulation or misinformation. Persuasion works somewhat better, but if we agree with someone or something only on the mental level of our being, it will not last either. Only real personal experience makes us truly change our beliefs and behavior.

"Setting an example is not the main means of influencing others; it is the only means." Albert Einstein [35]

When we accept people as they are, we accept what cannot be changed anyway. We will have surrendered the urge to be in charge. We can now live and let live. Others will feel our sincere unconditional acceptance and that simply works wonders with our getting along nicely with people. Instead of potential conflict and trouble we will have gained a solid base to work and play together in both productive and pleasant ways.

All is or will be well when we surrender in love and with trust. The more we do, the more we will be taken care of. It is a bit like the helpless child that is looking up to his or her mother with very loving and asking eyes, while a second child is going out into the world to chase his fortune, all determined, perhaps to the point of being a bit stubborn and proud. And perhaps too proud to ask his friends for help, not to speak of asking God.

Whenever we are able to fully surrender we will also become easily aware of our *eternal reality* (see also chapters *Love your Self* and *Be your Self*). In the act of surrendering we let go of our limited minds and meddlesome egos and yield to the all-loving and healing presence of God. And thereby *we are aligning our true desires and wishes with who we really are* and with all that is truly beneficial for us.

The ability to surrender is like taking a shortcut that avoids lots of unnecessary trials and tribulations. It is a humble yet merry way to go through the adventure we call life.

"There is something in humility which strangely exalts the heart." Saint Augustine

REALIZATIONS:

The world is good and getting even better

I accept people as they are

Everything happens at the right time

I love to surrender in love

Hope

Surrender is the passive principle to a successful and happy life, and hope is the corresponding active part.

Perhaps the most negative word respectively mindset in the world is 'hopeless'. And incidentally it is a word I have often heard from the very depressed; they frequently use that term in discussions. They even use it to describe themselves.

But when there is no hope, there is not much of a life left either… No hope, no future. But usually, plenty of anger…

"Hope is being able to see that there is light despite all of the darkness." Desmond Tutu [36]

Through hope we express our heartfelt desires in a humble way. It is a gentle way of asking for a desired outcome. Hoping is very different from expecting.

When we expect to receive or achieve something very specific, and possibly at a very specific time, we are setting ourselves up for disappointment. And the corresponding anger that follows.

Anger kills joy instantly. We can't be both happy and angry at the same time, no matter how hard we try. When we are angry we frown instead of smile, we scream instead of laugh, we feel tense instead of relaxed, we have a higher instead of lower blood pressure. And so on.

People are generally not attracted to angry people, even if their anger is righteous or justified. Because there is (d)anger in the air. And because it reminds us of our own sub-conscious anger potential that could become activated at any moment, robbing us of our peace of mind, vitality, and joy.

There seems to be no lack of anger in today's world. And that could very well be the understatement of the year, even decade. When we read or watch the news we can witness anger all the time. We get to hear about crazy or atrocious incidents that are mostly if not always a by-product of anger.

Growing anger is so prevalent today that even the very rich and famous are affected. They seemingly lack of nothing. They live a life of comfort and luxury most people can only glimpse in a movie. Their every desires and whims are taken care of instantly by a little army of people. And yet we can witness their outbursts of uncontrollable anger in public appearances, events or Tweets. [37]

How come? From a broader perspective it is simply this: The more we individually, and collectively as a society, distance ourselves from our spiritual heritage, the emptier we will feel - despite the external goodies and pampering we may be able to enjoy. In other words, we are running our lives on flat batteries. Thereby we are not fulfilled at the very core of who we really are. And no material matter or 'stuff' can possibly satisfy this spiritual hunger. Fighting and competing for approval and other forms of trying to receive subtle energies subsequently serve as substitutes…

Not being happy within leaves a vacuum that will be filled by the demanding and angry outbursts of the insecure ego.

Another way to understand this seemingly growing anger in the world is that we simply have too many unfulfilled expectations. At first we are mentally and emotionally attached to something, or somebody, some situations or outcomes. We have certain very firm expectations. And those are very often not fulfilled. Thereby, our expectations are replaced by disappointment. And that in turn will lead us to become angry.

To have very specific and firm expectations is a disastrous recipe for happiness as disappointments are programmed in from the very beginning. And particularly so if we let them in turn affect our relationship with God. A great many people have turned away from God simply because of their disappointment in not having their prayers answered the way they demanded and expected:

Jesus answered him, "It is also written: Do not test the Lord your God." (Matthew 4:7)

Some philosophies recommend that we simply don't get attached to things, or people… but that is a difficult (impractical and perhaps a bit cold) proposition for most. A better way is to follow in the footsteps of Jesus and his first commandment. Once we do that and direct our love first and foremost towards God, we will have a very solid foundation. It is the ultimate and all-encompassing form of attachment.

A disappointment about a small earthly matter will simply not be able to shake our core as we will still have our thorough and utter attachment to God and all the peace and joy that comes with it. All we can imagine and much more is contained within God.

When we *love, hope, and surrender*, we will never really feel disappointed. Because there is always hope. By default it always continues. 'Hope springs eternal'. And it is flexible. Our hopes may revise and adjust with the changes that are happening every moment and every day; the inevitable changes that are part of life itself.

And because hope is always positive and optimistic, if something doesn't turn out the way we have hoped for, we just know and trust that there is actually something even better awaiting us!

Or we get to realize that our desire was perhaps not really for our very best, in accordance to the big picture view of our life's goals. Maybe we went down the wrong track and wished for something that would have been very much to our detriment. And by not fulfilling such a desire we were actually protected for our own good.

"Be careful what you wish for, for you may get it." Proverb

"We would often be sorry if our wishes were gratified" Aesop

To fully and absolutely expect something to happen is both a bit arrogant and aggressive. We are demanding that our will and way will be happening, without concern for anything or anybody else.

To demand and expect certain things from God, is neither our place nor function. Yes, we can make the argument that we are also parts and parcels of God and his creation, but we are just one of many minute parts. We are in the position of servants rather than masters, even if that is hard to swallow for an ego-dominated mind that sees itself as the center of the universe and relegates God to the status of a mail order service.

And likewise, when we expect others to do or give things according to our expectations, we are disrespectful of their freedom to choose. We can ask people nicely but in the end it is up to them to make their decisions the way they see fit. To always expect a lot of specific things or behavior from others simply means to set ourselves up for plenty of disappointments in life.

To hope is neither aggressive nor arrogant. It is a both humble and loving way to ask, to express a desired outcome. Without firmly and absolutely expecting things to go exactly our way, no matter who or what might get hurt or disadvantaged.

Hope is the realization that we people can make all kinds of plans, but we cannot control the outcome of our plans. It is the realization that we are not the supreme intelligence and instead, let ourselves be guided by the wisdom and grace of the ultimate divine presence.

"For man proposes, but God disposes" Thomas à Kempis [38]

Saying, *"Father, if you are willing, take this cup from me; yet not my will, but yours be done."* (Luke 22:42)

Hope allows us to *keep taking inspired action*, rather than just sitting back, relaxing but expecting things to happen automatically. And if they don't, to feel disappointed, perhaps to the point of feeling depressed.

"A man's heart deviseth his way: but the Lord directeth his steps." (Proverbs 16:9)

We can express our hopes and desires in either a more positive or negative way. It is better to hope in a positive and precise way than being vague or negative. The issue is not about 'not confusing God' since he is the supreme intelligence and knows all of our desires anyway - no matter if or how we express them.

The point of expressing ourselves in a positive and powerful manner is that it simply feels better. Because it contains more hope! By definition, positivity is an inherent part and parcel of hope.

So it is more uplifting for us to say what we *do* want, with love and trust, than to say what we *don't* want, with anger or disgust. In other words, we come to solely (or mostly) *focus on the solutions*, and not the problems. With a bit of practice we can actually become so good at this that we hardly (or ever) even think about 'the dark side' of life. We are simply too busy to see the world of lights through the eyes of love, with hope and peace on our mind.

"I hope to pass the exam!" or, "I hope I'm not going to fail the exam."

"I hope you will quickly recover!" or, "I hope you don't feel sick anymore."

"I hope they will get along nicely!" or, "I hope they will stop fighting."

"I hope for peace!" or, "I hope there is no more war."

Whenever we say "Stop war", we are fighting *against* something. But when we say "We love peace", we are quietly hoping and asking for something, in this case re-affirming and strengthening our desire *for* peace. We don't even talk about war, we just focus on peace and all the good that comes with it.

"I hope to see more love, peace and happiness in the world." or, "I hope to see less war, hatred and injustice in the world".

"I was once asked why I don't participate in anti-war demonstrations. I said that I will never do that, but as soon as you have a pro-peace rally, I'll be there." Mother Teresa

Anytime we are against something, no matter who or what it may be, we need to invest and display a bit of anger in order to be heard and (try to) make an impact. The anger is an important part of the picture, of the *complaining*.

But as we learn to always feel love within we automatically see what is good and just for all. There is no need to first complain or feel angry as we see the light that illuminates the best solutions. Love and the understanding that comes with it always harbors better ideas than any derived from anger and hate (not to speak of the associated problems like frustrations, high blood pressure, or worse).

"Hope is like the sun, which, as we journey toward it, casts the shadow of our burden behind us." Samuel Smiles [39]

"May the God of hope fill you with all joy and peace as you believe in him, so that you may overflow with hope by the power of the Holy Spirit." (Romans 15:13)

In conclusion, the merry way of life is to always:

Love, say what you want, do what you can, hope for the best, and surrender the rest.

"Hope is the thing with feathers

That perches in the soul

And sings the tune without the words

And never stops at all."

Emily Dickinson [40]

REALIZATIONS:

I love to feel hopeful

I love to hope for the best

I like to love, hope, and surrender

Breathe

This may sound easy and it is. Yet most of us 'forget' to breathe at times. Some forget to breath properly all the time. And instead it 'happens' only sporadically in a rather superficial and shallow way.

Breathing can be both an automatic or conscious process. We need to be more aware of it because it will help us to feel much better and therefore a lot happier.

When we breathe deeply, all relaxed, and feel in harmony with the happenings of the outside-world, our bodies are not only getting enough oxygen, but the lymph system is working better as well, helping to eliminate waste products and improving our health. Our breath is acting a bit like a big pump that helps us to be 'in the flow' of life, the rhythm of the universe.

Our breath is a real-life indicator of what's going right or wrong in our daily life, every moment at a time.

Whenever we feel anxious, nervous or stressed out, our breathing tends to momentarily stop. Notice it. And likewise, when we're worried, sad or depressed. Being fearful or afraid is not very helpful either, at least until it's a life-threatening situation where our 'auto-pilot' kicks in and the accompanying adrenaline rush will accelerate our breathing, ready for the fight-or-flight response (but even then some may experience the 'frozen-deer-in-headlights syndrome' that blocks their breathing too and prevents taking proper action).

Deep breathing in harmony is crucially important for both our physical and mental well-being. It is a side-effect of being in tune with God and the Universe. So any time you feel a bit tense for whatever reasons, notice the blockage and make a deliberate effort to re-start the natural breathing process.

One way to do that is to *focus for a while only on fully exhaling*. Don't even think about inhaling as that is bound to happen anyway. Just keep your focus on the exhaling part, push out the air completely and all the way while at the same time letting go of whatever bothers you. Stress, tensions, problems, pain, negativity. Exhale and let it go. Surrender and connect. Keep going until you feel again at ease and peace.

And The Happy Rabbit Says...

"Exhale and dismiss all negative thoughts - while deeply inhaling, focus only on happy stuff!"

Here's another 'first-aid' measure that helps if you feel 'totally stressed out': Hyperventilate or 'over-breathe' for a little while, until you feel the clearing away of the negative thoughts and emotions that are causing the temporary blocking of your breathing.

Breathe much deeper and faster than normal. Try to not think about anything except the breathing in and out as fast and as deep as you feel comfortable. Do this until you start to calm down, for as long as it feels like giving relief.

But stop it at the latest if you start to feel a bit light-headed! This is nothing to really worry about; it is caused by the reduction of the carbon dioxide concentration of the blood below its normal level. It makes the blood more alkaline by raising its pH value, and constricts the blood vessels that supply the brain with oxygen and other molecules. In a way, it quite literally shuts up our anxious and over-active mind.

If you have the time and privacy, pray or meditate for a few moments. Contemplate on what's really important in your life, the big picture. Enter into loving union and exchange with God. Surrender. All worries, sorrows or stress will melt away and our natural deep breathing will resume, relaxing our body and mind once again. And bring back at least a little smile on our lips.

Let me share here one full-body breathing exercise from my first book. This is how we should always breathe! It is how all mammals breathe when they feel safe, relaxed and happy. And it is a way of breathing many of us have forgotten as we rush and run around in our daily lives. Try to breathe again like this throughout the day. It will help you to relax and feel more energized.

At first, a good time to practice deep breathing is before sleeping at night and right after waking up:

Sit or lay down in a comfortable position, close your eyes and concentrate on your breathing. Breathe out naturally and completely, then wait until you feel the strong instinctive urge to inhale. It's a bit like an ignition spark that fires up. While inhaling, the stomach area should lift up first, then the ribs area and finally the chest area. Hold your breath for a little while, and when you feel like exhaling, do it once again in the same order. The stomach area deflates first, followed by the ribs and chest area. Keep it going in the same order.

The more relaxed our breathing becomes, the deeper it will get while the rhythm will slow down ever more. Watch your thoughts just like watching a movie, as if they were not really yours, and keep concentrating on your breathing. As it becomes slower and deeper, less and less thoughts will go through your mind.

Enjoy feeling great and all relaxed, comfortable and secure. Feel loved. Hope for the best. And surrender the rest. Ask questions and feel the answers. At night, fall asleep and wake up completely refreshed. In the morning, feel inspired, focus on the important events to come, get up and greet the day with a merry smile!

And The Happy Rabbit Says...

"Massage your palms, temples and neck several times today - and remember to breathe!"

Here's another breathing technique that you can do pretty much anytime and anywhere during the day, while sitting at your desk. Make sure you're sitting in an upright position, with a straight back, head and shoulders, yet feeling as relaxed as possible. Let your elbows comfortably rest on your desk. And close your eyes.

Now cover your right nostril with your right thumb, and inhale deeply through your left nostril.

Then cover your left nostril with your left thumb and exhale completely through your right nostril.

In the same position inhale deeply through your right nostril. Then cover your right nostril again with your right thumb and exhale through your left nostril. In the same position inhale through your left nostril. Then switch thumbs again to exhale though your right nostril. And again, inhale through your right nostril, switch thumbs to again exhale through your left nostril. Keep going - once inhaling and once exhaling through the same nostril before switching sides - for as long as you feel good, respectively have the time.

While breathing, connect and contemplate, pray and meditate. You will feel your thoughts slow down and a deep relaxing calmness spread throughout as both sides of your body and brain balance and align itself in perfect harmony.

And if you feel like experimenting a bit, try the following mental exercise in addition to the above. If appropriate it's good to take off your shoes (best would be to do this with naked feet on natural grounds). Imagine a strong connection from your hips going downwards to your thighs, knees and through your feet, extending your body all the way to the very center of the Earth, while at the same time feel the crown of your head stretching (like being gently pulled by a strand of hair) upwards to connect with the heavens above.

This anchoring or grounding exercise is particularly helpful for very sensitive and highly emphatic people [41] who overly feel and connect with the sorrows and pain of others. It's an easy way to release any external or homemade stress and tensions, let go of negativity and aggravations, clear the mind, and connect the heart with love and trust.

And whenever you're ready to get going again, gently withdraw and center yourself e.g. by folding and tightly pressing your palms together in front of your heart, focus on the next task, smile, open your eyes, and go for it with renewed joy, peace and strength!

REALIZATIONS:

I love to breathe calmly

I love to breathe deeply

Stay Kind

There are always people who mistake kindness for weakness. This is not surprising in a world that strongly distinguishes between winners and losers. Almost instinctively we have come to worship money, power and fame. And in the end it doesn't matter all that much how the fortune and fame was acquired. Only results seem to count in today's society.

It is therefore not surprising that a great many people live their lives akin to a game of football or a match of rugby. Fast, tough and ruthless. Even merciless. (Some sections of) 'The elite' likes to reassure themselves with the slogan "There's a sucker born every minute" [42]. They think that it's perfectly alright to take advantage of the sheep in the world, the naive, the lesser educated, or 'unwashed' masses of people.

According to some of the 'winners' I listened to it is noble, even necessary, to exploit the dumb or weak and meek so as to teach them a valuable lesson in life. To keep them in their places. And to perhaps also come to understand that the big fish always eats the smaller fish. And in a Darwinian society of 'eat or get eaten', it's better to be the one who's doing the killing. The cheating, ripping off, lying, and so on. So come to learn and join the winners too, if you can… is their logic.

"He that is kind is free, though he is a slave; he that is evil is a slave, though he be a king." Saint Augustine

Despite their great wealth I have not come across much if any happiness in such circles. A strong belief of superiority is needed to be able to have the arrogant and condescending attitude that allows one to be a predator. It's a lonely life of ego, that is only occasionally, reluctantly or suspiciously shared with other equally lonely wolves at the top of the food chain.

We can come to understand that ultimately, arrogance is 'only' a sign of masked insecurity and weakness by a cut-off and separated ego in a constant and more or less desperate fight for survival. All alone, against everyone, in a tough world full of bad people... So they feel the need to become equally bad or hardened up in order to protect themselves and to *survive* a keyword for every insecure ego.

The big catch is only that such a mindset and lifestyle is hard to bear for the real persons we really are - the eternal spiritual self (or soul) that has been pushed aside and neglected, often for a lifetime. Alcohol and drug abuse, loneliness and depression is usually the result. Their accumulated wealth may buy them some temporary physical comfort and external relief, but their hearts are crying out for real love (not the fake one money buys), true happiness and genuine peace of mind.

In my experience it is better to be happy with the fellow 'sheeple' than to fight or mingle with lonely wolves. It is smarter to laugh and joyfully work together than to struggle and viciously compete to the usually bitter end.

"A crust eaten in peace is better than a banquet partaken in anxiety." Aesop

It is wiser to emphasize cooperation and collaboration over competition and fighting. Maybe (but only maybe) one will thus get only a smaller piece of the cake, but that is still a happier and healthier proposition than having the whole cake and eat it all alone in misery, somewhere tucked away in a big house behind big walls - perhaps fearing the big bad wolves that might come and get them.

It is also far smarter to be kind - instead of 'giving back in kind'. Kindness attracts kindness, while the ruthless plant seeds of unpleasant things to come - for them. There will always be a stronger, faster or more ruthless guy to challenge them. If it doesn't happen while one is young and strong, it will happen when one gets older and weaker.

Stay kind even if others speak or act unkind. Mostly we don't know their situation or reasons why, but it safe to assume that in almost all cases their being unkind has absolutely nothing to do with us. It is their own thing. Some people easily take things personally, but they very rarely are. Always keep it kind - never take it personally, and never make it personal either.

And The Happy Rabbit Says…

"Nobody can really make you feel bad unless you agree with it - so don't do it and stay happy!"

Another thing I've learnt (the rather hard way…) is to never burn bridges. We might want or need to cross them once again, perhaps to finish some unfinished business we may have. Otherwise, a similar person or situation will come up in the future to remind and help us to (finally) learn what we need to learn.

The merry way is to always stay kind and keep the doors open. Never say never.

"Be kind to one another, tenderhearted, forgiving one another, as God in Christ forgave you." (Ephesians 4:31)

Being kind doesn't take any effort because it is a natural part of who we really are. It is the masking of our kindness behind a poker face of cold indifference that takes the *real* effort. Being cold and ruthless requires a constant fight against one's true nature - even if we are not fully aware of that fact. And that is simply not a happy affair!

Being unreal takes a lot of energy. First, to build an often elaborate illusion (or delusion) that is able to convince both one's own ego and the minds of others. And secondly, in order to sustain a purely mental and thereby fake construct, one has to live in the energy-deficient and lonely desert of 'ego country' instead of being perpetually invigorated by being real and living in God's infinite universe of ever replenishing strength and joy.

"But the fruit of the Spirit is love, joy, peace, patience, kindness, goodness, faithfulness" (Galatians 5:22)

Kindness is an expression of real strength simply because it is an inherent feature of every loving and lovable soul. As such it is better to let it shine than to suppress it by fearing the reactions of the presently tough and unkind, the seemingly strong and powerful.

In traditional Chinese philosophy water is always considered to be stronger than a rock. Over time water will erode even the hardest coastlines or turn a rough stone into a nicely rounded pebble. Soft but persistent power will ultimately prevail over the hard and strong, as unlikely as this may seem at first.

Hanns-Joachim Gottlob Scharff, called the "Master Interrogator" of the German Luftwaffe during the Second World War, was highly successful with his interrogation techniques that essentially was all about being kind. [43]

He never used torture or other physical means to obtain the required information. Instead he was friendly and kind, cracked jokes, took prisoners for walks in the forest, shared homemade foods or even the occasional beer and Schnapps. He respected their rank, was polite and compassionate, and always treated everyone as fellow human beings, regardless of their official enemy status.

In contrast, numerous studies have meanwhile confirmed that the worst results were obtained whenever interrogators were sarcastic, arrogant or otherwise disrespectful and demeaning to their prisoners of war. Kindness simply works wonders in even the most unlikely of situations!

From time to time we may still come across some unkind people, doing or saying unkind things. But the more we live in the world of love, the less that will happen. Occasionally, when it does happen, it will remind us of both the contrast *and* the remedy. It will reinforce what we already know, and may have forgotten for a moment or two. Being kind to others reminds them too of what they have learned to push aside, perhaps for a very long time.

Also, true kindness generally makes it much harder for others to be mean or otherwise do the wrong things. And yet, there are people with a predatory mindset out there and we need to always be aware and mindful what is happening around us.

When we meet and greet people for the first (few) time(s), it is wise to read and feel their current energy. To know where they come from at that given moment; their current state of heart and mind. It is not a judging and condemning with a critical mind, it is simply a feeling and acknowledging of someone's actual reality (of awareness). With love and respect and detachment, all at the same time.

Here's why: You can spiritually love a lion with all your heart, yet to go out and hug an actual lion is still not a great idea. It is better to love and admire the lion from a safe distance because, while it may share and respond to your love, it may also mistake your affection for an invitation to lunch - with you as the main course, that is.

Likewise, an otherwise calm and nice person may suddenly and for all kinds of reasons become totally drunk and/or high on some crazy drugs (like crystal meth, crack cocaine, 'bath salts', even prescription drugs), and temporarily be totally out of their mind, aggressive and violent. When we read 'Live' backwards it turns out to be 'Evil'… In the absence of love there is potentially anger and the corresponding danger.

Not every soul in a human body has (at all times) a truly human (or more advanced) consciousness. We all have the full spectrum of consciousness available to us, to explore and choose from. Some people are always aware of this fact and others not quite yet. Some make mostly very conscious choices in their lives whiles others often (re)act in more basic (or primitive) ways, without being fully aware of the implications of their actions.

But even very good people sometimes do bad things, under certain circumstances. Just like the very bad can do very good at times.

Most people both remember and respond to kindness. To generally assume the best in others is a merry way to go through life. And yes, there are times when the basic trust we freely give is getting abused. It has happened to me a number of times, and yes, it is a painful experience. But allow me to share here a word of wisdom of my dear father-in-law, one that I wholeheartedly agree with:

"I prefer to be cheated than to do the cheating." Kosaku Yamaguchi (1937 - 1998)

He got also cheated for a lot of money, several times, and yet he didn't change his ways and stayed true to his always kind and honorable strong self.

One simply feels better about oneself during the day, and sleeps very well at night!

Besides simultaneously maintaining an open heart and mind, it is best to also have open eyes and see things how they actually are at any given moment in time. And to therefore be able to recognize the 'wolf that hides in sheep's clothing'…

"Beware of false prophets, which come to you in sheep's clothing, but inwardly they are ravening wolves" (Matthew 7:15)

So sometimes it is necessary - in all kindness yet firmness - to say 'No' to people. To walk or stay away. Be a bit distant and less available. Otherwise busy. And to love and hug them from a distance. Love yields kindness, but it should never be of the naive kind that could potentially be endangering our own (physical) life and well-being. Speak softly but do carry a big stick. And use it if really need be. Be kind but of 'the strong kind'.

It is important to be fully aware of our surroundings. And to be prepared for eventualities. To feel and read energy - the energy of people, objects, and even places - at any given moment. The more we feel love within and apply it in everything we do in the external world, the quicker we learn to once again use this inborn intuitive ability. Continually without fail and error; it is a natural part of life to feel and know the truth.

These days we can often see people walking around totally absorbed in their digital devices while walking around, crossing streets and so on. They are obviously oblivious to what's happening around them, in the 'real world'. And that is potentially dangerous. My wife and I were spared more than a few times thanks to listening to the warnings within and thereafter paying close attention to our environment (e.g.

we had very close encounters with deadly snakes, an attacking crocodile, and more).

Intuition, or tuition from within (the Latin verb 'intueri' means 'to view'), is natural to anyone who really cares to know and understand. We don't need to learn it. All we need to do is take the time to ask and listen within. Inspiration, or 'in spirit' is also a result of being 'in tune', united in love with God and his creation. And suddenly, there is this great idea that simply pops up in our mind…

At any given moment in life we can and should distinguish, discern and discriminate. Not in the negative sense of fault-finding but in the positive spirit of choosing what is truly valuable and important for us. In the current here and now, while keeping the big picture in mind at the same time. The being aware of who we really are (see also chapter *Be your Self*). The pursuit of our true passion and purpose. The focus on what we have come to experience, learn and do.

We simply can't please every one, even if we tried to. Please God by following his desire, as expressed by Jesus in his first two commandments. And live happily ever after as all else will fall into its right place. Easily and naturally. And chances are very good that such a lifestyle will ultimately come to please all the people in our immediate life as well.

And The Happy Rabbit Says…

"Be truly kind to yourself - in all regards - and include as many people as you can!"

Some may witness our acts of kindness but nevertheless accuse us of having ulterior and selfish motives. They usually are the very same people who want us to change *our* ways to please *their* way… and yet *they* are so very quick to call *others* 'selfish'!

So no matter what, be kind anyway because ultimately you are doing it for yourself. Firstly, we are all connected, far more so than we sometimes realize. And, we too want to live in a kinder world. And being kind is our contribution to make it so. More and more.

Besides, when we are kind we cannot help but feel both good and merry; and that is our instant and just reward. Savor it and smile!

"Never lose a chance of saying a kind word." William Thackeray [44]

"We think sometimes that poverty is only being hungry, naked and homeless. The poverty of being unwanted, unloved and uncared for is the greatest poverty. We must start in our own homes to remedy this kind of poverty." Mother Teresa

REALIZATIONS:

I love to be kind

I love to learn

I love to grow

Mind your Mind

Our mind can be a wonderful friend and ally in our life, or a formidable opponent and foe. A calm and sharp mind will help to bring us more peace, joy and success while a scattered and confused mind can bring about plenty of mayhem. Trouble like anxiety, nervousness, fear, frustration, and depression to various degrees.

The good news is that we ourselves can decide what we want our mind to be - once we have become fully aware that we *can* choose. Once we know that we, the spiritual soul or self, can control and direct our mind - via our willpower and intelligence (see also chapter *Be your Self*) - and thus how we think and feel.

Through prayer, meditation and contemplation we can learn to get into the habit of watching and observing our mind just like a remote viewer looks at the whiter or darker clouds drifting by in the distant sky, all the while staying completely calm and unaffected.

We are not our mind and neither are we our thoughts. Thoughts come and go. And just like clouds they are sometimes very white and bright and at other times rather dark.

While observing our thoughts we can choose to indulge further in the ones we like. Following our pleasant thoughts will quite obviously make us feel happier than pursuing the sad or mad ones. It is our choice - once we are aware that we really can choose.

Psychologists define mindfulness as being aware of one's current experiences in a non-judgmental way. They recommend to become more mindful as part of their treatments. It's a modern-day confirmation of the age-old Christian wisdom of not falling into the trap of judging or blaming others.

A good way to hone this skill is to sit in a public place and do a bit of 'people-watching'. In some cultures and countries (like Italy) that is a particularly popular pastime. Just watch people and the world go by and *stay loving and happy, no matter what*. Regardless of people's different sense of style or fashion, their looks or demeanor, and so on.

Be accepting rather than judging. Complimenting instead of criticizing. Feeling humble and equal instead of condescending and superior (because of this or that, things we may observe).

At times that can be a rather challenging little exercise, yet we can learn to become very good at it. And to actually enjoy it! Besides, it's a relief not having to do anything for a while. *Being* rather than *doing*. To just live and let live. To lovingly surrender to every moment at a time. One by one. It is a form of 'real-world meditation', a way to clear and calm our minds. And be… well, merry!

Science has caught up with perennial philosophical and religious traditions and demonstrated in numerous studies that meditation is very effective to calm our often hyper-active modern minds. Even Wall Street bankers are now using meditation techniques in order to gain a competitive edge over fellow traders.

While there are myriad of ways to meditate and calm one's mind, there are also plenty of things in life to potentially disturb our peace of mind. Or worse, to get us off the right track and heading into the wrong direction.

There is a vast amount of information and knowledge available to us, and still, the sum total is growing incredibly fast every moment of every day. And likewise there are sheer endless numbers of our collective opinions and assorted beliefs 'out there'. There is seemingly nothing that doesn't exist in our thoughts and imaginations. Only a little fraction of it is comprehensible to us as an individual. And much more is simply beyond the fathomable.

One can argue forever about who is right or wrong. However, there is one irrefutable fact: Some beliefs make us happy and others don't. Some keep us well and healthy and others bring about only anger, sorrow or worse.

Some of the plethora of information, knowledge and beliefs we get exposed to is true, yet much of it is still incomplete, or completely wrong. Some truths are relative and change as we change our perspectives, learn more, or grow in our awareness. Yet there *are* truths that are absolutely absolute; they don't change no matter how we'd like them to, or how we twist and turn things around to suit our mindset, respectively the outcomes we desire.

One indisputable fact is that our minds are in a fallible state - no matter how hard that may be to admit. No matter how intelligent or knowledgeable we may think we are. We rarely know the full picture about much or anything at all. Smart people and true experts are fully aware that the more they know about any given subject, the more they realize how little they really know about it. They came to see how much there is yet to research, discover and understand…

"The whole problem with the world is that fools and fanatics are always so certain of themselves, but wiser people so full of doubts." Bertrand Russell [45]

Our mind is like a fine instrument or tool. And as such it needs to be looked after. Proper care includes giving it plenty of sleep and enough time out to rest and play. To contemplate and meditate. To admire, laugh and smile. And so on (see also chapters *Admire* and *Relax*).

Looking after our mind also means to protect it from harmful influence. There is a term in computer science, abbreviated 'GIGO': Garbage in - garbage out. [46] It stands for the fact that computers process input of nonsensical data without questioning it first… And that will result in the output of equally useless data.

With our human minds we do have the ability to discern and question input via our intelligence and by what we have learned and experienced so far in our respective lifetimes. And yet, even the sharpest mind will come to the wrong conclusions - or beliefs! - if the input given is incomplete, nonsensical, or plain wrong (for whatever reasons).

An already tired mind that is subject all day long to hearing (both actively and passively) commercial messages, hours of 'reality' TV that appeal mainly to our lower selves, playing violent or stupefying computer games, or simply watching lots of doomsday news padded with the latest directives on how we should think and feel about certain issues... well, all that has an effect on our mind, life and well being. Whether we like it or not, and even if we have deluded ourselves to think that we're so smart and 'above' such things.

Try to race cars on one of the latest computer games for an hour or two before going to bed and you will still see the game continuing in your mind, drawing your attention away from everything else. It can be rather difficult to switch it all off and peacefully fall asleep. Garbage in, garbage out...

With proper rest and sleep, and through reflection, meditation and prayer, we can somewhat digest and delete undesirable mental input and put it in the right perspective. But we should not make the mistake and think that what we put into our minds has no effect on our thoughts and feelings, our beliefs and behaviour. In other words, our life.

"The happiness of your life depends upon the quality of your thoughts; therefore guard accordingly." Marcus Aurelius [47]

Make your mind your friend and ally. Treat it nicely and protect it from nonsense and the like. Your mind is your personal treasure and as such it is solely your responsibility. If you let other people control what goes into your mind, it's just like giving a bunch of complete strangers the keys to your house - to come and go and do as they please.

It's a big world out there and there's a big competition going on for mind space - to own a piece of real estate on *your* mind. To find the 'soft spot' that will open the strings of your purse, or worse.

Corporations like to enter our minds with advertising messages with the obvious goal to sell us more of their goods and services. That countless billions of advertising dollars are spent is proof enough that it really works and that it makes us do things we would otherwise not do! Like, make us borrow money to buy things we don't really need in order to impress people we don't even know.

It is simply amazing how countless millions of people around the world have been persuaded to buy and drink caramel-colored carbonated water full of highly processed sugar (or worse, high fructose corn syrup) and other unsavory and unhealthy ingredients (like phosphoric acid - otherwise used as a rust remover). Advertising makes us believe that colas taste better than a cool glass of clean water that costs only a tiny fraction of the price.

Soda makers even claim that their products are great at quenching our thirsts even though sugary fizzy waters are actually dehydrating and depleting our bodies of both precious water and minerals. Besides wrecking havoc with our blood sugar levels, and so on.

Government agencies too like to own some real estate on our minds. And so do other organizations or people of all kinds, including friends and family. Give your mind some tender loving care, be discerning what you allow in, and you will ensure that the output will be to *your* liking and benefit.

The issue is far more important than simply about the matter of letting a company subtly decide what we like to eat or drink. When we give others control over what enters our minds, we allow them to not only influence our thoughts, but subsequently also how we feel. And it is our emotions that so often decide what we buy or what we do. Or don't (dare to) do. Ultimately it becomes a question of who is in charge of our happiness. Our health. And our wealth.

If you are convinced that you really really need that new Prada handbag or pair of Gucci shoes in order to be happy (or happier), you will not be satisfied until you actually buy these things. Essentially *it means to set a precondition* on our happiness. It is a purely self-imposed and thereby totally unnecessary limitation that only restricts us, or worse prevents us from feeling great in the here and now today.

It also means to have entered the realm of feeling needy instead of fulfilled. To experience lack versus enjoying abundance. Furthermore, we can thus be manipulated to become angry. Or to be jealous and envious. Or to judge and hate others. And obviously, such states of heart and mind are neither a happy affair nor are they pleasing to God. Very much the opposite.

Watch your thoughts; they become words.
Watch your words; they become actions.
Watch your actions; they become habits.
Watch your habits; they become character.
Watch your character; it becomes your destiny.
Lao-Tze [48]

Theological thoughts and religious matters have also occupied precious mind space, often in very detrimental ways to our health and happiness. Or even worse, to our longevity.

We people have discussed and argued about God for thousands of years. And all the squabbles have produced plenty of wars, tears and sorrows. We need to realize that such discussions are only happening on the mental level, and thereby they are not able to offer us any real insights or true understanding. Nor will they bring about more love as so forcefully requested by Jesus in his primary two commandments.

"On these two commandments depend all the law and the prophets." (Matthew 22:40)

Our beliefs can make or break us. Jesus is very clear: He wants us to love, and all will be well. Arguments and 'endless discussions' are neither required nor particularly welcome. Because after all, we are simply not just our minds or brains. And no matter how smart an individual mind may be, the spiritual world cannot be understood by the strength of our critical or analytical thinking alone. Spiritual truths must be felt within, beyond the world of mind.

Religion at its core is not about believing. It is about experiencing. Spiritual truths are either personally experienced, or not (yet). The word *religion* itself explains it very well when we look at one of its Latin roots: *re-ligare*, or *'to reconnect'* - i.e. re (again) + ligare (connect).

A connected and calm mind combined with a loving and caring heart will help us to discern, distinguish and differentiate between what is real and what is not, between what is truly important and what is not, between what is true and what is not. It allows us to see what is really beneficial in the big picture view of things, and to choose wisely in all aspects of life.

Only (feeling and tasting) love will be able to reveal the world of love. A mind that is illuminated by the divine love felt in our hearts is the key that will open the doors to the understanding of all spiritual *and* worldly realities. Love is the light that will dispel all darkness. It is the warmth that will melt all ice. Love is the understanding that will bring peace, justice, and happiness.

"The kingdom of God is within you" (Luke 17.21)

"When we are unable to find tranquility within ourselves, it is useless to seek it elsewhere." Francois de La Rochefoucauld [49]

God is love (1 John 4:8). So whenever we live in the absence of love, God is absent, and we are quite literally 'on our own'. The results of discussions or actions that are produced by such 'disconnected' souls cannot be very beneficial to anyone. Neither personally nor for our friends and family, or the world at large.

A mind 'enlightened' by love will present us with a firm anchor to go through life with ease and delight, with passion and purpose, with peace and power. Matters of the mind will become increasingly clear and comprehensible as we present them to the loving and guiding light within our hearts. And so will matters of this material realm.

"But the Counselor, the Holy Spirit, whom the Father will send in my name, will teach you all things and will remind you of everything I have said to you." (John 14:26)

As we live the ways of a merry Christian and become ever more joyful and settled in our spiritual understanding in the here and now, discussions and arguments about theoretical doctrine - about who is right and who is wrong - will not hold much attraction any longer. It's a bit like chewing gum that has lost its flavors after a short little while…

When we feel love and peace within, what is really left to argue about? Where is the need to do so?

Arguments are visible signs of a disconnected and insecure mind that prevent its owner both from experiencing divine bliss *and* discovering the many wonders of this material world. Insecurity and arrogance usually go hand in hand… Arrogance and other delusions of superiority are mindsets that only prevent the inflow of new or deeper knowledge, without offering gains of any kind.

My Wing Chun (kung fu) master or 'Sifu' (meaning 'fatherly teacher') used to put it this way: If you think your glass is full, nobody will pour you any water as it would only overflow, go to waste and make a mess. However, when you feel like your glass is empty, someone will surely want to fill your glass all the way to the top, thereby adding to your wisdom and knowledge.

In the same way, if someone (e.g. a scientist, scholar or clergyman) is very proud or outright arrogant about their accumulated knowledge and credentials, no one will bother to offer them any additional information or advice (not the least, God…). It would simply be uncalled for. Those who are actually more knowledgeable will most likely prefer to remain silent. And move on to happier pastures.

"Real knowledge is to know the extent of one's ignorance." Confucius [50]

"It is a thousand times better to have common sense without education than to have education without common sense." Robert Green Ingersoll [51]

Being humble is the key that opens the door that lets in more knowledge and wisdom of many kinds. Arrogance and pride are simply the outward symptoms of a separated mind whose owner has thereby limited it to slow or no progress. They are quite literally on their own.

"The larger the island of knowledge, the longer the shore line of wonder." Ralph W. Sockman [52]

Whenever we bathe our mind in love and light, it will become calm and clear. And thereby it will be able to mirror the endless wisdom and spiritual insights that come from our eternal divine source within.

"Dear God, let love illuminate my mind."

"Please let your love enlighten my mind"

Feeling and exchanging divine love is the easiest and most efficient form of meditation. It brings about the best of results, and in the quickest possible way. It delivers real peace of mind, and provides the ultimate insights that are well and truly beneficial to all.

Only love can completely satisfy the desires of our heart because it perfectly nourishes and sustains who *we really are*.

Living with love is truly a most pleasant way to go through life.

REALIZATIONS:

I love to feel calm

I love my silent mind

May love enlighten my mind

Love your Body

A great many people take very good care of their cars, houses or other worldly possessions and yet they neglect to properly look after their own bodies. Either partially or completely. How come?

A great many business owners too are spending lots of time and energy to nurture and grow their companies while eating and sleeping poorly, not to speak about not exercising enough, or worse, abusing their bodies and minds with daily doses of alcohol and/or prescription (and other) drugs.

I know plenty of people who throughout their lives pursued the accumulation of money as their first and foremost priority. And once they had lots and lots of it, they didn't get to enjoy it much. Or not at all. Because in the meantime their bodies have become too frail or sick to be able to go traveling around the world 'in style'. Or to otherwise do the things they were planning to enjoy - once they had accumulated 'enough' money… (The problem is that suddenly it is never enough!)

Instead, they needed to take all sorts of drugs to keep their bodies kind of functioning, part or full time nurses, or outright intensive care. In short, all their money couldn't buy back their lost health; all postponed joy and the pleasures that come from having a healthy body were suddenly 'replaced' by much agony and pain.

And The Happy Rabbit Says…

"Close your eyes and send positive, warm and loving thoughts to your entire stomach area!" (3 x 3 min.)

Abusing our bodies or not caring enough about our physical well-being means to be cruel or unkind to ourselves. For some reason or another we simply don't care enough for our health, until one day we are abruptly forced to deal with the more or less serious repercussions of our neglect. One or several of our body parts starts to show some symptoms of disease. Perhaps at first only giving us a bit of a 'wake-up call' in order to help us to reconsider our priorities and mend our ways. Some will listen to those signals, and others won't.

Some spiritually astute friends of mine were often quite blasé about their bodies, a bit indifferent to maintaining a good diet, or following some basic fitness routine. They knew that they are eternal souls and that it's 'only' their bodies that will eventually die. Sooner or later we all have to go anyway. So it's no big deal; nobody knows when their time is up, besides, plenty of people died young in perfectly healthy bodies…

That is all true. But the point of being healthy is not so much to prolong our life on planet Earth but to live life to the best of our abilities. So it is more about quality than quantity. It is simply harder to do what we want or have to do while our bodies feel sick and we are in pain. And likewise, it is not as easy to be merry.

Yes, it is possible to feel spiritual joy within even though our bodies may not be all that well. Yet being able to feel such inner peace and pleasure will certainly make the pain a bit more bearable, and very often help our bodies to recover more quickly.

Truly being kind to ourselves must include loving our bodies and providing all that is needed to function properly and nicely - just as they were intended and built to be.

Our bodies simply deserve to receive first priority - long before our companies or cars, boats or houses. After all, our body is the most important worldly possession we have. It's the only vehicle of the soul to travel in this material dimension. We simply need it to experience and achieve whatever it is that we have come here to experience, learn and do. Much more so than we need our cars and the like.

And The Happy Rabbit Says…

"Be very aware of your body today - enjoy eating healthy foods and drink plenty of clean water!"

Some Christians seem to have a tendency to neglect their physical health for a variety of reasons. For some it could be a misguided or unconscious attempt to make entirely unnecessary sacrifices, while others neglect their own bodies by giving their undivided attention and first priority to everybody but themselves.

Sometimes, not being kind to ourselves is also the result of feelings of open or suppressed guilt that 'wants' to ultimately express itself in suffering and pain, self-abuse or other forms of self-destructive behavior like substance abuse of many kinds.

Quite a few of us learn these unkind ways already as a child, more or less consciously. From parents, siblings, relatives, friends, school or society in general. We get used to alcohol abuse by watching movies or TV shows, even those that are rated as family-friendly. Very often the hero gets senselessly drunk upon hearing some really bad or sad news, or while otherwise facing trouble; our favorite actors will head straight to the nearest bar to down a few shots, one after the other in rapid succession, perhaps while clutching a bottle of 'rocket fuel', their imaginary friend.

So we learn from an early age that to get drunk is a perfectly acceptable coping mechanism in times of trouble. After all, movie stars and adults in real-life do it all the time, so it must be the right thing to do!

Regardless of the reasons for our neglect or abuse, it is important that we care for what's in our care. Our bodies are the first things we are entrusted to look after, long before we acquire our worldly toys (or responsibilities). A car that doesn't get properly serviced quickly falls apart and ceases to function safely and reliably, thereby serving no further purpose (other than recycling). And likewise it is with our bodies.

To be generally fit and well is only natural for the majority of people. For most that is true at least at the time of birth or in our younger years. Potentially, there are many causes of disease and suffering. Some are quite avoidable, others not so easily. Some of the origins are physical, while others are on the *emotional, mental or spiritual* plane (see also chapter *The Divine Deal*).

Physical origins can often be prevented and we will look at some of the things we can do. There are however environmental causes that are harder to escape from. Unless we actually moved our home and family to safer grounds. The unfortunate people who lived for generations in or around the Fukushima area in Japan didn't have much choice but to leave.

To live in a country or city with heavy air pollution will cause much suffering too and perhaps even lead to a premature (physical) death. Our health will also suffer when we ingest polluted food and water, or are otherwise exposed to unnatural and often very toxic substances.

Ultimately, environmental issues can only be resolved with better technology and a deeper understanding of how interconnected it all is. Water, air, food, radiation and weather patterns constantly circulate around the world. There are no places to hide. To succeed we really need to *cultivate a more respectful, loving and caring attitude* towards planet Earth and all of God's creations. And that of course is a state of mind that is only natural for a loving and merry Christian!

Let's look at a few things we can do to help us to keep or regain good health. There is much information 'out there' about what to do or eat, or not. It can be rather confusing to try to sort it all out as much advice is ever-changing and plenty is contradictory or self-serving. Not surprisingly the level of research and the various 'truths' presented to the public depends to a large degree on the sources. In other words, who has actually paid for the studies; he who has the gold makes the rules! 53a]

The following points are not meant to replace medical advice but are simply some personal insights and habits. Most if not all of it is really just 'common sense' stuff that is likely to work for everyone. The primary idea is to mostly focus on the positive things that we should be doing. There are however a few things that we should try to avoid as well as they are proven to be bad for our health and well-being. For in-depths details on the issues raised simply follow the links in the corresponding *Notes* since we can't possibly cover all the scientific aspects within these pages.

Drink plenty of clean water (preferably free of chemicals additives like fluoride and other neuro-toxic pollutants): Dehydration is a major cause of obesity, depression, and a huge array of other serious ailments. Furthermore, since the human brain consists of 73% water, it actually takes just 2% dehydration to negatively affect our memory, attention span, and other cognitive skills.

It is safe to say that a large number of people are suffering from dehydration without being aware of it. Knowing the symptoms we can actually observe this by just looking at people's skin and faces. I highly recommend the lecture of this book: *Your body's many Cries for Water* by F. Batmanghelidj, M.D. The byline reads: "You are not sick, you are thirsty! Don't treat thirst with medications." 53b]

Move your body an hour a day: The saying 'Use it or lose it' is quite true, as tough as that may sound. Yes, we may still live a long life without properly training and using our muscles but at the cost of impaired functionality and well-being. The choice is ours. Exercise doesn't need to be hard or should even be considered to be 'exercise'. Best is to do something that is actually fun at the same time. And it's not necessary to sweat a lot either; a light sweat a day or just an inkling of it is plenty already.

Regular light exercise works wonders for both our physical and mental health. Research has shown that exercising is far better for treating a depression than taking anti-depressants. Plus it comes without all the nasty side-effects too. Physical activity is also proven to help us better cope with stress and anxiety; it increases our analytical and creative thinking, and makes us generally feel more confident and optimistic about life.

Best is to do something nice and easy *before* breakfast or heading off to work. That way it is done and out of the way. There is no need to think about it anymore (or come up with excuses, respectively feeling guilty later in the day). And it simply feels great to have one's body all warmed up nicely, feeling all stretched and supple, ready to go and have a great day!

Put together your own personalized gymnastics routine that moves your joints in every direction, uses all muscles in a relaxed and easy-going way, and let's you wake up gently and nicely. Perhaps incorporate a few Yoga moves, Tai Chi, Chi Gung, or the like. Make sure that you find it all very pleasant and that you are therefore happy to do it every morning. 20-30 minutes is all that it takes.

Remember to breathe and think some positive and uplifting thoughts. And of course, feel grateful and blessed, looking for and thereby seeing all that is good in your life. Or the day ahead.

Then during the day or evening go for a walk (or better, two walks) for another 20-30 minutes. Walk a little bit brisk at times, a bit slower at other times - always as fast a you feel comfortable. Let your arms swing all relaxed. Keep your head high and your back straight. And of course, whenever possible, walk somewhere really nice and beautiful.

Another good way to 'exercise without exercising' is to get into the habit of taking the stairs instead of the elevator or escalator. Or to stand up longer than necessary, say to read a book or your tablet computer.

Mind your posture: That may sound easy and yet it can be a bit tricky at first. Look around you and notice how many people walk in a slouching manner, bent over, and with otherwise rather shocking postures. Unfortunately this is also very true for a great many of today's young people; folks that are supposed to be at the peak of their physical abilities. Yet they grow up with their eyes and heads facing down and their necks kind of permanently strained forward (a.k.a. the 'chicken look'), even while not staring at their clever computers or smart phones. And nobody, including friends and family, seems to care or dares to tell them that their incredibly bad postures are equally bad for their health (besides, it's not looking particularly smart or cool, to say the least).

After all, our bodies were simply not designed to spend most of the day staring into gleaming little plastic boxes. That is simply not natural.

Having a good posture is most important for the healthy circulation and flow of our blood and oxygen, plus the proper functioning of our lymph, digestion and nervous systems. Besides, our posture also reveals a great deal about how a person truly feels the majority of time.

From the downtrodden to the outright depressed, from the seemingly to the truly confident, from the sad and downbeat to the youthful and cheerful; it all shows in the ways we walk, stand or sit. And while age may be a factor for some, it doesn't need to be. It's mostly a matter of how we think and feel most of the time. The proof is to see many of the young with horrible postures while quite a few of the elderly folks are still able to maintain great poise and stride.

It is *well and truly* worth the effort to make a conscious decision to maintain a good posture *at all times*. Even if nobody is around to see it. Do it for your own's sake. It is perhaps *the best way to continuously exercise our bodies* and burn lots and lots of calories without actually making much of an effort or even breaking a sweat. It helps to lose excess weight, and particularly so in those 'troublesome' places that got neglected by well, having a bad posture!

Initially it may take a little bit of an effort because certain underused muscles and ligaments need to work harder to get the body back into its natural upright shape. Wearing a wide belt or other tight clothing that supports our skeletal system can be helpful to get us going. And so is asking our loved ones to give us a friendly reminder whenever they see us 'slumping and slouching around' (Yours truly is most grateful to his dear wife for pointing it out to me whenever she catches me!).

Once we have achieved a great posture on an ongoing basis we will notice how easy and effortless it really is simply because our bodies were designed to be and move this way. The simple measure of minding our posture will improve life in so many aspects; it is simply amazing.

Be flexible: A supple and flexible body is a youthful body - regardless of its physical age. Some people are all stiff and hardened up despite their youth while many seniors are still soft and supple.

While much of it has to do with our state of mind, it is important to stretch one's body in every direction, on a daily basis. Best is to do it in a really relaxed and unforced manner by simply letting gravity do its work, all the while breathing deeply and joyfully. Stretching should never hurt even one tiny little it. To the contrary: It should actually feel great! We can even do it while watching a movie. An improving of our posture and stretching at the same time kind of thing works very well.

For thousands of years traditional Chinese doctors have pointed out that the harder and more brittle our bodies become the closer we will be to our (physical) deaths, regardless of our actual biological age. And in turn that a soft and supple, all relaxed and flexible body is proof positive of a youthful personality and is very likely to result in a healthy and long life.

Let nature nourish you: The quicker it takes for naturally grown food to reach us the better it is for our health. It means that our food is in a more natural state and less processed. It therefore contains far more still active ingredients (like vitamins, enzymes, minerals, etc.) to nourish our bodies, and at the same time none of the chemical additives that 'at best' slow down our metabolism and at worst poison our systems with toxins that need to be eliminated (if at all possible).

Non-stop from the farm or garden to our kitchen and mouths is always best; the less detours and delays the happier and healthier our bodies will be!

Much of today's industrial food is not even food anymore in the true sense of the word. Even 'Ninja', our little Chihuahua boy, knows the difference: He just loves to eat a nice Brie cheese made in France in the traditional old ways of the cheese-making craft, but adamantly rejects what may pass as cheese at first sight, but essentially fails a dog's discerning nose test: 'Modern' heavily factory processed cheese is often just a rather strange concoction of whey proteins and cheap but nasty (hydrolized) vegetable oil or fat.

Much the same can be said of modern meat products, and so on. Many of today's factory foods don't even rot or otherwise go bad for a long long time. Of course that is by intent and design in order to make them last longer for shipping and storing, respectively to increase their shelf life in the supermarkets. While these goals may be well-intentioned and certainly make much commercial sense, the flip side is that it goes against nature itself.

Our bodies are part and parcel of nature and as such we simply can't feed it plastic products or worse and win in the long run. Sooner or later it will show; the epidemics of modern-day diseases are simply very telling. Trying to outsmart something that is already perfect, designed by God's infinitely superior intelligence, purely for commercial gains for a few while destroying the health of many, does not sound particularly smart to me.

The best way to keep the doctor away is to eat a good balance of healthy natural grains, fats, fruit and fresh vegetables every day. A high-fiber and vegetable-rich diet will maintain healthy blood-sugar levels and protect our bodies from a whole range of 'lifestyle diseases' (e.g. hypertension, obesity, coronary heart disease, type 2 diabetes, epithelial cell cancers, autoimmune disease, and osteoporosis), besides slowing down the aging process.

The problem with eating highly refined factory or other types of industrial fast food is twofold. First, 'empty' or useless calories are not actually nourishing our bodies; nothing of real value is added to our cells (and that is why we don't really feel satisfied, respectively will quickly be hungry again).

And perhaps worse, these often indigestible materials also deplete our bodies of existing energy including stored vitamins, minerals and enzymes. Because now our organs have to work hard trying to get rid of all these useless and harmful substances. At best man-made items our body can't even recognize are finally excreted. Yet some of it will get deposited in fat cells, the liver, and other equally undesirable places to be dealt with later, one way or the other.

So a healthy little rule is to avoid eating anything that has a lot of chemical ingredients that are hard to spell or pronounce; chances are simply very high that those things just don't belong inside our bodies!

And likewise, it's best to also stay clear of any and all artificial sweeteners and use only natural ones, like raw sugar (beet root or sugar cane), honey, maple syrup, blackstrap mollasses, coconut sugar (coconut sap), and stevia.

While it may be tempting to stop by that fast food (a.k.a. fat food) joint 'on the fly', it is always far healthier (besides more economical) to cook or prepare our own meals. Even if we feel that we may not be very good at it. That is usually only an excuse anyway. Cooking can be lots of fun, whether we are alone or do it together as a family or among friends. Very soon it will simply taste best!

Plus it's the only way to really know what's inside. When you make your own yummy sauces you will not only eat better, healthier and cheaper, but also avoid all the nasty ingredients of commercial ones - that are mostly full of hidden MSG (monosodium glutamate) and other chemical ingredients that are essentially detrimental to the natural functioning of our bodies, no matter what industry-paid research may show.

For many years commercial interests have claimed that there is no difference in traditionally grown organic fruit and vegetables compared to modern farming methods. Yet a new study by Newcastle University, UK, "has shown that organic crops and crop-based foods are up to 69% higher in a number of key antioxidants than conventionally-grown crops", which translates into eating a couple of extra portions of fruit and vegetables a day. Another significant finding was the almost 50% reduction of toxic heavy metals like cadmium, lead and mercury. [54]

It simply makes a lot of sense to whenever possible grow, buy and eat organic foodstuffs. While it's true that it often costs a bit more one also does not have to worry about the toxic side-effects and eventual health and well-being costs of eating foods laced with petrochemicals - chemicals made from crude oil and gas.

Industrial-style agricultural, food and drug production fully relies on petrochemicals or coal derivatives; these unsavory chemicals are used in fertilizers, pesticides, preservatives, artificial colors and flavorings, wax coating on various produce (like citrus fruits, eggplants, cucumbers, bell peppers, and potatoes) and perhaps surprisingly, in man-made vitamins (fat-soluble vitamins like A, D, E and K keep accumulating in the body) or common drugs like Aspirin (acetylsalicylic acid) and a great many more.

To sum it up, our food can and should not only nourish and sustain our bodies, but be medicine at the same time! To repair, heal and revitalize every single cell. Imagine your great health if every bite would be so naturally full of God's goodness that it is constantly healing your body, besides tasting great. That is indeed the normal way as it was always intended. Designed by divine intelligence. Let nature nourish you and be well. Naturally.

Add bio-active food to every meal: Modern factory food lacks enzymes as they get destroyed at fairly low temperatures. While our bodies produce certain type of enzymes we also need to ingest them with our daily food to help with digestion and to maintain overall good health. So even if we do indulge in food that we know are not the best for our health (and who doesn't), we can dramatically improve its digestion by simply adding little bits and pieces of food that is still raw and therefore naturally endowed with enzymes and other still beneficial compounds.

Things like raw garlic, onions, spring onions, chives, ginger and turmeric roots. And fresh herbs like basil, oregano, rosemary, thyme, and so on. Or other living food like alfalfa and broccoli sprouts (or cress, mung beans, mustard, radish, etc.). Freshly-squeezed orange or grapefruit, lemon or lime juice is another great natural additive to salads. And so is raw honey, or natural and raw nuts of any kind.

By eating these type of 'living foods' with *every cooked meal* (and especially those that are a bit 'naughty') we can make a huge difference in our well-being. The naturally still intact compounds of many kinds speed up both digestion and the overall metabolism. This simple step alone is sure to help many shed some of the extra weight they may be carrying around.

Other bio-active food we should try to eat at least once a day are probiotics; they are a great help to further improve our digestion, lower blood pressure, and strengthen the immune system. Eat daily some sauerkraut, kimchi and other type of fermented vegetable pickles, or yoghurt, kefir and kombucha. And use miso to make delicious soups or add it to sauces of many kinds. Another easy way to eat probiotics is to take some organic spirulina or chlorella tablets or add some powder to a fruit and/or vegetable juice before the main meal. [55]

Spend daily time in nature: Connecting with God's nature is relaxing, healing and invigorating at the same time. It's a must do just like a fish needs to be in water to stay alive. Spending too much time indoors, in air-conditioned and artificially lighted buildings, sitting down most of the day, or think and do stuff that is far removed from what is naturally best for us, is simply not very conducive to great health and happiness.

And yet it is often a part of our modern lifestyle or work requirement that we cannot easily avoid. But a daily escape to nature is still something we should strive for on a consistent basis. Even if it's just for a little while, it's far better than not at all. It will keep us grounded and keeps things both in balance and perspective.

Taking a walk in the sunshine (the sun is shining even on a cloudy or rainy day), breathing fresh air (even if it's somewhat polluted), taking in the natural beauty (we can find it even in the city) is something that will make and keep any of us happy and healthy. It's simply so by divine design.

Drink responsibly: Some Christians have a bit of an ambivalent relationship with drinking alcohol. On one side it is kind of spurned yet most likely there are more Christians who drink daily than go to Church weekly! Besides, quite a few of the old saints did not seem to mind a bit of ale or wine. And neither did Jesus.

"The Son of man has come eating and drinking; and ye say, Behold a gluttonous man, and a winebibber, a friend of publicans and sinners!" (Luke 7:34)

"No longer drink only water, but use a little wine for the sake of your stomach and your frequent ailments." (1 Tim. 5:23)

Paracelsus, the famous Renaissance physician, taught that 'The dose makes the poison', so it all depends on the quantity we consume. In other words, even the most beneficial substance may become toxic if we overdo it. And likewise, ingesting potentially harmful substances may be fine if we indulge only occasionally and with moderation.

Alcohol can certainly be classed as a poison, particularly as it dehydrates our bodies and quite obviously and rather quickly impairs our nerve and brain functions. How often and how much we drink is a personal decision. Obviously, the less we indulge the better it is for our physical health. And yet there are certain (including some social) occasions where it can be fun to have that little bit of extra.

"Every man serves the good wine first; and when men have drunk freely, then the poor wine; but you have kept the good wine until now." (John 2:7-10)

"Everything in moderation, including moderation." Oscar Wilde [56]

No matter our individual habits and dispositions, these two points are well worth considering:

1. Drink a large glass of water alongside every alcoholic beverage. That will help the liver assimilate the alcohol and keeps the body from dehydration, the cause of many potential health issues (and headaches).

2. Drink only when you feel happy. To drink when one is already merry can make us even merrier. But the opposite is true too: Drinking when one already feels down or upset (for whatever reasons) is likely to make us only more depressed and/or angry. So it would be far better to meditate, contemplate and pray about things before opening that bottle (or smoke that joint; because the same thing can also be said about using recreational drugs).

While for some readers the inclusion of the above points about alcohol or recreational drugs may be somewhat surprising, it is also important to realize that alcohol has been around since time immemorial. And that for us humans (while in flesh and body) it is also quite natural (besides very common) to desire different states of mind. Or put differently, wanting to feel a bit intoxicated at times, or otherwise trying to alter and expand our consciousness and thus our experiences, is absolutely normal. After all, to be curious and searching, wanting to go beyond and learning ever more, is simply a natural trait of every soul at its finest!

Having said that, what is the solution for curing substance abuse? Quite obviously, and as history has shown, to solely promote abstinence does not work. If someone has a problem and keeps going beyond their healthy and happy limits, one cannot just offer empty words or platitudes. Or put them in jail. Or drug them out further with some unsavory prescription drugs that come along with a multitude of negative side-effects.

Best is to replace an unhealthy habit with a healthier and happier experience - by discovering a new lifestyle that is more satisfying and fulfilling than the one we were used to. How can we do that?

When we (start to) focus on experiencing more love - as discussed in chapters *Love God, Feel God's Love, Love your Self, Love All* - in our lives, the 'dark side' of self-abuse will gradually (and sometimes instantly) fall away as it is superseded by ever more uplifting experiences that match the increasingly loving vibrations we feel within.

The love we feel will guide us to take up a new hobby, sport or passion. Or we may find new friends or that special someone we were looking for. And so on and so forth. Good things happen when we live a life of love. Jesus knew that very well and therefore wants us to put love *first*. And *everything* else will follow easily and nicely!

Feel innocent and deserving: Whether one drinks alcohol or not, the main point is to not feel guilty about it. Which leads us straight to a 'biggie' about health matters: One big cause of not being at ease - and having a disease - is to feel guilty. This can be true for anyone yet some Christians are particularly prone to be affected.

The inducing of shame or guilt after all is a main curriculum in many congregations. In fact, this is a central 'feature' of many if not most of the world's creeds. Yet once we truly feel the all-embracing nature of unconditional love we will also know that this is very unfortunate and entirely groundless. Since time immemorial inciting both guilt and fear has been the primary tool of scrupulous manipulators; be aware of any such attempts (including by friends and family) and keep smiling anyway!

The fact is that we are only responsible for what we do personally as an individual:

"The person who sins will die. The son will not bear the punishment for the father's iniquity, nor will the father bear the punishment for the son's iniquity; the righteousness of the righteous will be upon himself, and the wickedness of the wicked will be upon himself." (Ezekiel 18:20).

Jesus wants us to be pure again like little children. And that of course would not make much sense if kids were already born as 'big bad sinners who need to repent or end up getting roasted for all of eternity'… The following two verses make that rather clear:

"Truly I say to you, unless you are converted and become like children, you shall not enter the kingdom of heaven." (Matthew 18:3)

"They shed innocent blood, the blood of their sons and daughters." (Psalm 106:38)

To feel guilty and therefore to consider oneself as not deserving of God's grace is one major cause of suffering and pain. The 'idea' is to somehow or another make up for the guilt we feel. And being sick is one of the mechanisms that will seemingly allow us to remedy our guilty feelings.

Of course, perhaps for the majority of people that 'decision' is made purely on a subconscious level.

Nevertheless, the end results are just the same as if we would decide it consciously and flog ourselves as some people like to do (see also chapter *The Divine Deal*).

And The Happy Rabbit Says…

"You truly deserve to be healthy - feel this truth deep within - and look after your body and mind!"

Once we fully experience the love of God however we also realize that God does not wish us to be sick and suffer - despite our shortcomings, mistakes and lapses. We will know that God wishes us to be healthy and happy. For most, to be fit and well is indeed the default condition. It is the way our bodies were designed and built; with so much divine intelligence, love and perfection that it can be rather hard to grasp for our usually limited and often doubting minds.

An important part of being able to feel innocent - and thereby deserving of good health - is to not engage in the 'blame game'. It's a game that is widely (and often rather quickly) played throughout society, on a personal level, within our families, among friends, in politics, or the corporate world.

The ultimate form of the blame game of course is to criticize God for our trials and tribulations; funnily that is often (but not exclusively) played by militant atheists who don't believe in anything other than their own smartness. They like to blame a God they don't believe in to tell us that he doesn't exist, more or less consciously hoping that doing so will increase their own happiness.

A related and perhaps funny question one could ask is "Why do insurance policies and corporate contracts have an 'Act of God' excuse for not paying up?" when the officially sanctioned and prescribed worldview denies that there is such a 'thing' as God anyway? The answer of course is that it's simply a very convenient excuse to save some money and thus increase profits.

So why do we play the blame game? Quite simply, we like to spread and assign guilt in order to feel more pure and innocent ourselves. That way we feel more deserving and are thus able to enjoy more of whatever it is that we want to enjoy. Feeling ashamed and guilty is simply a big bummer or letdown.

The age-old game is also played by various individuals and organizations as a tool of manipulation or social control; beware and don't get caught!

Best is to never (or at least not easily) point the finger at others. After all we mostly don't know all the issues involved in any given situation. Besides, we all make mistakes! A far better and merrier way to go through life is to praise more and blame less; to consciously stop being a fault-finder and instead turn into a seeker of excellence.

To cultivate our inborn habit to look at the virtues and successes of people rather than their mistakes and shortcomings means to make the quantum leap from blaming to praising, from feeling guilt and misery to experiencing satisfaction and joy. It simply feels wrong to play the blame game and deep down we all know this to be true.

Once we abstain from playing this rather destructive game and therefore don't feel 'duly guilty' anymore, we will start to notice a markedly improved physical health and general well-being. It is that important, and yes, being healthy can be that simple!

"Appreciation is a wonderful thing: It makes what is excellent in others belong to us as well." Voltaire [57]

Focus on love, peace and happiness: Instead of trying to negate or avoid the negatives, it's best to shift our focus to what is truly pleasing. But that is sometimes not so easy, and particularly if we carry along lots of old emotional baggage. Carrying around such old and unresolved stuff only weighs us down, and offers no benefits at all. It literally blocks us from feeling *God's loving and healing energies that are both omnipresent and freely flowing.*

And The Happy Rabbit Says…

"Both sickness and healing originates in your heart and mind - strongly desire to be whole and healed!"

The well-researched Placebo effect with success rates up to ninety percent is proof positive of the power of our mind in the healing process. And of course, the flip side of that power is the Nocebo effect whereby negative attitudes and beliefs will result in harmful consequences, even to the point of premature death (placebo - Latin for "I shall please"; nocebo - "I shall harm"). [58]

Past disappointments and anger are such powerful emotions that they may bring about serious health issues like anxiety and depression, high blood pressure and headaches, and worse.

And The Happy Rabbit Says…

"Instead of becoming sad or mad, choose to be amazed or puzzled - and stay happy within!"

Love God, your Self and All will once again prove to be the perfect solution. Because when we love we will come to *understand* why something has happened, respectively has not happened. Immersed in love we can come to easily understand why a friend or family member has behaved in a particular manner, and why we felt disappointed or angry in return. Seeing through the eyes of love we can perceive hidden motives like fear and insecurity, or past trauma and present pain.

In short, this is the merry Christian's formula for successfully and permanently dealing with all the anger we may have accumulated over time:

Love, Understand, Remember the lesson(s), Let it Be.

Regrets is a form of anger directed at ourselves. Love your Self more and thereby understand more. Appreciate what you've learned from a past experience and see how it has actually helped you to grow and become a much more loving and kind being.

And The Happy Rabbit Says…

"You can't change the past - accept it and let resentments go, but remember the lesson(s)!"

It's important to always feel and live in the here and now of every moment. If you're sad or mad about the past, you are unlikely to be healthy now nor likely to be in the future. As you sow so shall you reap. And while we worry about the future, we only create an unhealthy present and more than likely, a less than perfect future.

"Yesterday is history, tomorrow is a mystery, today is a gift of God, which is why we call it the present." Bil Keane [59]

A real biggie or *major source of pain and disease* is when we unwittingly indulge ourselves in a victimhood or 'poor me' attitude. It is a fundamental state of mind that is far more widespread than widely realized because it goes so very deep. And because we all have it to a certain degree. That may sound strange yet even those whom we would normally classify as 'winner types' (in terms of wealth and power) are not immune; indeed it may be their very motivation in life.

And unfortunately, quite often feeling sorry for one's self will result in unloving and unkind behavior towards others. It is a powerful negative emotion that easily allows us too justify the taking advantage of others. Some do it consciously, others unconsciously. Because bad things have happened to us, now 'it's our turn' to be winners and grinners. It's 'my time to shine', after all "I have suffered so much so now they can suffer some too!"

The thing is that *we all* have reasons to feel sorry for ourselves - in the same way we all have reasons to be grateful for. To be able to truly move forward in life it is very important to realize one's own natural tendency to feel like a victim at times. And, as a first step, to *make a very conscious decision* to let go of all notions of victimhood consciousness - thereby stopping the vicious downward spiral of negative anticipation that is only 'inviting' more bad stuff to happen.

The second part is to forcefully decide and strongly agree within to once and for all change our focus to experience ever more love, peace and happiness in our life. To make a conscious switch from the coming to expect to be disappointed (which only leads to having a 'continuing supply' of reasons to complain and feel self-pity) to always noticing and experiencing ever more causes to be grateful and happy.

And The Happy Rabbit Says…

"Have confidence that you can get what you want without first playing the "I'm the victim game"!"

Here's a little meditation that may be helpful to make that permanent switch. Make it a deep and personal pact with God and ask for his help to remember your fundamental choice in times of trouble:

Today I let go of all that caused anger and pain, sorrows and grief, disappointments and tears.

I fondly remember the joyful experiences, the achievements earned and the lessons learned;

I happily keep the best and lovingly surrender the rest!

From now on I welcome and accept all that brings joy, satisfaction and success.

I'm grateful for everything that adds to my health, wealth and wisdom,

I joyfully focus on all that increases my love, peace and happiness!

Let love heal you: While science and medicine has made large improvements over time, we need to also recognize their negative sides. Side-effects like dramatic weight gain are all too common in all too many people who take prescription drugs. While that is bad enough, often there are quite many additional and even worse side effects to be worried about (as per the manufacturer's own admission; simply visit their websites or read the inserted warnings).

A study by the prestigious Mayo Clinic and Olmsted Medical Center found that nearly 70 percent of all Americans are on at least one prescription drug, more than half take two, and a whopping twenty percent are on five or more prescription drugs. "Antibiotics, antidepressants and painkilling opioids are most commonly prescribed, their study found."

While Americans account for only five percent of the world's population they consume over 50 percent of pharmaceutical drugs, including 80 percent of all prescription painkillers (according to the Centers for Disease Controls every day in America 44 people die from an overdose of prescription painkillers). To read more absolutely shocking information about the using and abusing of legal drugs, and in particular the dangers of antidepressants, just follow the links in Note: [60]

No matter what slick advertising or paid advocates say, to be a 'pill-popper' constantly looking for a quick fix is a sure way to an early grave. The bottom line is that unless it is *really really really* necessary (as in 'life or death' situations) it is probably smart to avoid pharmaceutical products of any kind and look for alternative solutions. There are a great many ways to use natural remedies and holistic methods instead; all it takes is a bit of research and choosing wisely.

Speaking of which, it may not always be easy to find the best approach at first since there is lots of sometimes confusing or contradicting information out there. But when we ask God sincerely for guidance we will definitely receive it. One way or the other the necessary people and/or advice will suddenly come forward and all we need to do is to recognize and follow it.

"The art of medicine consists in amusing the patient while nature cures the disease." Voltaire

Moving beyond even natural remedies, *pure love* is still a rather underestimated respectively neglected medicine, yet it *is the most powerful healer* of all. Its healing properties go far beyond even the power of the mind (that is amply demonstrated and proven by the aforementioned Placebo and Nocebo effects) simply because *love directly affects the very nature of who we really are.*

The healing qualities/vibrations of love will resonate throughout the various energetic levels of our being and filter 'down' to the level of our physical bodies, to do its wonders even at the very core of the individual cells. We don't really need to be fully aware of the exact workings or mechanism. Yet we can still recognize and realize that love works miracles.

"Miracles are not contrary to nature, but only contrary to what we know about nature." Saint Augustine

In our quiet moments of prayer, reflection and meditation, before falling asleep or upon waking up, whenever we consciously tap into and feel divine love, we can send its healing light to every nook and cranny of our body. From the top of our heads to the tip of our toes. And in particular to those places that are currently aching or in pain. Ask and you shall receive:

"Dear God, let love heal my body."

"Please let your love heal my body"

Take a bath of love. Let it shine throughout your body. Get well and stay well. That is the divine desire. We can come to realize and feel this reality every moment of every day.

Feel love and feel healed. *Feel God and feel good!*

By the way, what about *looking* good? Quite a few of us are a bit concerned about getting older and more or less desperately try to preserve or restore our youthful looks. After all there are plenty of studies that show that good looks have a rather large influence on actually getting that job or not, respectively earning more or not. So do we need to 'invest' in expensive creams and potions or even more radically, submit our bodies to surgical knives and the like?

Well, let's consider the perennial words of wisdom of a saint, spoken over six hundred years ago:

"Since love grows within you, so beauty grows. For love is the beauty of the soul."
Saint Augustine

Love literally shines and its glow and associated smile will make even a wrinkled face look most attractive. Another beauty aspect of love is that it nourishes us at the core of our being and thereby it will at first reduce and eventually eliminate the need to binge-eat empty calories. The kind of eating where we stuff our bodies full of things that are not actually nutritious but only add to the unnecessary inches here and there and finally everywhere...

The best beauty advice *and* permanent way to lose weight is to follow what I like to call 'The Love Diet': It will reduce the unhealthy cravings for food that in reality are a craving for love. The love diet is most effective simply because it solves the problem at its very core. And contrary to all the many commercial 'solutions' out there, its only side effect is to become ever happier and healthier!

"A merry heart is good medicine: but a broken spirit dries up the bones."
(Proverbs 17:22)

Below is a quick summary of the discussed. It includes *Breathe consciously* and *Take your time to sleep and relax*; much can and should be said about both subjects so we are covering them in their own separate chapters (see *Breathe* and *Relax*).

What we have discussed here is deliberately kept as short and concentrated as possible - to focus on what really matters. Of course, good advice on achieving and maintaining good health could easily fill a book of its own. After all there is so much to learn - and sometimes *unlearn* - about health and nutritional matters.

It is also not easy to generalize since we all have different body types and situations to adapt to in our individual lives. Much depends on our particular lifestyle, state of mind, and finally, our beliefs. Yet incorporating the above thirteen principles will surely help most everyone improve their health and well-being as they cover essential aspects of every mind, body, and spirit (soul). All without nasty side-effects, but lots of extra happiness! In summary:

Love your body and…

Drink plenty of clean water.

Move your body an hour a day.

Mind your posture.

Be flexible.

Let nature nourish you.

Add bio-active food to every meal.

Spend daily time in nature.

Breathe consciously.

Take your time to sleep and relax.

Drink responsibly.

Feel innocent and deserving.

Focus on love, peace and happiness.

Let love heal you.

REALIZATIONS:

I love to feel fine

I love to be healthy and strong

May love heal my body

Be your Self

Who are we? Where do we come from and where do we go to? Since time immemorial these perennial questions have been asked and attempted to be answered by a great many people.

"Who am I?" is a smart question and ultimately we all need to find our own answers within. There are essentially three general ways to approach this subject. And for total clarity and absolute certainty on the subject it is of course best to adopt and combine them all.

First, *we can use our intellectual abilities*; consciously trying to make sense about things through the various forms of reasoning. With our analytical and logical thinking we can verify and establish facts, and attempt to find the original causes behind observed effects. In essence we use our limited brain power or rather more accurately, our minds, in our attempts to determine the truth. Sometimes we get it right, but mostly we get it only partially right, which means that many of the other parts are actually wrong. And that in turn could very well mean that the overall sum total of our conclusions is mistaken too.

We can read the deliberations and conclusions of famous philosophers and study a multitude of spiritual self-help, personal development or metaphysical books on the subject. And of course, quite many of us learn and follow the insights and conclusions of materialistic scientists, perhaps not realizing that their theories are often based on mere assumptions, incomplete knowledge, and yes, beliefs (e.g "something came out of nothing").

Or we could contemplate things within; think about what makes most sense to us, look at where and why others may have gotten it wrong, and perhaps come up with altogether new theories and explanations. For example, through meditation and observation we are able to notice and to some degree control our thoughts. And thereby we can partially control our bodies (yet much remains beyond our direct control, like blood pressure, hormone production, digestion, and so on).

Many elite athletes or accomplished martial artists know full well that they are able to direct the mind and control the body to keep going - way beyond the normal limits of what we would commonly consider to be feasible. And not just in desperate survival mode but purely in order to win a medal or otherwise achieve a personal dream.

Here we enter the domain of will and willpower. The purpose of our will is to direct our thoughts, intentions and desires. So now the question arises, *who wills?* Who is the person in charge of exercising this willpower that can drive us to achieve the seemingly impossible?

Secondly, *we can get inspiration* from scripture and read the personal accounts of the mystics and saints. These days we could also watch one of the amazing interviews and testimonials given on YouTube videos about near-death experiences (NDE) or out-of-body experiences (OBE). [61] This is in essence the faith-based approach; upon reading, watching and meditating, we feel something to be true because the revealed knowledge resonates deeply within and therefore we henceforth believe that indeed it is true.

The final and ultimate confirmation of anything, including spiritual truths, however comes when we actually *experience reality for ourselves.* This is the perennial path of the saints and prophets of the Christian mystical tradition and otherwise. Firsthand experience will fully confirm and totally authenticate our knowledge beyond a shadow of a doubt. It means to gain absolute certainty above the spheres of our limited minds. And that in turn will allow us to speak with authority on what others would call matters of faith.

We should all strive to incorporate this level of certainty and trust in our spiritual understanding; it will reverberate far and wide with only the most beneficial effects for everyone.

To fully get to know oneself is quite an adventure and ultimately, a perhaps rather rare achievement. It is not always easy to get to know who we really are or what our true passions are in a world that likes to mould and shape us to become more or less like everybody else. Society as a whole prefers us to think and behave along similar and thereby easily predictable 'safe' lines.

"No one should part with their individuality and become that of another." William Ellery Channing [62]

The totally new and outstanding proposal may sound outlandish at first. And an extraordinary idea is often frowned upon until it obviously produces such amazing results that it can simply no longer be ignored or ridiculed; at this stage it will become generally accepted and applauded as its great benefit to all of us has simply become self-evident.

Similarly, outstanding personalities and quirky characters get all too often criticized or belittled. The 'tall poppy syndrome' is still well and truly alive in our present-day societies; "the tallest flowers in the field need to be cut down to the same size as all the others." [63]

This goes on in school and later in professional life up to the point where, again, things have become self-evident. In Australia we now like to call Nicole Kidman *'our* Nicole' but only since she has become world famous as an outstanding actress. Likewise in Switzerland, Roger Federer has evolved into 'our Roger' upon winning countless tournaments all over the world. We people truly are a 'funny bunch' at times!

"The most difficult thing in life is to know yourself." Thales [64]

How many of us *dare to follow the dreams of our youth*? As a kid our dreams came naturally, without the need to make any effort. We just imagined to become a hero of one kind or another; we had visions to do and become great; we nursed high hopes for a happy life; and somehow we still fully believed in ourselves and the goodness of it all.

To not have followed and realized one's dreams is one of the greatest regrets people have on their death beds; while contemplating about their passed life the dying often lament to have mostly followed the expectations of others rather than daring to be themselves and do what they originally came here to experience and learn. [65]

Well-meaning parents, friends and teachers may convince us to take 'the safe way' and learn a profession that earns a stable income rather than following our 'pipe dreams' that *they* fear will only lead us to a life of lack and misery.

To be true to ourselves instead of trying to meet the expectations of others takes quite a bit of courage. To discover one's self and the infinite world of God is also not widely encouraged in a society that wishes us all to become 'productive units' for 'the greater good' (of more and more economic growth and higher profits). Yet taking some time off to find out who we really are and what we truly want to do and achieve in life should be a most encouraged, even mandatory, task.

Both in the big and small picture view of things it is far more important to be true to oneself than not to be authentic in order to please or impress others. At the end of our lives on planet Earth no one will thank us for having denied ourselves by living a 'fake' life trying to please everybody but ultimately nobody.

And The Happy Rabbit Says…

"Be(come) very comfortable within yourself - because you will always be closest to yourself!"

No matter our age we can and should begin to dream again, to once again connect with our younger selves and remember the things that were important to us then. And to perhaps start to implement a seemingly long lost idea whose time has now finally come.

"Keep true to the dreams of thy youth." Friedrich von Schiller

To remain genuine and thus be able to stay passionate and adventurous in life, to discover ourselves throughout the various dimensions of our being, to keep learning exciting new things, and to dare to follow and realize one's dreams is not just important for us individually, but ultimately it will be of great benefit to everybody else (see also chapters *Respect* and *Do it with Love*). We all have our very own individual mission in life that neatly fits into the big puzzle of God's majestic universe.

"Each of us is meant to have a character all our own, to be what no other can exactly be, and do what no other can exactly do." William Ellery Channing [66]

Taking some time out and reflect on life is time well spent. It helps to put or keep us on our personal path, true and well anchored to ourselves and our individual purpose. It's a good idea to write down one's dreams and hopes in a quiet moment, all the while making sure that these are really our own dreams and hopes, and not the desires, doubts or projections of anybody else.

"The number one reason people fail in life is because they listen to their friends, family and neighbours." Napoleon Hill [67]

"Vision without action is a daydream. Action without vision is a nightmare." Japanese Proverb

Once done, we could make another list and write down our core beliefs and values. The idea is to compare them with the list of our dreams and hopes to see if there are any areas of conflict. Are our dreams and hopes in line with what we believe and value? If not, we need to make changes on either side in order to be able to well and truly move ahead in life, without undue impediments and difficulties.

"The only way to discover the limits of the possible is to venture a little way past them into the impossible." Arthur C. Clarke [68]

Living an authentic life will also enable us to more easily discover our true eternal self, besides increasing our core happiness. The more we can be true to ourselves in everything we do and say, the further we will be able to move beyond the world of scholarship, science and faith, into the world of actual experiencing and *knowing.*

"The words printed here are concepts. You must go through the experiences." Saint Augustine

"The true basis of religion is not belief, but intuitive experience. Intuition is the soul's power of knowing God. To know what religion is really all about, one must know God." Paramahamsa Yogananda [69]

There is a vast difference between believing something purely based on hearsay or the mere learning of past conclusions, and well and truly *knowing* it upon having made the actual personal experience or experiment ourselves. This is both true for spiritual and scientific matters. Because the worst case scenario is always that we faithfully believe something that is actually totally wrong and only the repeating of old dogmas or assumptions that serves someone else.

"Opinion has caused more trouble on this little earth than plagues or earthquakes." Voltaire [70]

Funnily, blind faith is perhaps more common in the realm of science (and in particular among the fundamentalist proponents of New Atheism) than in the world of religion where people really do make the very real and obviously positive experiences that keep them going. Studies have shown that atheists are far more common in social sciences (e.g. economics, political science, psychology, sociology, anthropology, jurisprudence, history) than in the fields of natural science (e.g. physics, astronomy, biology, chemistry) whose proponents more often than not turn out to be (or become) theistic scientists. [71]

"The first gulp from the glass of natural sciences will turn you into an atheist, but at the bottom of the glass God is waiting for you." Werner Heisenberg [72]

"Small amounts of philosophy lead to atheism, but larger amounts bring us back to God." Francis Bacon [73]

History is full of examples of visionary scientists who were derided and worse simply because they were, well, right! Yet fallacy and arrogance in 'official' science continues into the present-day: Close-minded (or corrupt) skeptics cling to outdated models and dare to ridicule foreign concepts that they have no idea about simply because they are too afraid to actually investigate and think, or experience and experiment, for themselves.

"The existing scientific concepts cover always only a very limited part of reality, and the other part that has not yet been understood is infinite." Werner Heisenberg

Regardless of their often fancy titles, people like this are simply followers who repeat what they have heard or read and are thus not really freely thinking or genuinely inquisitive individuals. Fact is that nothing new, exciting or beneficial has ever come from uncritical adherents and propagators of outdated models who seemingly like to stop progress of any kind. And worse, even if they do find out that they had it all wrong, some may still prefer to stick with the erroneous status quo simply because it benefits their bottom line:

"It is difficult to get a man to understand something, when his salary depends upon his not understanding it." Upton Sinclair [74]

The only way to truly and permanently elevate our consciousness is if our new insight is grounded upon our own personal experience. Nobody else can do this for us, otherwise the past enlightened souls would have enlightened us all already and there would be no need for it any longer. That would also mean that the world is full of love, peace and happiness already. But we all know that this ideal is work in progress to which we all need to contribute.

"Knowledge gained through experience is far superior and many times more useful than bookish knowledge." Mahatma Gandhi [75]

Imagine for a moment that you have lived all your life in a totally remote jungle in the Amazon or Papua New Guinea. You are one of the still existing tribes who have never had any contact with modern civilization, indeed, outsiders of any kind. Someone could now suddenly appear and tell you that chocolate ice cream tastes really great, that it's absolutely divine food 'made in heaven'. But since you have *never ever* tasted any ice cream before you'd have to make of these three choices:

1. You believe it on faith because you somehow trust that the visitor speaks the truth.
2. You don't believe that there is such a thing as chocolate ice cream or that it tastes good.
3. You make the smart choice and try some for yourself. That is the only way you will know for sure. Because obviously you will have made the actual personal experience yourself.

It is clear that the individual choices we make in our lives will greatly influence the overall quality of life. Indeed it will also affect what happens day in, day out. The same can be said for what we choose to think, believe and know.

What is the best way to discover the truth? Any truth including the truth about who we really are? The short answer is to *become a lover of truth*. In other words, a truth-seeker.

Nowadays, knowing the truth can be a complex endeavor as discussed in various places throughout this book. Yet there is one simple remedy, a method that is *guaranteed* to work:

Be always truthful to yourself within and only speak the truth.

People who lie or tell fibs first and foremost punish themselves. Lying is a form and sign of unkindness; being unkind both to oneself and to others. With a bit of intelligent thought many realize early in life that being untrue is never actually necessary in the first place; it is far better to simply remain quiet or to only reveal certain (true) parts of a story. After all we don't really have an obligation to always justify ourselves to others, or to easily reveal our innermost thoughts and feelings.

Besides, it is far easier to always live and speak the truth than having to remember fake and false stories all the time. Eventually the truth will always come out; most of us learn this lesson already as a child. And yet, when we look at our modern societies, truth has been mostly substituted with deliberate falsehoods, empty promises in advertising, and a constant flow of propaganda by a myriad of organizations.

These days we sure get to 'enjoy' a great deal of fake journalism and fictitious news, fabricated food and bogus medicine, politicized education and politically correct religion, counterfeit money and fraudulent markets, make-believe 'quality' products and a myriad of fake body parts. We could also add corrupted democracy and phony human rights to the list. Are these all symptoms of an honest society that well and truly treasures truthfulness and sincerity?

"Three things cannot be long hidden: the sun, the moon, and the truth." Buddha [76]

To be truthful is the happy way to go because the truth itself is an inherent and natural part of every spiritual soul. There are no lies in heaven. Fact is that with the exception of psycho-or sociopaths we all feel at least unconsciously bad if we tell something we know to be false or not quite true. And of course that would show in our body language too, respectively is intuitively felt by those who actually do live a life of truth, both within and without.

Telling the truth attracts the truth, thus *enabling us to recognize and know the truth* whenever we come across it. And likewise, we will instantly know it when someone is trying to tell us BS, lies or otherwise attempts to sell us something that is not in the least to *our* benefit. No matter how fancy the charade, we just instinctively know what is really going on and we can simply and merrily move on to greener pastures with a polite "Thanks, but no thanks!".

"Treat those who are good with goodness, and also treat those who are not good with goodness. Thus goodness is attained. Be honest to those who are honest, and be also honest to those who are not honest. Thus honesty is attained." Lao Tzu

Being honest to ourselves means to acknowledge both our strengths *and* weaknesses. After all we are all not perfect while here on planet Earth. So let's face it and accept it, warts and all. And improve whatever and wherever we can. To be our authentic and genuine selves is actually quite a relief for anybody who dares to be themselves. When we don't need to hide or pretend anymore we also allow others to do likewise. Despite our imperfections we are all lovable. And those who don't like and accept us the way we are will naturally fade away and enrich our lives with their absence.

"Insist on yourself. Never imitate." Ralph Waldo Emerson

Ultimately *the honest journey both within and without will enable us to realize who we really are*, eternally. And that in turn will help us to *conquer fear*. Not just any and all fears, but the original and ultimate one: The fear of dying, the dread that we may cease to exist - forever.

"God is spirit, and his worshipers must worship in the spirit and in truth." (John 4:24)

Are you afraid of death? Or at times even feel a bit insecure about life? Like being frightened to not have enough money to survive or retire with? Many Christians believe in the afterlife, upon judgment day. Yet at the same time so many of even the most devout people still believe in materialism, the belief "that matter is the fundamental substance in nature, and that all phenomena, including mental phenomena and consciousness, are identical with material interactions." [77]

"And ye shall know the truth, and the truth shall make you free." (John 8:32)

So "Who am I?" It's a great question to ask God in deep prayer. And as always the sincere heartfelt question will be answered. In due time and perhaps in ways that may surprise us. Like in our sleep or during a deep meditation we will just know. Somehow or another we may receive guidance and come across the evidence that will further confirm what has already been revealed and experienced.

"Meditation is the dissolution of thoughts in Eternal awareness or Pure consciousness without objectification, **knowing without thinking***, merging finitude in infinity."* Voltaire

"With God's help, I shall become myself!" Soren Aabye Kierkegaard [78]

Solely for the purpose of our discussion let's categorize human consciousness into the following three general schools of thought or awareness. Since consciousness goes beyond mere thinking, analyzing and reasoning, we could call them the three main modes of experiencing the world, or perspectives:

1. The Materialistic Perspective - hereafter referred to as *'Machine Man'* or *Homo Machina*

2. The Religious Perspective - *'Believing Man'* or *Homo Credo*

3. The Spiritual Perspective - *'Mystic Man'* or *Homo Mysticum*

Of course, the three categories are both very broad and fluid. For example, it is certainly possible to be a religious person but also believe in mainstream science, up to a point. And likewise there are a great many scientists who believe in God; not every scientist is a radical atheist even though persons of that flavor are regularly promoted by mainstream media and government departments.

Mystic Man too can be deeply devout while at the same time be very interested in the latest progress of science - albeit they have the natural tendency to come up with a far broader interpretation (say about Quantum Mechanics) than a typical materialistic scientist or mainstream doctor.

By making the above distinctions we certainly don't wish to assign any value. That would be irrelevant anyway as quality of life, the underlying beliefs and our overall consciousness is a most personal experience. And as such it is beyond criticism by external parties (for as long as one does not attempt to harm others). Besides, even scientific reductionists can invent something that is truly beneficial to all of us, and so on. But let's see the difference between the following general perspectives:

1. *Machine Man:* People who *think* that they *are* their body - ruled by a more or less intelligent brain, aided and abetted by a better or worse set of DNA. This is the purely materialistic perspective, incessantly propagated and promoted by academia, governments, and the mainstream media. According to *Homo Machina*, "We are just smart animals." Adherents of this belief system think that when they die, well, they will be dead. Forever. They believe that *they* basically cease to exist, respectively *turn to fertilizer* and worm fodder.

2. *Believing Man:* People who *identify* themselves as their body but *believe* that they *somehow* or another *have* a spiritual eternal soul. It is s*omewhere*, deep down or within themselves. This is the religious perspective and it is based mostly on scripture, faith, and cultural traditions. *Homo Credo* mourn their dead yet at the same time believe (to various degrees) that the deceased person continues to exist as a soul, hopefully in heaven.

3. *Mystic Man:* People who *know* that they *are* the eternal spiritual soul, but are temporarily having a human experience in a body made of flesh and blood. This is the mystical perspective, *based on real personal experiences made or insights gained*. People who truly know who they are may also deeply miss the soul that has passed away and will honor their dead bodies, yet they continue to feel connected with a beloved person through their

eternal bands (and means of communication) of love. They are *totally sure* about seeing their loved ones soon again (knowing full well that time, after all, is very relative), and they are already looking forward to it. This state of consciousness literally helps to live more fully and aware in the current here and now while taking away any remaining fear of dying and much of the heartache of losing a loved one at the same time. It is therefore a recipe for real freedom and great happiness!

The ways we think, talk and feel are all influenced by our overall consciousness or perspective; it literally determines how we see and experience the world we live in today. And of course it will also influence how we act; the kind of things we do and equally the things we *don't* do!

We can observe the above three modes of consciousness in the different ways people talk about those who have passed on:

1. "He is dead". Full stop. That's the end of it. "Too bad and sad but get over it and accept reality! Try not to think about it and move on." *Homo Machina* well and truly hates to talk about death or the dead; it's a mortifying even frightening subject. No wonder they often do get depressed in life; it is a rather depressing philosophy!

2. "May God have mercy on his soul". Hopefully his soul will go to the right place (heaven). "I miss him so much and really hope to see him again." And yes, it will happen, for sure! (see also chapter *Love in Separation*).

3. "She's a most beautiful and loving soul. And I very much look forward to seeing her again when my time has come. In the meantime we will remain connected in love."

The way we write is equally revealing to how we perceive the reality of life and death. See how the following snippets all talk about *a soul as something other than themselves*, a separate 'inner being' that is different from who they are (or rather, who they think they are) :

- Bared his soul

- Looked deep into his soul
- Searched his soul
- A weekend retreat for your soul
- Helping to discover their soul's purpose
- The deepest stirrings of your soul
- Speaking to my soul
- Wake up your soul
- I had sold my soul
- Your soul is possessed
- I feel it in my soul
- She has a carnal soul
- Chicken soup for the soul
- SOS - save our souls
- We have an eternal soul that will never die
- I am the captain of my soul

You can also observe the different insights or perspectives in historical sayings; the first one is by a famous German philosopher, and the next one by an Indian Hindu monk who inspired many Westerns teachers and writers:

*"There is one thing one has to **have**: either a soul that is cheerful by nature, ßor a soul made cheerful by work, love, art, and knowledge."* Friedrich Nietzsche [79]

*"You have to grow from the inside out. None can teach you, none can make you spiritual. There is no other teacher but **your own** soul."* Swami Vivekananda [80]

Strangely or perhaps funnily, quite a few of both historical and contemporary books that deal with spiritual themes (religious, personal development, self-help etc.) display this lack of insight into who we really are. While these authors surely have other interesting and helpful messages to convey, their core perspective is about 'being a physical body but having a soul somewhere'. In other words, they write about the beliefs of *Homo Credo*.

In contrast, here are some sayings by some of history's greats who did indeed know that they **are** the spiritual soul who lives forever - rather than being a physical body who **has** a soul as a separate and mysterious entity (that is 'somewhere', and 'somehow' able to teach you, the body…)

*"If it be a sin to covet honor, I **am** the most offending soul."* William Shakespeare [81]

*"I **am** a soul. I know well that what I shall render up to the grave is not myself. That which is myself will go elsewhere. Earth, thou art not my abyss!"* Victor Hugo [82]

"The end of life is to be like God, and the soul following God will be like Him." Socrates [83]

"I do not believe…I know. I have had the experience of being gripped by something that is far stronger than myself, something that people call God." Carl Jung [84]

Not knowing one's true self means to only be able to repeat a cherished belief learned from an equally unaware mentor or teacher. Yet by definition a person with a fundamentally materialistic consciousness cannot possibly reveal anything meaningful or truthful beyond that particular perspective, no matter how well-intentioned they may be. The simple fact is that we cannot get clarity about who we really are from people who are still confused themselves.

The way we think, feel and express ourselves always reveals our core perspectives and beliefs. And those in turn do have great repercussions for the quality and direction of both our immediate *and* infinite lives.

What do the holy scriptures say about who we really are?

"And I say to you, my friends: Be not afraid of them who kill the body, and after that have no more that they can do." (Luke 12:4)

"I declare to you, brothers and sisters, that flesh and blood cannot inherit the kingdom of God, nor does the perishable inherit the imperishable." (1 Corinthians 15:50)

"For we know that if the earthly tent we live in is destroyed, we have a building from God, an eternal house in heaven, not built by human hands." (2 Corinthians 5:1

"Meanwhile we groan, longing to be clothed with our heavenly dwelling," (2 Corinthians 5:2)

"Therefore we are always confident and know that as long as we are at home in the body we are away from the Lord. We are confident, I say, and would prefer to be away from the body and at home with the Lord." (2 Corinthians 5:6, 5:8)

"That which is born of the flesh is flesh, and that which is born of the Spirit is spirit." (John 3:6)

"Do you not know that you are God's temple and that God's Spirit dwells in you?" (1 Corinthians 3:16)

These Bible verses are very clear that while our bodies are perishable we are made of spirit and do not even need to fear the killing of our physical bodies. And that indeed we, the eternal souls, also have a natural 'heavenly' body which is spiritual in nature too.

"The body that is sown is perishable, it is raised imperishable; it is sown a natural body, it is raised a spiritual body. If there is a natural body, there is also a spiritual body." (1 Corinthians 15:42,44)

We, the spiritual souls, cannot be destroyed. Ever. We are always alive.

Once we not just believe but know this to be true *we will have conquered the origin of all fears*. Death, the great equalizer that brings about more meaning to our life on planet Earth. Every fear we can possibly dream of or be scared about is related to this original fear. It's the fear that we may cease to exist. It is an entirely needless fear and yet it is being promoted in so many ways, and for so many (sales) reasons.

Indeed death in its supposed finality is the key ingredient that we find so entertaining in our books and movies, computer games and so on. Throughout history and to its present day *fictional* death is portrayed in endless shapes and forms, usually the crueler or more 'colorful' the better. Yet in 'real' life the subject is most often a total taboo that no one dares to talk about.

"If you realize that all things change, there is nothing you will try to hold on to. If you are not afraid of dying, there is nothing you cannot achieve." Lao Tzu

So what do the scriptures of other spiritual traditions say?

The Vedas - thought to be among the world's oldest sacred texts (going back 1500-1000 BCE) - describe our spiritual nature in various of their holy books:

"Never was there a time when I did not exist, nor you, nor all these kings; nor in the future shall any of us cease to be." (Bhagavad Gita 2:12)

"Know that which pervades the entire body is indestructible. No one is able to destroy the imperishable soul." (Bhagavad Gita 2:17)

"Only the material body of the indestructible, immeasurable and eternal living entity is subject to destruction; therefore, fight, O descendant of Bharata." (Bhagavad Gita 2:18)

"The soul can never be cut into pieces by any weapon, nor can he be burned by fire, nor moistened by water, nor withered by the wind." (Bhagavad Gita 2:23)

In other parts of Vedic scripture, the spiritual soul is described even further, including its very size:

"When the upper point of a hair is divided into one hundred parts and again each of such parts is further divided into one hundred parts, each such part is the measurement of the dimension of the spirit soul." (Svetasvatara Upanisad 5.9)

"There are innumerable particles of spiritual atoms, which are measured as one ten-thousandth of the upper portion of the hair." (Srimad Bhagavatam)

A typical *Machine Man* 'insight' says that "no one escapes alive". And of course this is only true if one erroneously identifies with their physical bodies, their external 'clothing'. We all keep living, but someplace else. The actual person, the spirit soul, is simply leaving. And it is 'just' our bodies that stay behind in this material dimension to which its atoms and molecules belong.

The reason why some people believe in having a soul that is a separate 'thing' or entity from who they are is because they still identify themselves as their physical bodies. So perhaps funnily, both *Homo Machina* and *Homo Credo* have something rather profound in common: Their materialistic worldview.

Whether one believes that we are just a complicated concoction of atoms and molecules, or that we are our bodies yet also have, own or possess a soul somewhere essentially means the very same thing: It is the erroneous identification of ourselves as something that we are not.

The following quote shows a good example of the confusion or dilemma of Believing Man:

*'If you die you're completely happy and **your soul somewhere lives** on. I'm not afraid of dying. Total peace after death, **becoming someone else** is the best hope I've got."* Kurt Cobain [85]

You could not possibly be your physical body and when that dies, you - the dead body composed of unconscious particles of matter - suddenly and mysteriously become something or somebody else; the spiritual soul. It's a rather absurd concept and yet many *Homo Credo* do believe just that: The now dead and decomposing body morphing into something suddenly alive and forever so. That is as much fantasy as *Machine Man* with his belief of nothing turning into something; dead and unaware particles that suddenly appeared out of nowhere and by sheer chance turned into living and conscious beings.

In contrast, *Homo Mysticum* knows full well that it is *us* who *are* the individual spiritual souls who live eternally. Here are two examples of the insights of Mystic Man:

"Thou art a little soul bearing about a corpse, as Epictetus used to say." Marcus Aurelius

"We are not human beings having a spiritual experience. We are spiritual beings having a human experience." Pierre Teilhard de Chardin [86]

To get to know who we really are does matter. And very much so. As the benefits are both many and important. One benefit is the discarding of all fears, including the origin of them all; the fear of dying. Another is that we will better be able to cope with grief, the deep pain that comes from losing loved ones.

Regardless of our personal perspectives, losing a loved one is always a profoundly sad and life-changing experience. This is true no matter how 'enlightened' or knowledgeable we are about our spiritual nature and so on. We will still miss the dearly departed ones until we will be once again reunited.

Yet in a perhaps not fully appreciated way, loved ones that have passed on ahead of us can actually make it easier for us to understand who we are. And once we are fully 'self-realized' the dearly departed do make our own passing a lot easier because we are absolutely sure to see them again when our time has come, and indeed are already looking forward to it even while living here to the fullest (see also chapter *Love in Separation*).

"That which is so universal as death must be a benefit." Friedrich Schiller

We do live forever albeit not in our present temporary bodies. This is true for all of us, even the 'bad guys', people who have strayed so far away from who they really are and the eternal dimensions of divine love that they 'are able' to do abhorrent things to their fellow brothers and sisters. That may be 'news' to those Christians and non-Christians who 'believe' that one has to *earn* eternal life by being a good person and so on.

Yet once we know full well about our eternal reality we simply know better. This truth was actually acknowledged by the rather conservative Pope Benedict XVI in a 2015 discussion with Fr. Jacques Servais, SJ. [87]

While everybody lives forever the question still remains where exactly, in which dimension? We all go to different places and that all depends on our consciousness (see also chapter *The Divine Deal*).

"I thought of the soul as resembling a castle, formed of a single diamond or a very transparent crystal, and containing many rooms, just as in Heaven there are many mansions." Saint Teresa of Avila

"I know a man in Christ who fourteen years ago was caught up to the third heaven. Whether it was in the body or out of the body I do not know—God knows. And I know that this man—whether in the body or apart from the body I do not know, but God knows—was caught up to paradise and heard inexpressible things, things that no one is permitted to tell." (2 Corinthians 12:2-4)

Knowing who we really are will also make us better people in terms of our behavior, no matter how hard militant atheists claim and pretend otherwise: If we believe the philosophy of *Machine Man* that the physical death of our bodies is the end of everything, we will focus solely (or at least mostly) on material aspects of life. Because that's all there is for them. Survival of the fittest for as long as possible. For them there is no love but only chemical illusions as part of the breeding process (respectively the continuation of their particular set of surely superior genes).

"Chance is a word void of sense; nothing can exist without a cause." Voltaire

Ultimately for *Homo Machina* there is no need for moral or ethical behavior because the primordial soup that supposedly produced us doesn't know the difference between good or evil anyway. And since, according to them, life is only the random combination of dead matter (an amazing oxymoron) that is somehow preoccupied with self-preservation, why should morality matter for the 'enlightened' atheist? Survival of the strongest and smartest or richest and most ruthless might do just fine…

In a conversation and a perhaps rare moment of truth ('in vino veritas'), a humanist atheist actually acknowledged that there is no real basis for humanism other than desiring that their offspring will also be able to live in a more or less civilized society where certain rules and regulations govern our conduct. Which in turn increases their chances of living a long life. Yet when pressed on the matter he kind of sheepishly admitted that he would kill a hated adversary if he would be *absolutely sure* not to ever get caught. In such a scenario he would have no moral qualms whatsoever.

While that may sound extreme, and it sure is, we need to be(come) fully aware that our deeply held beliefs do matter a great deal; they hugely influence our lives, from the big all the way to the small, from the very positive to the very negative, from the uplifting to the outright depressing.

Popular memes and acronyms among many of today's younger generations seem rather self-explanatory: YOLO stands for "you only live once", while DILLIGAF means "do I look like I give a f***?"

Should we really be surprised about such attitudes when we all get incessantly reminded by 'officialdom' about being smart animals only that will turn to worm fodder soon? Why should we care or behave morally? The beliefs of *Homo Machina* do not sound to be particularly enlightened or civilized when we consider their real meanings and practical implications. To put it mildly.

"Our ideas about death define how we live our life." Dag Hammarskjöld [88]

Once we realize and know full well that we *are* the eternal spiritual soul we are again a truly *whole* person. And how could we possibly 'misbehave' in this or that way? To be fully self-realized and still be unloving or uncaring or worse is simply a very unlikely proposition!

Once we see ourselves and everyone else as fellow children of God - kindred spirit souls with overall rather similar hopes and dreams and fears - it will become very difficult to be unjust or mean to one another. Love after all is the nature of spirit, the nature of God. And once we all feel this truth within we cannot help but act accordingly in our daily lives!

"Knowing others is intelligence; knowing yourself is true wisdom. Mastering others is strength; mastering yourself is true power." Lao Tzu

With a clear spiritual perspective we will also lose much if not all of our seriousness that is really uncalled for. The gravity of life and death loses its power and we become once again more light-hearted and yes, merry! At the same time we will also be more energized and enthusiastic about our life while here. To learn and grow. To love and laugh. To achieve and assist. And so on.

There are millions of people around the world who had a mystic experience that led to deep spiritual insights about their real nature. A great many people had a more or less voluntary out-of-body experience (OBE) respectively an always involuntary near-death experience (NDE). The descriptions of their experiences have much in common - despite them living in different parts of the world. Despite their differences in language, culture and creed they all realized that they are not their physical bodies.

And this most happy of realizations fundamentally changed their outlook in life; they are now very strongly motivated to be the best person they could possibly be. And knowing of their eternal nature yet the temporary and relatively short time available here, they all have a deep and heartfelt desire to help making the world a better place.

"For those who are led by the Spirit of God are the children of God." (Romans 8:14)

Imagine the kind of world we would live in if we all just knew... We would have conquered all our fears... We would cooperate more and compete less... And we would be too preoccupied with living a life full of love, peace and happiness to even think about fighting wars that benefit only the very few to the detriment of the very many...

"For God has not given us the spirit of fear, but of power, and of love, and of a sound mind." (2 Timothy 1:7)

"Our deepest fear is not that we are inadequate, our deepest fear is that we are powerful beyond measure. It is our light, not our darkness, that most frightens us. We ask ourselves, 'who am I to be brilliant, gorgeous, talented and fabulous?' Actually, who are you not to be? You are a child of God. Your playing small doesn't serve the world. There is nothing enlightened about shrinking so that other people won't feel insecure around you. We are born to make manifest the glory of God that is within us. It is not just within some of us; it is in everyone. As we let our own light shine, we unconsciously give other people permission to do the same. As we are liberated from our own fear, our presence automatically liberates others." Marianne Williamson [89]

Merry Christians are never really afraid of dying, being fully aware that we all have to go one day in the same way we know while vacationing that our holidays will come to an end. We have booked the hotel for two weeks and when the time is up we'll have to check out and go back home, to our normal real life. Part of why we enjoy our vacations so much is because they are limited in time.

An endless holiday may sound good at first but it is likely to become a bit boring after a while. We are born in this particular world to be active, to do, learn and experience things that are only possible in this rather unique environment, the world of polarities and contrast.

"A beautiful soul has no other merit than its own existence." Friedrich von Schiller

To discover the various dimensions of our existence, to experiment and experience all there is to explore, will not only make our Earthly lives a lot more fulfilled, but also ensures a happy 'going home' when our time has come. And most likely with our contributions of love in action we will also leave the world a better place for future generations.

Being asked by the Pharisees when the kingdom of God would come, Jesus answered them, "The kingdom of God is not coming in ways that can be observed, nor will they say, 'See here!' or 'See there!' For indeed, the kingdom of God is within you." (Luke 17:20,21)

Discover your Self. Dare to be your Self. And stay mostly merry!

REALIZATIONS:

I love to know the truth

I love to truly know my self

I love to be my original self

God wants me to the best I can be

Follow Love

Perfect advice is the advice that brings out the best possible outcome for everybody - for the asking as well as all others involved in an interaction or transaction. Perfect advice always creates win-win situations for everyone. As impossible as that may sound at first thought, it will make everybody happier.

The skeptic might ask if there really is such a thing as perfect advice? And if so, how or where would we get it? Or how would we actually be able to *recognize* perfect advice upon hearing it? After all, we live in a world where we all have a great many opinions. Besides, there is certainly no lack of people or organizations trying to tell (or sell) us what to believe, think and do.

Many Christians engage in political battles of all kinds. Some ask 'what would Jesus do' and then discuss and speculate, or worse, argue about the answers. However, since we are not Jesus, how can we know for sure what *he* would do? What is the best *we* can do in any given situation or moment?

Always finding the perfect answer can be very easy: Jesus asks us to love God - first and foremost - with all our heart, soul, and mind. And then, to love our fellow brothers and sisters as we love ourselves.

God is Love. If we desire to live our life in harmony with God, being connected and united in love, we will also need to act with love. And this will happen automatically the more we embrace and feel God's pure love for us.

All we need to do to receive the perfect answer to any question, no matter what it may be, is to sincerely ask while feeling divine love within our hearts and minds.

What would love do?

What's the answer of love?

How does love see this?

What's the advice of love?

Unconditional pure divine love has certain inherent attributes or built-in characteristics:

Love never wants to see suffering or violence. Love does not order punishment of any kind.

Love is not partial nor does it discriminate against anyone.

Love is healing. Love is supportive. Love is nourishing. Love is understanding. Love is peace. Love is just. And, love is joy and happiness.

Or put in a bit of a cheeky way: Love is being a merry Christian!

All we have to do is to follow Jesus by living according to his first and second commandments. Live immersed in love and be merry! Listen to the love within our hearts and act as we feel inspired.

Here we will not discuss the various aspects of today's political and social issues that we are confronted with on a daily basis. There are already plenty of religious and political leaders 'out there' who want to be heard and tell us what we should think or how we should behave. Their prescriptions, preferences and admonishments however are solely based on their own beliefs, interpretations, and personal interests. Having reached exalted positions of any kind won't necessarily make them true and right.

The question is always what do they *really* sow and advocate - both in their private and public lives? Is it love and understanding, compassion and joy that speaks and acts there - or is it the very absence of it? Will there be more love, peace and happiness in the world thanks to their words and deeds - or will there obviously be less?

Best is to always see and taste the fruits. That is far better than to be a sheep and blindly follow the wolf in sheep's clothes into the spiritual abyss that only leads to a cold, dry and lonely desert…

We have to be aware and beware the tree that produces only hatred and division, discord and war, suffering and pain. Recognize the false prophets. And simply *ignore them!*

Jesus was very clear about those hiding behind complicated rules and unnecessary regulations, the ones huffing and puffing, playing pious in public only, or feigning moral outrage purely for personal gains.

"Not everyone who says to me, 'Lord, Lord,' will enter the kingdom of heaven, but only the one who does the will of my Father who is in heaven. Many will say to me on that day, 'Lord, Lord, did we not prophesy in your name and in your name drive out demons and in your name perform many miracles?' Then I will tell them plainly, 'I never knew you. Away from me, you evildoers!'" (Matthew 7:21, 22, 23)

"Going to church doesn't make us a Christian any more than standing in a garage makes us a car." Billy Sunday [90]

Jesus is love. He lives it, and he commands it. And love speaks a very clear language that we can all understand very easily. Why? Because love is an inherent part of all of us. It is part and parcel of the very fabric of a spiritual soul.

"The kingdom of God is within you." (Luke 17.21)

We all immediately recognize love when we feel and witness it in action. No one needs a translator. Or a teacher, preacher, guru or the like. Love is simply self-evident. Self-illuminating and radiating just like the sun.

The contrast becomes very clear in the following table, and so is the choice for merry Christians:

Love	*The Absence of Love*
Love	Anger
Spirit Soul	Worldly Ego
Unity	Separation
Understanding	Condemnation
Accepting	Judging
Agreements	Arguments
Taking Responsibility	Apportioning Blame
Healing	Hurting
Patience	Impatience
Cooperation	Competition
Respect	Disrespect/Ridicule
Peace	War
Supportive	Undermining
Strengthening	Weakening
Generous	Avarice
Compassionate	Careless
Kindness	Indifference
Joy & Happiness	Greed & Gluttony
Praising	Criticizing
Confidence	Insecurities
Creating	Destroying

Things really become quite easy when we distill them all the way down to their very essence. Yes, there are always shades of gray in between, but ultimately, there is still black and white at the polar ends. Certain things are either good or bad. Right or wrong. Healthy or not. Likeable or not. And so on and so forth.

Children usually know this from the very beginning. We were all born with a conscience and a inherent moral compass that guides us through life. The majority of crooks knows full well when they do something wrong!

The stark contrast of the polar opposites helps us to distinguish between the many potential choices and thus serves to illuminate the roadmap ahead. Where are we now and where are we heading to?

As we have discussed in the chapter *Love All*, love can be found in virtually all shades of gray. In most interactions love is present - to various degrees. From the very minute to the all-encompassing.

On one end it's unconditional pure love (represented by the saints of the world) and on the very other side it is the complete lack of it. The very absence of love is the totally selfish ego 'love' (egocentricity) that is solely concerned with satisfying the lower instincts without any regards for others (as represented by the psychopaths, respectively sociopaths. It is estimated that about one percent of the general population falls into this extreme end of the scale, and 3-4 percent among certain professionals). [91]

Whenever love is present, the spirit of God is equally there to the quantity and quality of the love expressed. The more the merrier!

When we feel and live a life of love we will truly help to make the world a better place. That is most pleasing to God. And it will make our life much happier because we are living just like we are supposed to live. Because love, peace and happiness is our natural state of being, desire and purpose.

Living life as a merry Christian will make life much easier too. Simply because we won't need to carry around so much excess weight. The world of ego has literally endless demands and desires, complications and aggravations. As we leave it further and further behind, there is simply less and less reason to struggle or feel stressed out.

Simply surrender to the infinite presence of love and trust in the ultimate go(o)dness and wisdom of its advice. We can't go wrong. Love is the best adviser and it won't cost us a single cent!

REALIZATIONS:

I love to follow love

I love to let love guide me

Respect

We all have the desire to be respected. At least by our peers. And most if not all of us know how it feels to be slighted or otherwise not respected. Disrespect is very often the cause of lots of dramas and upheavals in life. Sometimes it even turns into acts of violence with all the corresponding sorrows and pains that inevitably follow.

The need to feel validated and respected is inborn in every baby already. Some of us are lucky to receive plenty of validation, love and respect as a child while others are not so 'lucky' and often chase it in the outside world. More or less desperately. And more or less successfully.

Respect plays an important part in leading a successful and happy life. It is also an important ingredient in the harmonious functioning of society as a whole. Realizing this and living accordingly has only benefits. First, we eliminate a lot of problems, from small to potentially very serious ones. And second, it makes our life a lot smoother. When people we interact with feel wholly (holy) respected, they are likely to give us respect in return and otherwise be more positive and constructive. Whether that's in private, corporate or public life.

A lack of respect corresponds directly with a lack of happiness, both within our own hearts and minds and externally in the 'outside' world we seemingly share.

Some people lament the growing lack of respect in today's world, particularly in the public arena, in politics and (often not so) civil life, within families, between colleagues at work, and even among friends or otherwise loving couples.

Psychologists say that this is partly a consequence of the growing narcissism we can witness (and measure) which in turn is partly fueled by the widespread use of social media, besides the overly pampering by some parents who have elevated their offspring to a kind of God-like status... Their kids are always best and great, no matter what. The problem is only that such sentiments are rarely shared by the world at large, thereby introducing a whole range of usually negative consequences into their later lives.

For many of us 'kids of all ages', social media has quickly turned into a 'Fakebook' kind of thing where we strive to present ourselves only in the very best of light. This is certainly understandable when we consider the pressures we may face to get a decent job or otherwise move ahead in life.

So nowadays our public portrayals have often not very much in common with reality, to the point of friends not recognizing each other in those thoroughly attractive yet totally faked (photo-shopped) pictures. Even supermodels feel the need to make themselves look (even) skinnier, delete bags under their eyes, or hide a little cellulite, before sending out their Tweets! Whatever it may be. Whatever it takes... These days seemingly everyone has to have the profile of a superstar. Yours truly included, of course!

The internet has thus enabled the portrayal of a dramatically augmented reality that is often only wishful thinking. A battle of our insecure egos. To see who is prettier, smarter, more successful. Or to compare who leads a more glamorous and fun life. Who is richer and has all the right, cool and flashy toys? Who has more so-called friends, is more popular, influential, or famous?

We participate because we all want to be winners; nobody wants to be seen as a loser - as defined by the majority 'in' mob of essentially followers who rally around the latest popular (weird?) decree of the day without actually thinking for themselves. The first question we need to ask when examining any heavily promoted issue is always 'Qui Bono?' - who benefits?

This battle nobody dares to call a battle creates even more insecurities and anxieties in people less apt at leading (or performing) such a wonderful and successful life - in public. In many of the 'losers' it can bring about outright depressions, upon seeing themselves as so very ordinary, compared to their flashy 'friends'. After all, not everybody is inclined or good at showing off their attractive sides. Or perhaps more accurately, prone to lie to themselves and others just to feel a bit better. Temporarily…

We are all champions. Or feel the need to be one. And strangely, or funnily, we really are…

We are all special simply because we are all unique. It is never really a matter of who is superior or inferior in this or that way. Such are just external man-made distinctions, attributes or assessments that easily come, and easily go. To the heavens of hot air.

The reality is that every one of us is unique and thereby special. So we don't really need to chase external respect and approval. We don't need to do anything to achieve it. It is already a given. It's a gift by God. All we need to do is to recognize, understand and embrace it. And to be thankful and happy about it!

Our DNS is a once in the entire universe kind of thing, and so are our fingerprints, the retina of our eyes, our thoughts and feelings, our experiences in life, our dreams and desires, our set of social environment (nobody has the same friends, family and colleagues as you do). We all have our totally unique story to tell.

And yes, what we do while we are here - our individual purposes and passions - are also totally unique. Everybody is important. In some way or another. To someone or to many. No matter how high or low our job or social position may be, we are all equally needed. Otherwise we would not be here, or exist at all.

Some may say that the captain of a cruise ship is the most important person and without him (or rarely, her) 'the show couldn't go on'.

Well, the same can and must be said for everybody else on that ship: Each passenger pays for the privilege and pleasure to be aboard and makes it all possible in the first place. The stewards, the machinists, the navigators, cleaning crews, and so on are all equally important as their functions are crucial for the successful operation of a ship.

And so were the engineers, designers, builders and investors that built the ship. Each one of the great many people involved in the complex enterprise we call life is here for good reasons!

And The Happy Rabbit Says…

"Know and feel that you're a unique part of the Universe - and just as special as everyone else!"

One 'funny' fact about respect is that once we fully respect ourselves within we don't really need to chase it in the external world. We just don't have that urge any longer. Or not that strongly anyway. And yet, perhaps strangely, we will at the same time receive more respect from others. Without asking or yearning for it. It is the inside world getting mirrored externally. Like attracts like.

"When you are content to be simply yourself and don't compare or compete, everyone will respect you." Lao Tzu

Another plus about feeling respect within our own hearts and minds is that we don't get totally mad or deeply sad about someone being rude. We can simply shrug it off, simply assuming that they had a bad day, and silently wish them all the best. It's a both respectful and respectable way that yields much goodness and happiness.

The key is to respect yourself as the eternal spark of God you are. And likewise, give others this same basic respect as a fellow child of God. It's a seeing of things with our spiritual eyes. Instead of the demanding of respect as a separated and insecure 'little' ego that looks for the external approval and confirmation of its importance and specialness.

"I see God in every human being. When I wash the leper's wounds, I feel I am nursing the Lord himself. Is it not a beautiful experience?" Mother Teresa

It is often those who sternly and loudly demand to be respected by others who at the same time have the habit of treating others in rather condescending and disrespectful ways. Their urge to show disrespect is only a sign of insecurity and should be understood as such. There is never really a need to take offense. And thereby become unhappy. Best is to understand and overlook. Because it can and does happen (in the best of families) if we don't yet know and therefore respect ourselves as the person we really and eternally are (see also chapter *Be your Self*).

And The Happy Rabbit Says…

"Don't expect to receive approval, respect or love from those who don't yet know themselves!"

Some might question the idea of giving respect to the various disagreeable characters 'out there'. The people who do bad, sad or mad things. That is surely an understandable sentiment, and yet even they deserve to receive some basic respect as they are also unique and have their purpose in the big picture of things. Even if we don't understand any of the reasons why.

It is rarely up to us to know it all. And therefore it is never up to us to judge or condemn a person as much as we may object to their actions or lack thereof. After all, every saint has a past and every sinner has a future.

They might end up doing something extraordinarily great at some later point in their life. Something that benefits us all. It could be the saving of the life of a young still unknown saint or scientist to be. Or the invention of a medical device that will improve the lives of millions of people. Anything is possible by the grace of God.

"Do not judge, or you too will be judged." (Matthew 7:1)

Best is to always see and respect others as fellow children of God - even if they themselves don't yet see it that way, respectively they don't behave as such in any way, shape or form. By doing so we will make it easier - and more likely - for them to come to that point of realization and behavior. Sooner or later. After all love is the only way to nurture and bring about more love, not to judge and condemn, or worse, to feel disgusted and superior.

Relating to others as the kindred spirits they truly and eternally are will bring about the best in all and surely keeps us happy, healthy and humming in the meantime. If we recognize and see others as fellow travelers on planet Earth and the spiritual brothers and sisters they are, so will you be seen too. Sometimes on a conscious and at other times 'only' on a sub-conscious level. Nevertheless, much good (God) will happen!

"For in the way you judge, you will be judged; and by your standard of measure, it will be measured to you." (Matthew 7:2)

By doing so we are building a bridge to who they really are. It's the most direct and positive way to relate to each other. Soul to soul. Thereby we do our bit to strengthen a person instead of pulling them down to the level of their egos, thereby weakening and degrading them.

When we see others in a loving and enlightened way we will make it easier for them to behave as such as well. When we respect their abilities, achievements and eternal identities we are connecting to all their positive and good energies. And that simply feels much better than to subtly link to their lower selves or activities.

"Until you have learned to be tolerant with those who do not always agree with you; until you have cultivated the habit of saying some kind word of those whom you do not admire; until you have formed the habit of looking for the good instead of the bad there is in others, you will be neither successful nor happy." Napoleon Hill

To love people also means to let them grow unhindered at their own time and leisure. To force things however is just like pulling on a plant to try to make it grow faster. It will simply get uprooted and die. The kind way therefore is to always respect other people's right to have their own opinions, thoughts and beliefs even if we don't agree with them in any shape or form.

"It does not require great art, or magnificently trained eloquence, to prove that Christians should tolerate each other. I, however, am going further: I say that we

should regard all men as our brothers. What? The Turk my brother? The Chinaman my brother? The Jew? The Siam? Yes, without doubt; are we not all children of the same father and creatures of the same God?" Voltaire

At times that may sound like a tough act to to follow. Particularly in times of trouble or disagreements of any kind. Or worse when there is an active conflict or confrontation of some sorts. How can we possibly keep our peace of mind and continue to feel love within our hearts? In theory it's all good and easy to understand, but depending on a situation we may 'lose a fuse' in the heat of the moment. And especially so if we know deep within that we are not at fault in this situation.

The point is that even if we are one hundred percent right, the moment we start to actively and profoundly disrespect a person for their activities or behavior by expressing it more or less loudly, we will feel an inner uneasiness and upheaval.

The following thoughts and expressions are a respectful way to disagree with someone quietly within our own minds only, or to directly but nicely voice our displeasure to the person concerned:

I respect the spiritual person you are, yet what you did was wrong.

I respect the spiritual self you are, yet I don't like what you did.

I respect the spiritual soul you are, yet I am not pleased with this.

By keeping the big picture view of things like this we are able to transcend a conflict and keep the peace. Both within ourselves and externally; things will start to quickly calm down and turn out to the best for all. That may sound unlikely at first, but give it a try!

"In every person who comes near you look for what is good and strong; honor that; try to imitate it, and your faults will drop off like dead leaves when their time comes." John Ruskin [92]

One way to always keep a respectful attitude to others is to be fully aware of the fact that we can truly learn something from *anyone* we come to meet. Even from the most unlikely of persons. And it doesn't really matter whether we meet a person in 'real life', over the phone, or via cyberspace. Everybody we meet or come across has something to teach us. Sometimes it is a positive lesson and at other times a negative one.

We can learn how to do something better, or we can learn how better not to do it. Good and bad examples are equally instructive and valid. The smart and merry always maximize their life-long learning and recognize the essential positive messages that are contained in *every* of our interactions with others. To anyone with this awareness and attitude many great insights and pearls of wisdom are bestowed, on a daily and constant basis!

And The Happy Rabbit Says..

"There is something we can learn from everyone we meet - listen carefully and find out what it is!"

For the reasons outlined above and to sum up this chapter we can say that to *respect it all* makes and keeps us happy! And the opposite is true as well; to feel and express our disrespect feels rather bad and sad, because it is fundamentally based on the erroneous consciousness of identifying with our ego, instead of staying calm and merry by being firmly situated in our eternal reality.

So as strange as it may sound at first thought, we don't really do others a favor by being respectful to them; in reality it is simply in our very own best self-interest!

Holiness is not the luxury of the few; it is a simply duty, for you and for me, because Jesus has very clearly stated, "Be ye holy as my father in heaven is holy."
Mother Teresa

Ultimately, to respect it all includes not just the people in our immediate and distant environment but respect for all of God's creations; the big spaceship we mutually share and call home, planet Earth and all its inhabitants. We can and should respect nature in all its beautiful and glorious manifestations.

REALIZATIONS:

I love to give respect

I love to feel respected

I respect myself as I am

Admire

We live in a wonderful world full of beautiful people. Wow, that is quite a statement! And a great many people would very much disagree with it. Nevertheless, it is the truth. Yes, there are quite a few essentially man-made problems in our world, and not everybody behaves in a civilized and kind way. To put it mildly.

And yet things are a lot better than most people would think or acknowledge. Why is that so?

The short answer is that it all depends on who is telling or selling the story...

At first we need to realize that the mainstream media has a real need (and therefore the motive) to make things look a lot worse than they really are. They like to sow a bit of fear and anxiety, or otherwise appeal to our lower instincts - simply to get more of our time and attention. That will then translate into selling more advertising or subscriptions. They do this very deliberately; it is a fundamental commercial decision, an inherent part of their business model.

In short, it is institutionalized negativity. Since the very dawn of newspaper publishing the traditional formula for selling more copies has been: "If it bleeds, it leads." And now of course that very same concept is also being applied to all forms of electronic media, in particular the emotionally stirring worlds of *television programs* (= visual programming from a distance).

So much of what masquerades as news these days could safely and happily be ignored. Perhaps even most of it! There are many better ways to spend one's time and energy than reading, listening to or watching the latest gory stories of mayhem and crime, accidents, biased opinions, corporate or governmental press releases and other assorted propaganda pieces, besides the plethora of celebrity 'revelations'.

The main issue with the general media is not just the wasting of time, but that it repeatedly stresses the convictions of self-interested parties that the world is about to come to an end - unless we do as we are told - or that the world is a sad and bad place full of angry and mean people.

We will run out of this or that soon, it is dangerous to be alive and the next major catastrophe is 'just around the corner', according to the fear-mongering crowd. And of course, history has shown that people that are afraid or feel generally insecure and hopeless can all too easily be manipulated and controlled (see also chapters *Hope* and *Mind your Mind*).

The thing is that our internal and external views are mirroring each other. It goes both ways; one side affects the other, to various degrees. [See Note 93 to learn more about the interaction and interconnection of *All There Is* on the quantum mechanical level; Heisenberg's uncertainty principle, the observer effect, and quantum entanglement]

"The atoms or elementary particles themselves are not real; they form a world of potentialities or possibilities rather than one of things or facts." Werner Heisenberg

While there is mutuality in effect, the individual mind gets usually far more influenced, even dominated, by the strongly held convictions of an entire community, or society as a whole.

And mainstream corporate media, owned and/or controlled by a few oligarchs, claims to know and interpret what 'We the people' feel and desire. It tells us all the time what we should or shouldn't believe and do. Christianity, of course, is totally 'out'! That is only for the feeble-minded, stubborn dinosaurs that need to be extinct, the sooner the better. Or so they wish…

The question is whether we want to believe their overall assessments and attitudes, and follow their prescriptions, or not. The directions and directives offered are more often than not of the self-serving kind that only serve a narrow group of beneficiaries. Another aspect is that the media in general is more interested in keeping the flames of arguments going rather than finding the kind of lasting solutions that would actually be beneficial to all of us.

One effective first-aid measure to combat feelings of depression and hopelessness is to *switch off* the never-ending flow of unnecessary bad or sad news. With the advent of the internet and modern always-on gadgets lots of us have become addicted to tuning in to that constant flow of mostly negative or trivial input. And that can easily overwhelm our minds to the point of totally burying our inner equilibrium. Indeed, and sometimes quite literally, we can come to lose our sanity by being more or less angry and aggravated all the time!

Not wanting to miss anything or 'lose out', we simply *have to* check our mail every few minutes, or instantly know (or publish) social media updates, respectively swallow the latest titillating gossip or shocking news; it's truly a never-ending story. The big issue however is that it all boils down to this:

If you see the world as a frightening, dark and hopeless place you will not be able to feel peace and hope in your mind. It will make it much more difficult to be optimistic in your own life if you adopt the rather pessimistic platitudes of the general media or other doomsayers. And therefore it will be much harder to advance in life, and expand to be the best you can be.

Put differently, if you see the world as 'going down the drain' you will most likely go down the drain with it! At the very least it will make your life needlessly harder and less fulfilling. It is simply better to be a hopeful person than to become a hopeless one! One will surely make a positive difference, the other is rather unlikely to. One is easily and mostly happy, the other perhaps occasionally only.

One is essentially a rather complaining and ungrateful way of going through life, the other the appreciative and thankful. Criticizing and fault-finding versus praising and admiring. Both mindsets are equally easy to live and experience, but not equally rewarding. It is our choice, once we are aware of it.

God loves us and wants us to be the best we can possibly be! And that is very hard without having strength, purpose and hope. How could we ever live up to our fullest potential - in all aspects of life - if we have given up already without even trying? Or if we don't know what *we* really want or why we're here in the first place?

What is the true purpose of our life, the kind of things we would very much regret not having done whilst lying on our deathbeds? Who in his or her right mind would have wished to spend more time at the office or alone and lonely in front of the computer?

A negative outlook in life is quite often a sign of listening to the wrong people, the ones with a purely materialistic and mechanical view of life. People who identify themselves and all others as their bodies only (theirs with a smarter brain, of course). Disconnected egos that claim to know it all, or at least, know it best - not just for themselves, but everybody else as well.

Corporate media is not the only culprit. Governments or government sponsored institutions (like schools, colleges and universities) too teach only a materialistic way of life. Their understanding of humanity is limited to us solely being the smartest animal on the planet. As such the big fish eat the small fish. It's a matter of survival of the fittest. Alternative views and philosophies have absolutely no space, time or money allocated in our modern 'enlightened' world, where growing numbers of people are becoming disillusioned and depressed.

"Small amounts of philosophy lead to atheism, but larger amounts bring us back to God." Francis Bacon

God is not welcome anywhere in 'officialdom' except for some photo-opportunities for politicians showing up in churches (usually just before elections only). The very concept of a God is utterly and completely rejected by increasingly technocratic governments and bureaucracies around the world, simply because that would entail *unwelcome competition*. Our modern hearts and minds have to be enamored of our respective governments that promote themselves to be a true rather than just an 'imaginary friend'... That's the idea or plan anyway.

Is it really any wonder that so many people feel ever more depressed? There simply is a very strong correlation between the incessant promotion of 'scientific materialism' and the growing numbers of depressed people who are subsequently persuaded by their doctors (or via promotional media stories and advertisements) to swallow dangerous psycho-active concoctions of chemicals in order to live a 'normal' life. Never mind the fact that the very same drugs admittedly *cause* depression (as per their *Important Safety Information* and black-box warnings), besides dramatic weight gain and a host of other most unwelcome side effects. [60]

Thankfully, an increasing number of especially younger people have started to ignore materialistic propaganda of any kind. Instinctively we feel and just know that there is much more to life than what is portrayed in officially sanctioned and promoted philosophies. Many of today's young are shunning the mindless accumulation of 'ever-more stuff' and are more into *experiencing the world and its many wonders.*

Reality is that most people in the world believe in God, no matter what is being said or done trying to change that. Most people do know the difference between what is right and what is wrong. After all, conscience and introspection is inherent in our very nature (with the apparent exclusion of psychopaths/sociopaths, estimated to make up one percent of the general population).

"Deep within every one of us lies a natural understanding of good and evil. That is why one man can tell the truth convincingly, but it takes the entire apparatus of the state to peddle a lie, and propagate that lie to new generations." Gandhi

Reality is that we live in a wonderful world full of beautiful people. The world is (already) good, and it is getting better every day. This is the merry way to look at things. And it truly is so.

"The fact is that people are good, if only their fundamental wishes are satisfied, their wish for affection and security. Give people affection and security, and they will

give affection and be secure in their feelings and their behavior." Abraham Maslow [94]

God created this planet and all its inhabitants, indeed this galaxy and *trillions* more, in perfect design and order. It was perfect the way it was before we arrived, and it will remain perfect after we have left. There is harmony even though we may doubt it at times (particularly upon reading the news in corporate media). The world looks imperfect only because of our limited perception that results in our (temporarily) partial understanding.

Yes, there are quite a few issues in the world that really can and should be improved. But we need to always keep the big picture in mind. Like our spiritual heritage and identity. The endless beauty and goodness of it all. And stay in the ever-present flow of love, being merry all the while. In such a state of mind we can and will more easily find the best solutions to any current or future problem 'out there'.

Indeed, it is safe to say that virtually all problems humanity faces today are man-made (and yes, sometimes they are only imagined respectively 'packaged' or marketed problems by various interested parties that stand to benefit from the impositions 'offered'). And as such we will also come up with the solutions. We always have and we always will.

"Necessity is the mother of invention." Aesop

History has amply demonstrated that we will always invent whatever is necessary to survive and thrive. Sure, at times we let things slide until the very last moment. We do this both individually and collectively. Apathy and laziness (sloth) are simply part of human nature. Yet no matter the problem, it actually *pays* to find solutions and make things better. Quicker. Easier. Cleaner. Quieter. More efficient. And so on.

In most aspects of life the world has become an ever better place. More peaceful. Healthier. Wealthier. Smarter. More comfortable. Fairer. More compassionate. Even more fun. Imagine this to be true… then see for yourself that it really is so! Despite the dire warnings of gloom and doom prophets virtually any area we care to look at has seen vast improvements.

Most of our ancestors could not even imagine the comfort and amenities we nowadays take for granted. Washing machines and driers. Microwave ovens. Cars. Airplanes. Smartphones providing us with instant communication, worldwide. Or equally instant and mostly free access to the world's accumulated knowledge, libraries, recipes, entertainment, and so on.

We are now used to eating food from every corner of the world, delicacies that were previously unknown even to kings and queens. We can order products and services with a few clicks of the mouse and get them delivered straight to our homes, sometimes within minutes or a day. Almost anyone can afford to travel pretty much anywhere in the world, quickly and easily.

There is less poverty in the world now than at anytime throughout recorded history or indeed, just a few short decades ago. Less war. Less hunger or malnutrition. Less child labor. Less rape, or domestic violence. All despite the incessant headlines saying 'the end is nigh'. We could go on and quite easily fill an entire book outlining all the evidence. [95]

Yet the 'funny' thing is that the better the world becomes the more we get mad at the issues that are still bad, unresolved or otherwise in need of improvement. In short: Since time immemorial and continuing to the present day there were plenty of doomsayers of many different persuasions yet they had one thing in common; they were all wrong! And still are.

No matter where or how we look at things, the overall progress we have already made over the course of history is simply amazing. Of course we can and will improve things ever more. And yes, there were setbacks as we've introduced new problems like pollution and so on. But as we continue to learn and grow, becoming ever wiser and more loving and compassionate, the necessary solutions will present themselves. For sure.

"All I have seen teaches me to trust the creator for all I have not seen." Ralph Waldo Emerson

All problems already contain the seeds of their solutions within. And God is the ultimate innovator who constantly reveals new ideas and intelligent solutions to those searching and asking. Many of mankind's greatest inventions were actually made (or received) at the same time by different people from different parts of the world. [96] Somehow or another they all had the same great idea pop up in their minds! How come? Or better, where from? (see also chapter *The Divine Deal*)

"All matter originates and exists only by virtue of a force… We must assume behind this force the existence of a conscious and intelligent Mind. This Mind is the matrix of all matter." Max Planck [97]

Sceptics and cynics may say that we have polluted the world beyond hope and that we need to not only dramatically reduce our ecological footprint but a large part of the human population altogether. While there is a lot more to be said in response than space allows within these pages, let's just have a quick look at recent promising developments that illustrate the optimistic points made above:

Scientists have found an easy and permanent way to turn heat-trapping carbon-dioxide into rock; a newly discovered species of bacteria produces a plastic-eating enzyme that completely breaks down PET film (polyethylene terephthalate) after six weeks; glucose biofuel cells may revolutionize medical technology; genetically engineered bacteria, including E. coli, are coaxed into producing hydrocarbon chains that can be turned into gasoline, respectively produce hydrogen; besides eating plastic, asbestos, cardboard, jet fuel and radioactive compounds, researchers have now discovered that some fungi (mushrooms) also eat radiation itself; a newly discovered species of microbe is rapidly breaking down oil from oil spills; 3 type of newly evolved superworms were found to eat poisonous heavy metals such as zinc, copper, lead, and arsenic; the Desulfitobacterium was observed to produce electricity as a by-product of breaking down toxic waste. [98]

Anywhere in the universe and everywhere on planet Earth we can notice an amazing intelligence behind and inherent in everything. We all learned that every cause produces an effect. So likewise, we have to conclude that behind every intelligent effect there must be an intelligent cause. Even atheistic scientists observe and acknowledge this perfect intelligence wherever they look, yet insist (without producing any evidence) that it all just happened randomly by pure luck or chance, something that serious mathematicians conclude is statistically (besides logically) impossible!

The more people feel grounded in the spreading consciousness of love, peace and happiness, the better our individual and collective future will be; it will enable us to identify and introduce only those solutions that are truly beneficial for all of us. In contrast, a purely or mostly materialistic consciousness will bring about only more separation and loneliness, besides further jostling and fighting over resources and a better 'place in the sun'.

"Where love rules, laws are not needed." Annie Besant [99]

When we live a life of love, peace and happiness we automatically admire more. And of course, what we greatly admire we also tend to protect and conserve.

To be able to sincerely admire what is good and great is an inherent gift. Every little child has received it and it often shows. Some of us still practice the art of admiring every day, and others don't. Perhaps they are too busy being grownups, making money, or they simply see the world as destitute and 'broken'.

"The soul that sees beauty may sometimes walk alone." Johann Wolfgang von Goethe

It is a great to once again learn (respectively decide) to be amazed. To wonder about the incredible dimensions of our infinite universe. To admire our world of breathtaking beauty. To be aware of its glorious abundance. To celebrate nature's delightful diversity. To treasure the absolute perfection of all of God's creations. And the amazing harmony that prevails in all exquisitely intertwined systems, constantly interacting on the macroscopic and microscopic levels, most of it far beyond our ability to comprehend.

As kids we may have often looked up to the stars on a cloudless night and were simply and totally in awe about the sheer vastness and overwhelming beauty of it all. But as we grow older we tend to forget about it, perhaps only noticing it occasionally, on a holiday to the mountains or while walking on the beach.

Scientists don't know the full size of the universe and admit that it may very well be infinite - a concept that seems impossible to understand with our finite minds. Thanks to ever improving telescopes and the like we get to read every year that the universe is far larger than previously estimated. And yet it is expanding further at the same time, at an accelerating rate.

The known universe of ordinary (baryonic) matter which includes all atoms, stars, galaxies, and life only accounts for about four percent of its content (4.9%). Dark matter (26.8%) and dark energy (68.3%) are thought to make up the difference; *the nature of both is still unknown.*

Imagine this and try not to be simply amazed: Just the *observable* (visible) universe is about 28 billion parsecs or 91 billion light-years in diameter at the present time (one light-year is about 10 trillion kilometers, respectively 6 trillion miles). It contains an estimated 300 sextillion or 300,000,000,000,000,000,000,000 stars - that is a three followed by twenty-three zeros. That number is thought to be more than forty times the number of grains of sand on planet Earth. [100]

On a smaller scale there is so much to admire about our own bodies and it's amazing abilities; no matter which aspect we look at we have to conclude that the intelligence and perfection behind it is both incomprehensible and *inimitable* (no matter the hopes of ardent *believers* in transhumanism who'd like to live forever in this dimension; they - random chunks of dumb organic matter that accidentally assembled itself into them - the smartest representatives of their species, to be further augmented by the latest technological gadgets, to rule forever over the poor and dumb).

An adult human body is made up of about 7 octillion atoms (a seven followed by twenty-seven zeros), which is an even greater number than there are stars in the observable universe. Yet quantum physics has shown us that an atom is mostly empty space and that its nucleus would be comparable to the size of a fly in an otherwise empty cathedral. Without all that empty atomic space our bodies would fit into a cube less than 1/500th of a centimeter on each side.

Our bodies actually contain more bacterial than human life; there are around 10 trillion of human cells but 10 times more bacteria. There are about 500 species of bacteria with most of them living in our intestines; they are responsible for making over 30 neurotransmitters including serotonin (with over 100,000 neurons, the intestines form a kind of 'second brain').

The human brain is equally awesome; besides being far more efficient, it has also much more raw computational power than the currently fastest supercomputer; the Tianhe-2 in China has a peak processing speed of 54.902 petaFLOPS (one petaFLOP is a quadrillion, or one thousand trillion, floating point calculations per second) yet our brains are calculated to operate at least one thousand times faster at 1 exaFLOP (1 quintillion calculations per second).

Put differently, it took the world's 4th fastest supercomputer forty minutes to complete the same number of calculations of just one second of one percent of human brain activity. [101]

The natural world too is simply amazing no matter how we look at it; it contains about 8.7 million species (excluding bacteria and other types of micro-organism) yet the vast majority have neither been identified nor catalogued, a task scientists say may take more than one thousand years. So far only 14% of the world's species have been identified and only 9% of those in the oceans. In other words, a mind-boggling 86% of land species and 91% of marine species are still undiscovered. [102]

We can also just marvel at the level of our collective knowledge, regardless of the fact that we still know so little about so much. Yet still, over the centuries past we have accumulated an incredible amount of knowledge in ever expanding new fields. Of course we can also say that some of the things we do know are actually detrimental to our self-interest. The everpresent threat of nuclear Armageddon is one example. Another is that we have learned many more ways to kill one another than to love each other, respectively to express our love in words and deeds.

Nevertheless, we can and should acknowledge the amazing knowledge that already exists 'out there'; it is far greater than we could ever come to learn and know on an individual level. This existing and ever expanding pool of knowledge is ultimately a gift of God, whose knowledge is absolute and complete. And as we seek further and deeper knowledge so it will be given and revealed. Everything happens at the right time.

"Grant that we may not so much seek to be understood as to understand." Saint Francis of Assisi

There is much to admire about people too, both as a whole as well as individuals: The resilience of people in difficulties, the endurance of the sick, the hope of the downtrodden, the bravery of police, firemen and emergency operators rescuing others at the risk of their own lives, the fearlessness of those who defend their loved ones from danger and stand up for their communities in times of trouble, the generosity of many and especially of those who give even though they have very little for themselves, the dedication to the common good of whistleblowers who risk career, liberty and life to warn us about wrongdoings, the attention and care of dedicated teachers, doctors and nurses, the selfless acts of many quiet heroes, the unconditional love of mothers and fathers, the ingenuity of problem solvers, the creativity and tenacity of authors (there are more than 32 million books and 61 million manuscripts in the US Library of Congress alone), the expressions and performances of artists, the courage of entrepreneurs, the loyalty and dedication of a great many employees, the achievements of outstanding athletes, the culinary skills of great chefs, the devotion of monks and nuns, the intelligence of inventors and innovators, the patience and focus of scientists, the benevolence of charity workers and volunteers, the innocence of the newly born, the honesty of the young, the beautiful smile of lovers, the joy of happy people, the kindness of strangers, the goodness of most people, and so on and so forth.

"Who is the happiest of men? He who values the merits of others, and in their pleasure takes joy, even as though they were his own." Johann Wolfgang von Goethe

Yes, there is simply so much to admire in people! Most if not all of us are not just good but actually have the potential to be great, and particularly so in times of trouble and need. While we all have our shortcomings, and imperfections, injuries and pains, sorrows and fears, we also have character traits and abilities that are well and truly outstanding, inspiring and helpful.

Marvelous things happen when amazing people work together for a common cause. Just see the great many fantastic man-made creations, from great works of historic or contemporary architecture to the wonderful achievements of science and technology. We have built machines and devices that make our lives so much easier than ever before, besides far more productive.

We have created societies that are not yet perfect but overall are actually working mostly fine and keep the peace. And while we have come a long way already, we have barely started yet: The number of scientists and engineers that have graduated in the last two decades alone is quite possibly far greater than all of history's preceding ones combined. And all of them want to become rich and famous by coming up with the next big thing!

And The Happy Rabbit Says…

"Give as many compliments as possible - but only honest ones - and include yourself!"

It is only natural to admire and praise whom and what we love. But perhaps it's even more laudable to seek and find the admirable parts in those people we otherwise don't quite like or generally don't agree with; that is not only a great exercise in practicing our tolerance and ability to feel pure love, but also *most helpful in acquiring those very same desirable attributes in our own lives.* In addition, it emphasizes and strengthens the good parts of a person to the detriment of their bad parts; as the light expands the darkness disappears.

"Appreciation is a wonderful thing: It makes what is excellent in others belong to us as well." Voltaire

To admire beauty is perhaps the easiest and most enjoyable way to connect with God. There is so much beauty to discover and enjoy, both in the natural and man-made worlds. We can admire it *everywhere and all the time* as there is great beauty to be found even in otherwise desolate places.

While we were all born to admire beauty it may still become necessary for some of us to be reminded to actually do it. As in every day, and every moment.

Some people simply do not have the mindset or take the time to look at and admire even the most spectacular scenes life presents to its connoisseurs. Recently in a restaurant, my wife and I were thrilled to notice and marvel at the mysterious and exhilarating beauty of a rainbow right in front of us, clearly visible across the entire bay for about ten minutes. Yet until we pointed it out our otherwise not at all busy waitperson just did not see it, no matter how obvious it was.

And likewise also recently, upon landing in Japan while en route downtown in a large airport limousine bus, only a few people noticed the magnificent all red sunset in the hills above Osaka; everybody else was obviously way too busy doing something on their smartphones. Some started to look too once they noticed us admiring the fantastic display of beauty, yet seemed to wonder 'what's the big deal?' upon taking a quick glimpse, before immersing themselves again in cyberspace.

"Everything has beauty, but not everyone sees it." Confucius

To admire all that is beautiful and great is both an easy and enjoyable way of worshiping and staying connected with the divine; we can do it every day and all the time simply because there are so many things to cherish and adore! To admire doesn't even require any effort; it is simply a lifestyle choice that richly rewards its practitioners with so much joy, continually renewed vigor, and a great enthusiasm for life. Even though it's entirely free!

"There are only two ways to live your life. One is as though nothing is a miracle. The other is as though everything is a miracle." Albert Einstein

"Never lose an opportunity of seeing anything beautiful, for beauty is God's handwriting." Ralph Waldo Emerson

Best is to always:

Live in a constant state of wonder.

Be less angry and more amazed and amused.

Feel less anxious and aggravated and admire more instead.

It will help to make the world a better place and keep us merry at the same time!

REALIZATIONS:

I love to admire beauty in all its forms

I love to admire all that is good

I love to admire all that is God

Wish well

A connected and thus merry person naturally likes to wish everybody well. At first and in some particular situations that may sound like a tough proposition. But start wishing well anyway. Include at least the immediate people in your life. Like family, friends and colleagues. With a bit of practice it will become ever easier and we will get ever happier at the same time. The results will simply speak for themselves!

Let's first discuss the reasons why and then a bit more about the how, particularly in those somewhat 'challenging cases'. You know what I mean.

We have already looked at how we are all connected on so many levels. Throughout the physical, mental, and spiritual dimensions. Emotionally we are also influencing each other or are getting influenced. Most likely we are connected on other vibrational levels as well even though we may not be aware of it.

The other part we need to be aware of is that all the people we come in contact with are there for a reason. Even those we meet only fleetingly. We have somehow attracted each other to meet sometime. And there is always an exchange of energy taking place. Give and receive. We can't stop that even if we really wanted to. We are part of 'All There Is' whether we like it or not, whether we know it or not.

In essence, if we are partial by wishing some of the people well and others not, we also exclude ourselves from the ever-present flow of love and well-being. With the ones we explicitly exclude we obviously have a problem with. We think that for whatever reasons *they* don't deserve to be happy and well.

By doing so we assert a usually not very important problem and make it into a real issue - for as long as we hold such a restrictive belief about that person. From a spiritual perspective a great deal of problems are really non-existent as they only occur between illusory and easily hurt egos, the world of labels that is descriptive but not really real.

The key is to always be aware that everybody deserves to be happy and well. We all deserve all good. That may be hard to accept in every single case or situation but we should try to go with it anyway; wishing everybody well even if it's initially for our own sake only.

Start with yourself and wish yourself well. *Wish yourself all that is good*, all that you want to experience in your life.

Make sure that you fully agree with the notion that you deserve to be happy and well (despite your occasional or even frequent mistakes and other perceived shortcomings). Desire to be the best you can be and realize that *you are worthy to receive all that is best for you* to accomplish your mission in life.

We all have different dreams and desires, but we are all deserving and worthy in the eyes of the universe as we are all parts and parcels of it, no matter how minuscule. Everybody matters. This is so even for those people we judge to be 'disagreeable' or 'bad'. Don't deny anyone this fundamental right. That's part of the 'big picture view'.

"Did not just one God create us all? Why then does humankind deal treacherously with one another? This betrays the teachings of our ancestors." (Malachi 2:10)

Wishing everybody well means to *reassert our own right and worthiness* to be happy and well. Denying that to people equals to putting ourselves above them. It is the thinking that we are better and thus deserving and they are just 'low life scum' or whatever and hence not worthy of any good (or God).

That mindset is a form of mental or spiritual arrogance, respectively ignorance. Arrogance and other delusions of superiority are always a sign of insecurity. It's the dis-connected ego view. Connected and thereby strong people live in the flow and have no need for putting themselves above anyone. If anything, quite the opposite. On a spiritual level such kind of thinking will only block us from the ever-flowing goodness of the universe.

It is easy to wish well to people we already like and love. And of course it gets ever tougher the more we dislike someone. But even that will get easier once we have decided to remember the big picture in life in everyday moments and happenings (see also chapter *Be your Self*).

So even if someone gets on your nerves or whatever, end up wishing them well as you depart or hang up the phone. And try your best to actually be sincere and mean it. The more so the better.

By sincerely wishing him or her well you will overcome or disconnect any emotional hang-ups and be able to move on whistling and singing in your heart and mind. It kind of closes the chapter even on an otherwise unpleasant encounter and keeps you in the flow. It reasserts your insight into who you really are, who we all eternally are. Fellow brothers and sisters on an epic journey through life. Real-world heroes doing their best, even if it may not look that way at times.

There is also no need to look for reciprocity. What the other person thinks and feels about you is really their choice and concern. And yes, it will determine how they feel within themselves. But sending even those folks who don't seem to like us very much a little spark of love (I call it 'Love Mail') and goodwill will do wonders.

We will continue to feel great for a start. And they will suddenly or gradually begin to feel better about us too, often without knowing the reasons why. They may also start to feel better about themselves as they resonate more with our better qualities, perhaps by remembering the good times we shared together in the past.

Miracles do happen when we send or receive love mail!

Mostly we wish people well directly in their presence, or by sending a written note:

"Have a safe flight", "I hope you will get well soon", "Godspeed", "Good luck with it", "Best wishes with your new job", "I hope you'll succeed", "I'm sure you will make it happen", "All the best", "Have a go(o)d weekend!", "Enjoy", "Have a very Merry Christmas", "Happy New Year!", "Speedy recovery", "I wish you lots of strength", "Happy holidays!", and so on.

At times of underlying or outright conflict however it is often more appropriate or beneficial to send our little sparks of love, good vibrations, and best wishes quietly within our hearts and minds 'only'. It is a humble and peaceful yet fulfilling and happy way. It will bring about amazing results because it is the most direct path of communication between people - *soul to soul*. And thereby there can be no distractions or conflicts of the mind and ego that all too often prevent us from making peace and getting along nicely.

Sending love quietly will certainly reach its destination and bring about positive changes in a relationship. At the core of who we are we can feel a person's love and sincerity, and that will sooner or later manifest itself in a better understanding and the resolution of outstanding matters.

May love enlighten your mind

May love heal your body

Some people are a bit reluctant to wish others well as they think that it may somehow reduce their own 'supply of good luck' or well-being. Like it is some kind of subtraction from one's score of brownie or good karma points. That is purely a mechanical or materialistic way of looking at life. It is the transferring of what normally happens in the material dimension (3D level) to the more subtle energy fields: If you give someone a hundred dollars you will have one hundred dollars less and the other person has one hundred dollars more.

However, when it comes to matters of the mind or heart it is a very different story. Wishing people well is an act of love. And there is no lack of love as there is no lack of God. Love keeps expanding. The more we feel love and pass it on the more we also have it in our own life for our own enjoyment and sustenance. As we wish well, love, and all the good that comes with it, flows through our hearts and minds to purify and uplift our own experience. Wishing well is a connecting with the endless supply of goodness and well-being that is God.

Of course, best is if we are able to wish others well out of love. Yet wishing people well purely for our own sake still feels good and brings great results in life. And over time, as love grows within, we just can't help but always wish people well. It simply becomes effortless and automatic. After all it is so very normal and natural to who *we really are*. And therefore it simply feels good and right.

The only caveat is that to be real and effective, wishing well must be done in the spirit of being equals, and never in the condescending way of feeling superior, or perhaps even worse, out of pity or a sense of obligation. Obviously, and as discussed throughout this book, such ego-based states of mind will not produce much good for anyone, including its originator.

And The Happy Rabbit Says…

"Send out positive thoughts only - to yourself, to everybody and everything!"

Being able to wish everybody well ultimately means that we are able to *transcend the lower vibrational forms of emotions to connect and relate with people on the higher platform of inherent feelings*. Like love, respect, peace, joy, and happiness. As such the ability to wish well is a practical application of our current state of mind. It is the litmus test of our consciousness, whether we are connected and happy, or not.

In *Yes I Am Happy Now!* [1] we made the distinction between the fleeting emotions of the ego versus the true feelings of our eternal spiritual identity. Emotions are not really real although they can surely appear to be that way in our daily life - whenever we are so fully immersed in our activities to the point of totally forgetting the big picture view of who we are and what life is all about.

Another point made is that both emotions and feelings can be expressed as energy that vibrate in different wave lengths or Hertz. 'Illusory' emotions are lower level vibrations compared to the inherently spiritual wave lengths of true feelings. Emotions like disappointment and anger; jealousy and envy; regrets and self pity; sadness and worries; anxiety and fears; guilt and blame.

We also discussed how we can escape the clutches of emotions - not by suppressing or compartmentalizing, but by transcending or 'checking out' of that vibration levels altogether by becoming more aware of ourselves and what is really happening within and around us on different energy levels. By focusing on experiencing our true feelings only, or at least predominantly.

The reason why escaping negative emotions is possible in the first place is simply because of the inherent nature of feelings. They are really real, forever and throughout all dimensions. The feeling of happiness is an integral part of our eternal reality. And so is true love and friendship. Or creativity and passion. Being relaxed, calm and confident. The unconditional acceptance and respect of each other. And lots of joy and bliss to the point of ecstasy.

Wishing well means to wish love and thereby send love. If we can't wish a fellow traveler well, it means that we have decided to have a problem with that person. Whether we have decided this consciously or not doesn't matter one bit. The effect is just the same. By denying well-being to others we deny it (to the same degree) to ourselves.

But if we can easily wish anyone well - even if we may not agree with someone in some way or another - we will have transcended all emotional smog issues and uplifted ourselves to ever-soaring new heights of love, peace and happiness. And that simply feels great. Do it now and every day!

REALIZATIONS:

I love to wish well

I wish myself all the best

I wish everybody all the best

Help

Christians have a long and noble tradition of being good Samaritans, of helping their fellow brothers and sisters in need, and protecting the innocent and vulnerable.

There are so many ways we can help. Like providing food and shelter. Or clothing. Helping to find clean water supplies. Giving comfort to the sad and depressed. Protecting the oppressed and exploited. Speaking out for more peace and justice. And yes, wishing well (as discussed in the previous chapter).

Praying for the well-being of the world and wishing all its inhabitants more love, peace and happiness is a most powerful way to help and do good. It will have a profound impact; we may not see its results right away in the big picture view of things, yet we will be able to instantly feel and enjoy its fruits within our hearts and minds.

Helping others is part and parcel of what makes a Christian. But not every way is equally effective or indeed helpful. To both parties, the helper and the helped.

Quite a few Christians believe that they need to personally share some of the suffering alongside the less fortunate in order to help and heal them. They feel (or are told) that this is an essential part of a Christian's 'job description': Suffering together.

Feeling empathy and compassion for a suffering soul is a completely natural and therefore good thing; indeed it is an inherent quality of every loving soul. But there is no point to 'share the pain' as this will simply not be helpful or diminish any of the suffering that someone is going through. Instead of actually halving the pain it will only add to the hardship simply because there are now two people who are suffering. So there is more of it and not less as we may have intended.

No matter what may have happened in the physical dimension of this world, to really be able to make a difference it is important that we stay connected and strong at all times. And on every level; spiritually, mentally, and physically. By being and staying united in love with God we are in the position to give real assistance and genuine comfort.

If we see someone who has fallen down a hole in the ground and is unable to climb out, we will not be particularly helpful by also jumping in. Then sit together at the bottom of the pit and share the misery. Of course it would be far better to find an easy way to pull that person out of the place so that both can continue on their merry ways.

Likewise we cannot alleviate poverty by becoming poor as well. The better way is to have plenty of money yourself with much to spare and share. In our modern world however it is mostly the mental and spiritual dimension where help and healing is sorely needed. We all need more appreciation, love and respect. And that we can only give by staying united and strong ourselves. Becoming also sad and depressed is not real empathy or help, even if that is what we are trying to do.

"There is more hunger for love and appreciation in this world than for bread." Mother Teresa

The most effective way to help often happens when we don't even try to help; it just happens naturally and without much effort. And sometimes going too far out of our way to help may only produce adverse results (unless of course it's a real emergency that requires our immediate attention). The same is true when we try to help but have the wrong motivation. Like feeling obliged to help. Or doing so only (or mainly) to evangelize. Or having other ulterior motives.

The best way to help is when we respect and help each other as equals. Just like real friends do. One attribute of true friendship is the desire to help each other through thick and thin. Because there is so much love and care. Besides, it feels good to be able to help; it is a very normal thing simply because it is so natural to who we eternally are. Among good friends one never even thinks about the reasons why. We are simply happy to help out. And don't actually expect a reward. Being able to help a friend is already its own reward.

"My friends are my estate." Emily Dickinson

While supporting and helping a friend is easy, ultimately we will come to realize that indeed we are all friends, regardless of our external differences. You know the old adage that 'strangers are only friends we have not met yet'. We are all in the same boat, on beautiful Planet Earth; the place we all call 'home away from home'.

"What you are doing I cannot do, what I'm doing you cannot do, but together we are doing something beautiful for God, and this is the greatness of God's love for us — to give us the opportunity to become holy through the works of love that we do." Mother Teresa

What about helping individual causes, whatever they may be; what is the best way to help? Or where? There are so many worthy causes we could support yet obviously we can't help them all.

Our ability to help in person may be limited at times for a variety of reasons yet we can always say what we wish the outcome to be. Like when we see war and hate or despair we can always wish to see more love, peace and happiness. It costs nothing, is easy to do, and makes us feel great too.

In some situations we may need to simply accept the things that we, as an individual, cannot change. There is a certain freedom and peace of mind that comes from accepting what we personally cannot change. We don't have to take on the burdens of the world as we are not the 'Big Boss'. But of course there are times when we really should take inspired action and help - whenever and wherever we *can* make a difference, even if it's seemingly only a very small contribution. Yet "It all adds up," said the little happy ant.

"We ourselves feel that what we are doing is just a drop in the ocean. But the ocean would be less because of that missing drop." Mother Teresa

What is inspired help and action? Or perhaps first, what it's not: When we do something solely out of a sense of obligation and duty, or because we feel guilty, ashamed, or worse, out of pity, the results will usually not be particularly pleasant or pleasing to anybody. If there is a lack in the right conviction or loving intention it will also lack in strength and effect. Motivation that is entirely directed by our ego, where we erroneously identify ourselves as something that we're not, can result in dramatically negative, even disastrous, results (see [Note 103 about the 'law of unintended consequences']).

Inspired action is when we feel united and thus in harmony with God and have a sudden strong inner knowing and desire to do something. And suddenly, somehow or another, a way or action plan will present itself. It could pop up within our hearts and minds. Or we may come across it externally in the 'outside world'. We will suddenly feel inspired and happy to go out and just do it. With joy and strength and purpose. This kind of action will produce only good results for everyone involved and affected.

Why is it so important to only take action and help when we feel *personally inspired* to do so? When it feels good and right within - versus only feeling energized and 'motivated' in the presence of one's peers, respectively in an agitated crowd? It is simply because we could easily fall prey to be active on behalf of villains and evildoers. There is no shortage of various parties in all kinds of areas who have a vested interest to get your support (attention and energy, money, or direct action in its many forms, usually done for free) for totally misguided policies and possibly worse.

Just because an organization is very skilled at appealing to our soft hearts and able to stir up a multitude of usually negative emotions does not mean that their cause is right and just. We live as much in an information age as we live in the age of misinformation where public relations and propaganda is being used all the time, mostly for selfish interests, and often for social engineering and other nefarious purposes.

In the USA ninety percent of what people consume in so-called 'news' is served up by six large corporations. [104] In other countries it's even worse. Whose interests do they have at heart? Yes, you are right; they serve their shareholders, top executives and clients (that include governments, both domestic and foreign, plus all kinds of related organizations).

That many of these mega-corporations profit greatly from propagating and promoting dissension, war and upheaval (besides a variety of rather unsavory investment choices or unhealthy food and health care endorsements, etc.) via both open and hidden but always paid-for ads and editorials may not come as a surprise to the well informed who dare to look and read elsewhere. Outside the recommended and approved channels. These days the question we always need to ask is 'Cui Bono?' - who benefits? Who stands to gain from this? Or what is the real purpose?

The problem of taking misguided action and helping out the wrong crowd is that it may result in a great deal of waste; the wasting of our energy, time and indeed, quite possibly our physical body. It could even affect our afterlife; whether we will go to a more or less heavenly place. Not all places are equally enjoyable and fun. Those who helped Hitler maim and kill others more efficiently are not likely to be able to hang out and have dinner with Jesus (no matter how 'saved' they may think they are). For example.

There is a big difference between feeling inspired and having great passion for a noble cause to turning into a brainwashed fanatic who rejects all other points of view, at best looks down to non-believers, and at worst is prepared to harm or kill infidels and heathens in the name of God, the all lovable and loving. Having no mercy in the name of God the all-merciful is obviously not something that is pleasing to God. And yet it happens when people don't know *who they really are* and let crooks indoctrinate them with anger, envy and hate.

There is obviously no lack in fanatical groups of all kind that would just love to get our (free) help and contributions. They come in all shapes and forms, presenting themselves and their cause as the one and only alternative to further mayhem. When in reality there are always a lot more than just the two false choices we are usually presented with; it's either black or white. Choose freely. As long as it's either black, or white.

Here is the fact that is not being mentioned or talked about: *Divine love and intelligence within all of us constantly inspires a myriad of innovative and beneficial solutions to all perceivable problems,* way beyond the artificially drawn boundaries that narrow down the dialogue to the acceptable level, as defined by a selfish group of people and organizations.

Some problems that are presented may not really be problems at all and are just attempts to increase market share and the like. One example would be the incessant promotion of ineffective and dangerous yet lucrative anti-depressants and other psycho-pills by the media and assorted lobbying groups, all paid for by your supposedly well-meaning pharmaceutical giants. [60]

"It has always seemed strange to me... the things we admire in men, kindness and generosity, openness, honesty, understanding and feeling, are the concomitants of failure in our system. And those traits we detest, sharpness, greed, acquisitiveness, meanness, egotism and self-interest, are the traits of success. And while men admire the quality of the first they love the produce of the second." John Steinbeck

Traveling and living around the world for over three decades, plus meeting and negotiating, respectively wining and dining, with many of its billionaires and movers and shakers, lead your author to a number of insights. One is the utter contempt some members of 'the establishment' have for 'commoners', the uneducated peasants without PhD's; the unwashed masses with little money, the ordinary crowd with barbarian tastes, the simple-minded still full of superstitious beliefs.

Unfortunately, quite a few members of the elite consider regular people to be infinitely dumb, good-natured and docile, just like sheep. And just like cows one can freely and generously milk their emotions and money.

We have already amply discussed the reasons for the need to feel superior and why that is always a mistake. And likewise, how such disconnected people are rarely if ever able to contribute to real and benevolent solutions of problems, sometimes of their own making. The problem with wrong beliefs is that they inevitably lead to the wrong action, no matter how 'enlightened' we may think we are.

"We cannot solve our problems with the same thinking we used when we created them." Albert Einstein

Fortunately, a growing number of us already realize that despite the obstacles we 'the little people' do have tremendous power to ultimately co-create heaven on Earth. Even when we consider things on the mundane level only, not to speak of the spiritual dimensions. While our democratic votes may not bring about that much change, or none at all in places where voting is denied to the people, we do have effective ways to bring about the change we want to see in the world.

We can vote with our attention; by giving or denying our attention we give or withdraw our energy. For example, by not reading or watching negative or misleading or outright false news and doing something positive instead. Our attention is worth a lot of money to advertisers after all. Speaking of which, by using our money to only buy goods and services that we fully believe in and are thus happy to support, all the garbage providers will either go out of business or adapt their ways.

Voting with our money works very well. And likewise, voting with where we hang out online, or what links we click on. Non-compliance with sad, bad or mad practices is a most powerful way to change things for the better. Just don't participate in the things you feel are really wrong. Fat food joints cannot exist if we stop eating their horrible concoctions. Before going out of business they will change their ways.

Each one of us can be the change we want to see in the world. And the more of us realize this and move beyond an indifferent or resigned state of mind the quicker we will create heaven on Earth!

The apathetic and uncaring however who let themselves be turned into sheep and cows by unscrupulous manipulators are obviously not only *not helpful* in bringing about a better world, but are likely to promote ever more division instead of unity, more discord than harmony, more fear than love, more despair and war than peace and happiness.

It is always far better to do nothing than to do the wrong things. Or to help the wrong cause. Or assisting the right cause but in the wrong way that harms others. It makes a lot more sense to only act and help if we feel well and truly inspired within our own hearts and minds. Feel the truth, know the truth, and act accordingly.

Sometimes we may be in doubt and not know one way or the other. When in doubt it is again best to *not do anything until we are sure*. There is nothing wrong with doing nothing at all for a while. Until we feel well and truly inspired.

That is true both in big picture things and in smaller day-to-day affairs. Like in 'the heat of the moment' matters, when things go a bit crazy, when everybody else is rushing around, or getting overly emotional to the point of hysteria. Before committing or panicking too, respectively before saying or doing anything at all, it is always best to first pause, exhale and take a few deep breaths, then quietly do the 'Love Test' within:

"Is it coming from love, or not?"

"Is my action inspired by love?"

"Will my action increase love, peace and happiness for all?"

If our action is increasing love and kindness in the world, it will certainly be pleasing to God and we will (continue to) feel great within as a result. Such action will be beneficial to all. Even to people who are not directly involved. If our action is without love and care however it usually results in more negative effects and feelings. Even if we'd have mentally convinced ourselves to only having the best of intentions. Yet without fail even serial killers and violent dictators think just like that. There is simply no end to the follies of a disconnected and thus self-deluded mind.

To put it in a simple formula: The more our intention and action comes from and with love the more God is present and the better the outcome will be for all. And vice versa: The more egoistic our intention and action the less God is present and the worse the outcome will be for all.

Or even shorter: *Where there is pure love there is God.*

The degree of our personal happiness is fully reflected in this formula. We simply can't act totally egoistical to the total exclusion and detriment of others and expect to be a very happy person. Yet by default, whenever we act with pure love we automatically include ourselves as well; our personal interests will inherently be included and taken care of.

Because pleasing God equals pleasing everybody. This is so even if we individually are not always aware of this fact. If we try to please everybody in our lives we are likely to end up pleasing nobody. But pleasing God who has only the very best of intentions for the entirety of his creation will instantly benefit all of its parts. And that obviously includes ourselves as well.

"that you may be sons of your Father in heaven. He causes his sun to rise on the evil and the good, and sends rain on the righteous and the unrighteous." (Matthew 5:44-45)

All (only) good will flow from a loving heart. Automatically. There is no reason to despair and no need to become a martyr or to otherwise make sacrifices and feel pain in order to make a difference. Or to advance spiritually. We don't need to bribe or compel God in any way or for any reason whatsoever simply because God already wants only our very best. Always.

This is the nature of unconditional love. Once we come to feel and therefore know and understand this everlasting reality we will feel very merry indeed!

REALIZATIONS:

I love to give help

I love to get help

Do it with Love

Every thing we do can be classified as either a 'love job' or a 'hate job'. An act of love. Or a compulsory act performed under pressure, with disgust, anger, or worse.

Instinctively we all know the difference while performing or witnessing different kinds of work. Few people may call or consider it that way yet we can easily see if someone pours their heart into what they do, or if they obviously don't really give a damn.

According to surveys these days only few people are actually happy at work. While there are many factors to consider as to the reasons why, on a deeper level it is most likely that many jobs are simply not particularly satisfying to who *we really are*. Often there is a lack of meaning, creativity, or appreciation - both emotionally and monetary.

A Gallup study concluded that only thirty percent of American employees feel engaged or inspired at their jobs, while seventy percent of U.S. workers are not reaching their full potential. The '2013 State of the American Workplace Report' estimates that widespread disinterest and unhappiness in the office is not only affecting an individual company's performance, but is costing the country as a whole between $450 billion to $550 billion a year. [105]

And that study doesn't even count the personal consequences of unhappiness plus the large follow-up costs of the related *extra* use of both legal and illegal drugs, respectively the excessive consumption of alcoholic beverages. We would also need to add the associated expenses of our unduly or prematurely deteriorating health, besides the many days of us 'pulling sickies' (Aussie slang for taking a day off as sick leave when one is not actually ill) or having a hangover.

"Choose a job you love, and you will never have to work a day in your life." Confucius

Most of us spend at least a third of our week at work and perhaps another third or so is taken up with sleeping. The remaining third is filled with personal hygiene and other physical chores, eating, commuting, and finally, trying to squeeze in as much fun times as possible. For leisure, sports and hobbies, meeting up with friends, and so on. All too often our 'happy time' (or happy hours!) only happens 'after hours'!

And that means that essentially a very long time and a good part of our overall life is spent being grumpy and unhappy. But being unhappy on the job is simply a huge waste of our happy potential. Therefore it simply makes sense to somehow or another find ways to enjoy our work to the best of our abilities. Or to at least amuse ourselves - somehow or another, no matter the dark or depressive sides of our jobs.

"Whether you eat or drink, or whatever you do, do it in such a way that the Divine can be revealed through it." (1 Corinthians 10:31)

As children we automatically know how to amuse ourselves even in the most unlikely of situations, as seen later from the perspectives of an all-grown up and seemingly mature adult. Yet with the proper mindset we can actually re-learn the art of amusing ourselves as adults - even without the use of fancy external tools and toys.

And The Happy Rabbit Says...

"Sing, hum and whistle cheerful songs - in the shower, car and kitchen!"

The key ingredient to do a great job and feel great at the same time is to feel love in our hearts and minds. In other words to feel happy within, being a merry Christian. All at ease and peace with ourselves and the world. Going from one moment of appreciation and amusement to the other, until all of a sudden it's time to go home. We all know the experience: Time seems to move faster while we are having a good time! Imagine if we can make it so even at the office or wherever work may be.

"The best way to appreciate your job is to imagine yourself without one." Oscar Wilde

Every little thing that needs to be done is worth doing. When we take a shower or brush our teeth, it is something that needs to happen at least once, preferably twice a day. Chores like washing the dishes, doing laundry or cleaning house, all that and more is important work. We may do it as a routine, perhaps feeling bored, even annoyed, or are otherwise not really into it, focused on something else, perhaps a worry or regret. And yet, with a loving (and lovely) attitude and a merry outlook in life all things will suddenly become enjoyable and fun.

"If a job's worth doing, it is worth doing well" (Proverb)

That may sound a bit much as there are plenty of dirty, boring or hazardous jobs that need to be done and indeed are getting done. And yet we all have different ways to think and feel about things, including what type of jobs we could and would enjoy doing. Some people find it exhilarating to clean the windows on a skyscraper while most of us would not even want to think about it! What we find scary others will find exciting. And so on and so forth.

Since my early teenage years I sure had my fair share of seemingly unpleasant jobs, yet I decided to focus on the bright side as the alternative simply sounded way too boring. Besides it would have negatively affected my happiness, something I wasn't ready to sacrifice just because I had to work!

So I looked at the positive sides of every job, like calculating the money I made per minute, thus literally turning every single minute into a worthwhile venture. The money earned was energy that I got in return for my efforts, but I additionally kept reminding myself that it also helped me to learn new things and thus progress further in life. Rather than being a victim I felt victorious being able to realize my immediate dreams (at the time 'grand' things like treating my girlfriend to a romantic dinner on a Saturday night).

While digging holes or shoveling cement I was quite happy to look at it as exercising. I tried to do every move with as much care, ease and efficiency as possible, and enjoyed the progress made in controlling my body, becoming ever quicker, better and stronger. I was also rather pleased that essentially I got paid to get fit! Plus I had more leisure time than most of my buddies who worked in a stuffy office all day long and had to pump up their muscles after hours - in a costly and smelly gym! (See [Note 106 if you'd like to see a complete list of my various jobs to date.)

The thought to be as grumpy and dispirited as many of my co-workers often or always were seemed like wasting time and opportunities to be happy. We were all doing exactly the same work for more or less the same pay, were 'locked' into the same place for up to nine hours a day, and had the very same often rather unpleasant bosses. And yet we all lived in a completely different world. Within our hearts we felt differently, different thoughts filled our minds, while different expressions appeared on our faces.

"Only those who have the patience to do simple things perfectly will acquire the skill to do difficult things easily." Friedrich von Schiller

At the very least we should decide to consider tough or boring jobs as simply 'not worth it' to affect our mood, well-being and ultimately health, in a negative way. And neither is an unpleasant boss. To give a company or a particular manager such power over our own life and happiness is simply a mistake! We need to re-claim this power and invest it in ourselves the way we see fit.

Once we truly treasure our health and happiness we will always want to see the bright side of things. In other words, we will have decided to always amuse ourselves, no matter what. In almost every single situation there is something amusing or funny going on. We just need to want to experience that reality. And then we surely will. That is living on the happy side of life!

"It is not how much we do, but how much love we put in the doing. It is not how much we give, but how much love we put in the giving." Mother Teresa

It is also a good idea to always remember that we are where we are and do what we're doing for a purpose. There are good reasons why even if we may not fully understand them yet. But the time will come when it will all make sense, just like a jigsaw puzzle that suddenly and perfectly fits together.

Life always prepares us for future situations, tasks and challenges. And with endless love and grace God ensures that we are more than capable of doing what we need to be doing at any given time. We will always have all the tools and talents we need. We are not alone. Unless we want to be…

Another way to think about it is that if we really needed to be or do something else in a different place, we would actually already be there and do that! The fact that we are who we are, where we are, and do what we do is prove in itself that all is as it should be. For now. It will change as it needs to change, and as we are ready or desire to change.

Every temporarily unpleasant situation is a necessity that will give us the experience and know-how to handle what is yet to come, or to learn what we still need to learn. So we can choose to always appreciate it as such and be happy anyway, regardless of the external challenges we may experience at the time. Very often, the sooner we accept and learn our lessons, the quicker and easier an unpleasant situation will turn into a pleasant one!

And The Happy Rabbit Says…

"There is no need to suffer when you're ready and willing to learn what you need to learn!"

Doing everything we do with love and care equals doing them with God. And naturally, that's the merry way!

REALIZATIONS:

I love to do it with care

I love to act with love

Relax

Nowadays a great many people complain about today's hectic pace yet feel forced to participate anyway. The pressures of our modern society clearly show. Just watch how many of the pedestrians in the street walk around with rather stern expressions, their stress, frustrations and anger seemingly engraved forever in a myriad of wrinkles, or otherwise showing by their rigid or resigned body language. One rarely sees relaxed and smiling people anymore. At least during the day.

Even young kids look grim, severe and stressed out already. Many of the young haven't learned yet how to cope with all the pressure and fear heaped upon them from an early age. Playtime is kind of frowned upon but study time an absolute must do; the earlier in life and the more, the better. Of course, one could also say that many parents are simply not able to show their children how to take it easy anymore. Because they themselves never knew how to or have simply forgotten it after years of stress and struggle.

In our materialistic societies one hears *Homo Machina* exclaiming: "I can sleep plenty when I'm dead" or "I can sleep a lot when I'm old and retired."

Sleep is considered to be unproductive time. In other words, worthless. Indeed, Science doesn't really know or understand why we sleep anyway. There is no biological or other reason that actually explains the need to sleep. So some scientists would just love to be able to get rid off this backward burden on our productivity.

Thankfully for them, new electronic gadgets are rapidly being developed to help us make our time, including our sleeping time, ever more effective. With biomonitors we can now record our pulse and hearth rhythm, besides the frequency and depth of our breath; the idea is to sleep more efficiently and regenerate quicker so that we have more time and energy to work. Be ever more productive and profitable is the name of the game; buy and use ever more stuff; there is no time to waste as life is short. Or so *Machine Man* says (see also chapter *Be your Self*).

The ever-present nature of our modern communication devices is often convenient yet 'robbing' us of our time to relax and recover; they force us to deal with work matters during our 'downtime' (manager speak for 'a period of time when one is not working respectively a piece of machinery is not in operation').

Modern technology allows us to both work and consume ever more, at a forever faster speed. The worldwide pressure is on to incessantly promote ourselves to our international peers, clients and employers via social media. We must always be online; to be offline is for losers…

We have built the almost always-on 24 hour and seven-day-a-week society that never really allows itself to rest. Playtime is usually only encouraged if it costs something and makes someone lots of money. So just sleeping is definitely 'out', an idea widely frowned upon already by the young. Even when we play we are in a bit of a hurry, trying to cram in as much pleasure and enjoyment in the little time we have allocated.

"Gotta be quick; something exciting might be happening, and oh horror, I could totally miss out!"

The only acceptable time out from our busy schedules seems to be when we are kind of 'passed out' from drinking too much. Here in Australia having a bit of a 'slow day' is the generally known code word for having a hangover. And many bosses are quite understanding in this matter as they themselves are also known to indulge from time to time, needing our sympathy in return.

To be mostly in the active mode is simply a recipe for disaster; both our health and happiness suffers when we are out of tune. And not sleeping and resting enough very much means to be out of tune; with yourself, God and the universe. The commandment to rest is rather clear and likely for good reasons.

"Remember to keep holy the Sabbath day. Six days you shall labor and do all your work, but the seventh day is a sabbath to the Lord your God. On it you shall not do any work..." (Exodus 20-8-10)

According to a study from the Walter Reed Army Institute of Research, sleep deprivation reduces our emotional intelligence, constructive thinking skills, and intrapersonal functioning (reduced self-regard, assertiveness, sense of independence, and self-actualization). Furthermore we have less empathy toward others, and lower the quality of our interpersonal relationships. Our ability to think positively suffers as well as our normal ability to control our impulses or make moral judgments. [107]

If that were not enough good reasons to get plenty of sleeping and resting time, here are further few negatives of staying up a bit longer just to watch some more TV, play a few extra computer games, or watch other people doing sports and exercise their bodies while getting paid big bucks:

- Increased risk of obesity and some cancers
- Higher risk of diabetes as well as heart disease
- The risk of a stroke quadruples
- More likely to have an accident or catching a cold

Sleep deprivation is both a historical and contemporary form of torture, yet perhaps funnily, most of us are doing it to ourselves. Voluntarily. Not getting enough sleep is also a recognized cause of depression and anxiety - both on the rise in Western civilization, which is perhaps hardly surprising when we don't really appreciate our bedtime.

Indeed we could say that there is a bit of a macho culture among those who consider themselves to be the intellectual or entrepreneurial elite; they just love to brag in person or via their autobiographies how little sleep they need to stay sharp and smart. Like three to four hours or so per night; the less they sleep the smarter they think they are, respectively would like to appear. Yet Albert Einstein, a man widely and greatly admired for his outstanding intelligence and sharp wit, was said to sleep ten hours per night plus take a couple of naps during daytime. Sounds pretty smart, doesn't it?

One reason some people don't like to sleep much is their actual fear of being by themselves; their conscience is literally disturbing their sleep to the point where they are afraid to let go (see also chapter *Surrender*). Their inner equilibrium is so out of tune that seemingly only copious amounts of booze and drugs will allow them some 'time out'. But of course that will only make matters worse, and particularly so over time.

The secret for a great night's sleep is simply a loving heart and the quiet mind that comes with it. We can all experience that if we really wanted to. It's never too late to get started. And of course it is totally worth it.

A good part of the Western world is based on Puritan work ethics with its doctrinal emphasis on almost constant work and little leisure, if any. Amusingly, atheists and agnostics are just as equally affected by this doctrine, perhaps without being aware of it. Essentially, having to work hard is not so much a concept that is based on necessity but one of fear and guilt instead of love and joy: *'Satan finds some mischief for idle hands to do.'*

Even in today's world where much of the traditional manual work is done by ever-smarter machines and robots, and we have therefore become so much more productive, one is still required to work long hours (and particularly so in mid-level management positions where nowadays weekends partly 'belong' to the company too).

This is of course because working long hours is thought to increase profits. Yet new studies show that this is not really so. For example, according to OECD statistics, Greeks are some of the most hardworking people, putting in over 2'000 hours a year on average. Germans, generally thought to be far more dedicated to their work, actually work only 1'400 hours per year. And yet, German productivity is approximately 70% higher, resulting in a generally wealthier country.

Another recent study demonstrated that even if we work more hours we don't necessarily work better. [108] Working less is actually likely to make us more productive. Decades of management consulting in various industries has convinced me that much of today's work is simply 'presence time' that only breeds feelings of resentments; most office workers of any kind or position are well and truly aware of the fact that they could achieve what really needs to be done in about four to five hours. And that the rest of the day is simply attendance time where the name of the game is 'doing your best to look busy and important'.

So of course most employees would rather go home earlier and do what they really want to do. Like look after their loved ones, take care of their home and garden, do some sports, be creative, and so on. That would be the honest and therefore good way to go. And productivity would not suffer thanks to a well-rested and motivated work force who appreciates their jobs and fully understands what actually needs to get done to keep their companies doing well.

With the advances in artificial intelligence where robots become self-learning systems, a great many hospitality industry and white collar jobs will increasingly disappear too and we will have to find new models of how we structure and run our societies and economies. Perhaps Bertrand Russel, the English philosopher, was right after all: In his 1932 essay "In Praise of Idleness" he already suggested that if we could manage our affairs in a smarter way, the average person would only need to work four hours a day to "entitle a man to the necessities and elementary comforts of life."

Russell argued that working less will guarantee "happiness and joy of life, instead of frayed nerves, weariness, and dyspepsia."

And The Happy Rabbit Says…

"Re-learn the Art of Being Idle, just doing sweet nothing - practice it as often as possible and be happy!"

John Maynard Keynes, generally considered to be one of the most influential economists of the 20th century, thought along the same lines in his 1930 essay, "Economic Possibilities for our Grandchildren"; he reckoned that people might need to work no more than fifteen hours per week by 2030.

"We live in the age of the overworked, and the under-educated; the age in which people are so industrious that they become absolutely stupid." Oscar Wilde

We, both individually as well as collectively, should choose to work smarter instead of harder. And learn to stay focused on what is really important in life. The big picture view of things. Like family and friends, love and compassion, cooperating and sharing, fairness and fun, and so on.

Running around and rushing through life like a 'headless chicken' may look all nice and busy, but it doesn't mean that much useful work is getting done. It is usually far better to first relax a bit and find out the best course of action (inspired action!) than to be in a hurry, work hard and think about it later. And perhaps having to clean up the mess or fix the costly mistakes that come from making bad decisions or being in a hurry.

There is always the smart and easy way in life versus the hard and complicated one. The smart and easy way is not just the happier way but often costs a lot less in terms of time, nerves and money.

Rest more, work less, and let go more. When we realize the amazing eternity and absolute beauty of things there is simply no need to rush around and hurry through life. We can take it easy - even if we actually have to work. With the right attitude we can do this even if things seemingly get hectic 'out there' and people around us are kind of 'freaking out'. We can nevertheless stay calm and relaxed and happy within, thus becoming a 'pillar of strength', besides coming up with better results. The boss will certainly notice it and is likely to reward it too!

"Life is ten percent what you make it and 90 percent how you take it." Irving Berlin [109]

In this material dimension we simply need to find the proper balance between the two polarities: Yin and Yang. Hot and Cold. Soft and Hard. Work and Play. Active and Passive.

But mastering the art of relaxing is not easy unless one makes the conscious decision to do so and keeps practicing. In our societies the big obstacles are guilt and peer pressure, besides fear and anxiety. We have already talked about how unnecessary it is to feel guilty and how to overcome it in chapter *Love your Body* (Feel innocent and deserving). And likewise about mastering fear and anxieties by living a life of love, peace and happiness.

And The Happy Rabbit Says…

"Take a bubble bath in candlelight with soft music - massage your entire body and RELAX!"

Feeling bad about not working hard enough is so very common throughout even wealthy societies; the very rich after all are just as affected as the 'regular' folks. Oftentimes even more so as they have to deal with a whole range of peer and other pressure that is unknown to most. Atheists who openly decry God also live mostly according to the Puritan work credos and a Christian sense of morality, perhaps without being aware of it.

A former neighbor (and proud card-carrying atheist) kept saying how bad and guilty he felt every single day for being retired and wealthy, about not being able to work and be productive anymore. He actually felt 'useless' (and indeed that was one of his favorite words, frequently used in conversation about people and things) and was always looking for a purpose and some work to do; he could simply not relax even while living in a place of amazing natural beauty.

Money can buy us luxuries and comfort, yet no matter how much we have, it won't buy us any real peace of mind; a mind that is not tormented by fear, insecurity and anxieties. Having lots of money is certain to introduce the unenlightened or unwise to a whole new range of fears and problems. And without a strong philosophical foundation in life it is also likely to eventually 'buy us' alcoholism and assorted drug addictions. This is particularly true for *Homo Machina* who ultimately has nowhere else to turn to in order to find serenity and peace.

Yet many *Believing Man* (or Homo Credo) are actually in the very same boat as *Machine Man*. Yes, they do have the potential to be at ease and peace without first 'knocking themselves out of their minds'. But only if they have become a God-loving person rather than a God-fearing one; it is simply very difficult to be able to truly relax when one is anxious and afraid of the wrath of an angry and vengeful God!

The ability to be or stay relaxed seems to be a rather rare achievement in a world that 'likes' to make us upset and angry, worried or afraid, always expected to be active and 'on the go', stressed out and tense. Yet once we are aware of the 'name of the game' we can simply choose to not participate in the rat race. And stay relaxed instead. Cool, calm and collected.

When others are jumping up and down or would like you to do so, just exhale, smile, and consciously relax every part of your body that seems to stiffen up. Take a step back (mentally and perhaps physically as well) and keep breathing deeply. There is usually no rush to reply quickly, so don't. Stay relaxed and loving. Things will thus calm down naturally. At least for you. And usually for others as well.

And The Happy Rabbit Says…

"Be truly aware of your body today - relax all muscles and let all tensions melt away!"

What is the best course of action when we're starting to rush around, feel uneasy about not being sufficiently productive, or making progress fast enough? In short, it is 'Non-action'. Besides meditation, these are two of my favorite 'exercises' in non-action:

Watch the world go by just like traditional Italians (or Spaniards and Greeks) love doing; they sit seemingly for hours in their favorite coffee shop, look at 'bella signorinas' or God knows whom and what; they occasionally take a sip of their beverage, chat with friends and strangers alike, read the paper, or just watch and see what's happening. There is always something happening!

Or try cloud-watching; lay down on a beach or lawn and look up to the clouds, watch them drift by gently but surely. Calmly and nicely. Admire their always changing yet beautiful shapes, forms and colors. Occasionally wonder about important questions like "Where do they go next? What will they see? Where did they come from? What kind of weather will they bring about?"

Such peaceful moments can bring about much calmness and clarity in one's own affairs; we will suddenly know exactly what to do, or not to do, about that certain matter at hand that has been troubling us. We will now see the best course of action, and also have the renewed energy to go out and 'just do it'! Quickly, nicely, and easily.

To relax is neither the same as being lazy nor is it a waste of time. To feel relaxed actually means to be really focused on the divinity of every single moment or insight at a time. And therefore to be totally ready for all eventualities. To be able to move fast one has to be in a restful state, both mentally and physically. A strained and stiff person needs to first relax their muscles. And mind. There is always a delay in our response when we are tense and tight.

Accomplished martial artists and other top performers in their respective sports or arts know this full well; they are able to stay all relaxed, no matter what. Cats and dogs (and other animals) instinctively stretch their bodies from time to time and otherwise stay totally flexible and relaxed. And therefore they are always ready to move. Fast. Without undue stress or using any more energy than absolutely necessary. Such is life in the flow when we don't put up artificial (real or imagined) obstacles and other man-made dramas.

Some people choose to play stressful or violent video games in order to 'relax'; sometimes for such extended periods of time that they literally 'amuse' themselves to death. [110] But their sometimes fateful attraction is just an illusion and not really relaxing but only exhausting them further; it is their addiction to the hormone adrenaline (epinephrine) that needs to continuously get excreted (by the adrenal glands and certain neurons) for them to feel well. It's the same with smokers; they feel relaxed upon getting a nicotine hit but were actually only tense because of their body's *constant craving* for this most addictive of substances.

And likewise it is for a great many of us modern-day people who are essentially addicted to being busy and stressed out, always 'running high' on adrenaline. More or less living in constant fear, respectively in fight-or-flight mode. Alternating between being excited or angry. Merrily multitasking away. Secretly thrilled to be terribly busy or much needed. Until we are totally exhausted. And breaking down. Having a burnout moment. With our adrenal glands and nervous systems screaming out for a break. Or worse, causing other related health problems (kidneys, thyroid glands, high blood pressure, heart attacks, etc.).

The 'well-being' (like a boost in mood or energy, quick thinking or sharp wit) that comes from being addicted to adrenaline or other stimulants is simply not really real or lasting, but the physical side-effects on our bodies may very well be. [111]

These days a great many people are so tense in every sense that they don't ever *really* relax. They may think that they are resting yet their bodies are still stiff and in a nearly permanent state of tension.

Of course there is much we can do to physically relax our bodies. Like taking a hot bath in candlelight while listening to some soft music and inhaling a blend of natural essences. Or gently massaging our hands and fingers with the other hand to soothe painful spots and invigorating yet balancing the entire nervous system (respectively acupuncture points and meridians).

Meditations and visualizations work well too, especially when combined with deep breathing techniques, and the conscious letting go of tensions in every part of our bodies. One by one until there are none.

Yet even the best natural methods won't help much if our minds continue to be tormented by assorted worries, fears and regrets. We could get a really great massage that will temporarily relieve some physical tensions, yet within a short period of time our muscles may be all tense and tight again. Simply because our minds are not well and truly relaxed and calm.

Real relaxation only comes with spiritual awareness and feeling connected in love. Being a surrendered soul at ease and peace with God and the universe. That in turn will lead to a calm and quiet mind. Which in turn will lead to a relaxed body. Spirit (soul, *who we really are*) over mind. Mind over body. It is that simple (see also chapters *Surrender* and *Be your Self*).

When you want to be truly more productive in life you simply need to rest, relax and recover more often; it's a great time to reflect and pray, to contemplate and meditate, to dream and know. And more often than not, this is actually the time we make the most progress. In all aspects of our lives.

Part of relaxation is to amuse ourselves; to be less serious and more playful. No matter our current age, we can learn to be playful again as it is part and parcel of who we really are. We can watch children play. Or observe and feel inspired by the playful nature of most if not all animals. Once their basic necessities are taken care of they all play and amuse themselves. Constantly. Unless they sleep. Happily. The pursuit of pleasure and joy after all is an inborn part of every soul.

Life becomes a lot merrier once we discover our immortal true nature and we therefore give ourselves the permission to be the eternal child of the universe we naturally are. We live in a loving, playful and plentiful universe. Despite other people's opinions or choices. Respectively their attempts to spoil the fun. Don't let them. Keep loving, smiling and playing.

"Dare to err and to dream. Deep meaning often lies in childish play." Friedrich von Schiller

Always take your time to love and be kind; to read and learn; to literally smell the roses and watch the clouds; to breathe and move your body; to stretch and relax; to eat with gratitude and joy, to be merry and have fun; to watch the world go by in peace; to play and amuse yourself; to sleep and dream; to think and contemplate; to help and do good, to be fit and well; to joke and laugh; to meditate and pray; to work smart and succeed; there is always much to do *and* just as much not to do!

Love God every moment

Appreciate God in happy moments

Trust God in difficult moments

Admire God in beautiful moments

Surrender to God in quiet moments

REALIZATIONS:

I love to rest and relax

I love to feel relaxed and well

In Summary

We have now walked and talked all the way of *The Merry Way*, covering twenty different yet connected parts. Congratulations and hopefully you already feel very much like a very merry Christian!

Of course, as with everything, practice makes the master. The more we apply and incorporate the outlined principles into our daily lives, the quicker that will happen. And all of a sudden we are just always - or at least most of the time - full of love, peace and happiness. Confident and strong. Smiling and laughing. Playful and joking. Seeing the humor in situations. Able to recognize and treasure the deeper lessons and hidden meanings of why things are happening, or have happened.

We have also become proficient at turning around situations that would have looked too difficult to cope before. More and more we are able to see the positive and the good in any situation. It is usually the small things in life that trigger so many unhappy moments or conflicts. And likewise, it is often the very same things that can make or keep us happy - once we look at them from a different perspective, with a connected heart and thus a more enlightened mind.

"I am more and more convinced that our happiness or unhappiness depends far more on the way we meet the events of life, than on the nature of those events themselves." Baron Alexander von Humboldt

Each of the twenty happy insights discussed will help us to stay connected with God and his creation. All of them are easy to apply simply because they are already natural parts of *who we really are*. There is no need to come up with artificial compounds or illusory techniques that will only confuse or hinder us further. We simply can't treat our heartfelt needs and desires by applying anything that by definition works only externally.

We also don't need to fight against anything or to focus on first eliminating 'things' before we are able to be happy again. All we need to do is to remember and apply the above positive and easy aspects and activities that are already and eternally a part of us.

Thus every single part of *The Merry Way* in itself will already increase our joy and happiness. And the combination of all of them together makes for a most powerful and merry mix. All twenty points are again summarized in the following checklist that you may wish to copy or write down somewhere for your easy reference.

Go through the points every day for a month or two and check them off one by one, just like pilots do in pre-flight planning to make sure that all flight systems are working perfectly alright and everything is ready for a happy take-off!

Read and feel it all before heading off to work, during the day as a reminder, or in the evening to better 'digest the day' - helping you to empty your mind of what is best to simply let go and be. And to contemplate and remember the insights gained, the lessons learned, the blessings received.

The Merry Way

1 Love God

2 Feel God's Love

3 Love your Self

4 Love All

5 Appreciate

6 Smile

7 Surrender

8 Hope

9 Breathe

10 Stay Kind

11 Mind your Mind

12 Love your Body

13 Be your Self

14 Follow Love

15 Respect

16 Admire

17 Wish Well

18 Help

19 Do it with Love

20 Relax

In the following six chapters we will discuss additional aspects that may be helpful in our quest. Some of them aim to cover questions that may have arisen from reading or while applying *The Merry Way*. Others offer additional thoughts and insights to live a happy life in today's rather complex and challenging world. Here's a quick overview of what is yet to come:

- *In His Words*
- *Obstacles to Love*
- *The Divine Deal*
- *Merry Money*
- *Love in Separation*
- *Merry Realizations*

In His Words

Who is Jesus? People have wondered and talked about him for over two thousand years (an amazing accomplishment in itself!). Many worship and love him, some follow in his footsteps, and others doubt or dislike him to the point of desiring to ridicule his followers.

It may sound strange yet even to Christians Jesus can be something of an enigma. And quite a few are so busy with arguing, speculating or promoting their own fantasies about him that they totally neglect to actually feel united in love and friendship as he wants us to be.

Despite much talk and deliberations, Jesus made it actually very easy for us to understand him. He preached love as being the ultimate solution to everything. Yes, everything. One side-effect of a loving heart is to have a more open and understanding mind. The more we love the more tolerant and forgiving we will become in our various interactions with 'the world'. In other words, we will have ever less reasons (or the desire) to judge and condemn others.

So who is Jesus? Perhaps the best way to find out is by concentrating on his essential quotes - in his words - presented here without much comment as they are forcefully self-evident.

About his origins and God the Father:

"If you loved me, you would be glad that I am going to the Father, for the Father is greater than I." (John 14:28)

"I came from the Father and entered the world; now I am leaving the world and going back to the Father." (John 16:28)

About his love for the Father, the source and authority of his teaching:

"But the world must learn that I love the Father and that I do exactly what my Father has commanded me." (John 14:31)

"For I have come down from heaven not to do my will but to do the will of him who sent me." (John 6:38)

"My teaching is not my own. It comes from him who sent me." (John 7:16)

"For I did not speak of my own accord, but the Father who sent me commanded me what to say and how to say it." (John 12:49)

"I know that his command leads to eternal life. So whatever I say is just what the Father has told me to say." (John 12:50)

Jesus keeps emphasizing his role and function as the obedient and loving son who teaches exactly as instructed. He never desires an exalted position, and always places the focus of his teaching and living example on loving God the Father.

About how to be able to fully understand his authority:

"If anyone chooses to do God's will, he will find out whether my teaching comes from God or whether I speak on my own." (John 7:17)

And likewise, when we choose to follow the will of God we will also be able to understand and live the glorious message of love Jesus was sent to demonstrate and spread. At any given moment we are free to feel either connected or separated, independent or in harmony, playing God or loving God. It's always our choice as we have been given free will.

About following in his footsteps:

"Whoever has my commands and obeys them, he is the one who loves me. He who loves me will be loved by my Father, and I too will love him and show myself to him." (John 14:21)

About his first and foremost commandment:

"Love the Lord your God with all your heart, soul, and mind." (Matthew 22:37)

About his second commandment:

"And the second is like it: 'Love your neighbor as yourself.'" (Matthew 22:38)

Jesus repeated it here:

"Love the Lord your God with all your heart and with all your soul and with all your mind and with all your strength." The second is this: "Love your neighbor as yourself." Mark 12:30-31

And once again he stressed their primary importance:

"On these two commandments depend all the law and the prophets." (Matthew 22:40)

About where to place our trust:

"Do not let your hearts be troubled. Trust in God; trust also in me." (John 14:1)

About doing God's will:

Jesus said to them, *"My food is to do the will of him who sent me and to accomplish his work."* (John 4:34)

"I can do nothing on my own. As I hear, I judge, and my judgment is just, because I seek not my own will but the will of him who sent me." (John 5:30)

"For I have come down from heaven not to do my will but to do the will of him who sent me." (John 6:38)

About being joyful:

"As the Father has loved me, so have I loved you. Now remain in my love. If you obey my commands, you will remain in my love, just as I have obeyed my Father's commands and remain in his love. I have told you this so that my joy may be in you and that your joy may be complete." (John 15:9 -11)

About being friends:

"You are my friends if you do what I command. I no longer call you servants, because a servant does not know his master's business. Instead, I have called you friends, for everything that I learned from my Father I have made known to you." (John 15:14,15)

About being united in love:

"If anyone loves me, he will obey my teaching. My Father will love him, and we will come to him and make our home with him." (John 14:23)

Jesus points out that there is no separation, disharmony or discord in divine love.

About being a child of God:

"But I tell you: Love your enemies and pray for those who persecute you, that you may be sons of your Father in heaven. He causes his sun to rise on the evil and the good, and sends rain on the righteous and the unrighteous." (Matthew 5:44-45)

"I tell you the truth, anyone who has faith in me will do what I have been doing. He will do even greater things than these, because I am going to the Father." (John 14:12)

Jesus obviously wants us to follow his example and do what he did. He even desires that we do *greater* things than him! While that may sound rather unlikely or impossible at first, Jesus evidently has both the insight and faith to know that indeed this can be so! Quite some food for thought, or better, motivation.

"For the Spirit God gave us does not make us timid, but gives us power, love and self-discipline." (2 Timothy 1:7)

To be able to truly follow in his footsteps requires us to be strong, instead of playing weak. It calls for us to be connected and united with God and one another, instead of getting separated and dispersed into countless squabbling groups of many names and sizes that seemingly 'love' to argue over mostly irrelevant doctrines rather than actually loving God and each other (as instructed).

"Be perfect, therefore, as your heavenly Father is perfect." (Matthew 5:48)

In the above verses Jesus makes it crystal clear who he is and what he expects us to do. Nothing really needs interpretation of any kind, by anyone. Nothing needs to be added either. In other words, *anything else* is neither necessary nor important. Any man-made and contradictory additions are at best a waste of time and efforts, and at worst will only point us in the wrong direction, thereby resulting in all kinds of negative consequences.

"But you, man of God, flee from all this, and pursue righteousness, godliness, faith, love, endurance and gentleness." (1 Timothy:11)

So all we need to do is to remember and apply the above few key verses. And thereby be(come) merry! Being happy is after all an automatic side effect, a by-product of living a life of love and all the good that comes with it.

Over the centuries lots and lots has been said and done in the name of Jesus. Or rather, claiming to be in his name while much if not most of it was very likely very displeasing to him. And so he warned us in no uncertain terms:

"Not everyone who says to me, 'Lord, Lord,' will enter the kingdom of heaven, but only the one who does the will of my Father who is in heaven. Many will say to me on that day, 'Lord, Lord, did we not prophesy in your name and in your name drive out demons and in your name perform many miracles?' Then I will tell them plainly, 'I never knew you. Away from me, you evildoers!'" (Matthew 7:21, 22, 23)

People who ultimately preach disgust and hatred or otherwise promote disunity and discord obviously neither experience divine love nor do they live by the principles laid out by Jesus Christ - no matter how hard they profess to do so in public. Otherwise their unkind words and unloving thoughts, words and deeds would simply not be possible. The fruits are always telling the nature of the tree.

"The matter is quite simple. The Bible is very easy to understand. But we Christians are a bunch of scheming swindlers. We pretend to be unable to understand it because we know very well that the minute we understand, we are obliged to act accordingly. Take any words in the New Testament and forget everything except pledging yourself to act accordingly. My God, you will say, if I do that my whole life will be ruined. How would I ever get on in the world? Herein lies the real place of Christian scholarship. Christian scholarship is the church's prodigious invention to defend itself against the Bible, to ensure that we can continue to be good Christians without the Bible coming too close." Soren Aabye Kierkegaard

Theological discussions are all good and fine - but only as long as they actually *increase* the strength and purity of our love and corresponding unity. And that very rarely happens, if ever...

Do our words and deeds lead to more or less love in our personal and collective worlds? Does our loving faith and living example strengthen or weaken our communities? Bring about more peace and prosperity or further war and destruction?

Both love and the lack of it result in many by-products. Some of them are only nice and sweet, the others sour at best and bitter at worst.

"The correlative to loving our neighbors as ourselves is hating ourselves as we hate our neighbors." Francis Bacon

Theoretical questions purely exist on a mental level. Within our hearts there is always clarity. Mind matters however tend to cause arguments and disunity. Different minds and egos simply have a hard time to agree on things as we (perceive to) have different interests. The language of love however is easily understood. No one can argue about what love is. We just know it when we feel it.

A limited mind will never be able to comprehend the nature of God. Yet a mind that is increasingly enlightened by the love of God will get ever more glimpses about all the Who's, What's and Why's.

Obstacles to Love

When we look at the splintered world of Christianity today we can come to realize that selfish or otherwise dubious interests have gradually and quite deliberately watered down the essence of what Jesus taught to the point of irrelevance and worse.

The greatest row in the history of Christianity hinged on the single word of 'Filioque' and on the doctrine of the Trinity. Ultimately it lead to the Great Schism of 1054 that split the Eastern and Western Church. As with every conflict, it usually is about power and control over people and their assets, no matter how nicely it is cloaked and packaged.

The teachings of the Holy Trinity (introduced in the 4th century AD) say that the God the Father, God the Son, and God the Holy Spirit are all like one. Christians who reject this teaching say that Jesus Christ 'only' became well and truly enlightened while living among us here, and that the path of love outlined by him is not only open to all of us, but that it is indeed the very thing desired by God.

Who is right and who is wrong? The short answer is that it doesn't really matter *once* we feel the love of God. But if this doctrine leads us astray, in the totally opposite direction of where Jesus wanted to take us, it does matter. And very much so.

As we know, the only thing that well and truly matters is, in his own words:

"Love one another, as I have loved you. By this everyone will know that you are my disciples, if you love one another." (John 13:34-35)

Quite possibly *both* ideas are true *at the same time* - a concept that is likely to be beyond the ability of our limited minds to grasp. Yet likewise, quantum mechanics has shown us that we can choose whether we see a rock as solid matter or as mainly empty space where super-tiny particles of energy rotate at lightning speeds. Both viewpoints are correct.

What we perceive to be true from where we currently are is (at best) only partially true when seen from the enlightened perspective of divine consciousness.

What differs may simply be a matter of different roles and functions. One way to look at this issue is to imagine some candles that always stay in their original condition, as new. Say there is one candle that has lit another one, which in turn lights yet another one. An observer will see three candles in a row. All shine equally bright, and all disperse equal warmth.

When we place each one of the candles in different rooms, how will we know which candle was which? One lights up the living room, one the bathroom, and the third one our bedroom.

No one could tell which one of them is the original candle. Thanks to Albert Einstein's relativity theory we know that time and space are relative concepts, confined to physical dimensions only (which include the earthly ones we can perceive and measure). Yet eternity has no beginning and no end, and that is a notion that our limited minds simply struggle to grasp. So the idea that there is perhaps no original candle at all is rather difficult to understand as well.

We could go further still and imagine there to be a great many more divine candles, perhaps all lit by the seemingly original candle; lots and lots of candles that each in itself is whole and complete. Yet each one has its own unique role and function to play in the whole of God's creations and plays.

After all, God is the ultimate truth and infinite in his endless energies and manifestations; as such it is only normal that he can have unlimited friends and children too. There are simply no man-made boundaries for God, even if we'd tried to restrict (or define) him with our currently rather narrow and ignorant minds. God needs to be felt and experienced. Love is both the connection and the goal.

Even on planet Earth we can see that every seed in itself is complete and whole. It contains all that is needed to grow, for example, into a mature tree. And yet, that tree will never be able to call itself the forest. A drop of water in the ocean is a complete yet separate part of the whole. Indeed, the word 'whole' and 'holy' contain the same root and meaning (holistic is also spelled 'wholistic').

In the previous chapter (*In His Words*) Jesus always talks about God as being the most beloved subject of his love. And about doing solely his will. He wants us to do likewise and first and foremost focus our love on God. Furthermore he asks us to become perfect children of God. Be 'Christ-like' too and do even better than he did!

"Be perfect, therefore, as your heavenly Father is perfect." (Matthew 5:48)

That alone should be our focus. All else will be added and become clear to us once we do so. Easy.

However, when our mental concoctions and worldly interests contradict the most important desire and commandment of God, as conveyed to us by Jesus, we actually do have a problem. We will go in the wrong direction and squabble over meaningless little details all the while disregarding the essential. Hence the many tens of thousands of Christian organizations, no matter their names or sizes.

Hopefully that will change. And it will once we all realize the above and simply be both loving and lovable at all times. In other words when we all become merry Christians! There is great strength in unity. And now the time is right to stand up and be counted. To let go of all the little nothings and focus on love, the very everything.

Jesus answered, "I am the way and the truth and the life. No one comes to the Father except through me." (John 14:6)

Quite a few people use and abuse this verse to deny God's love to non-Christians, to all the not converted, or 'saved'. Basically they are saying that anyone who did not have the good fortune of hearing about Jesus is denied the possibility of feeling God's love or loving God.

What kind of God or messenger of his would deny unconditional divine love to any of his children? The very thing that he clearly and repeatedly said is most important and desired?

Such folks cultivate and propagate various types of exclusionary and divisive cults that often also reject Christians of any other denomination or persuasion than their own. They like to proclaim to be the 'lovers' or representatives of Jesus yet at the same time they quite obviously don't follow his first and foremost commandments: The lack of both love and joy is simply there for all to see. Love *never* breeds hatred or associated words and deeds. Not for any cause, reason or justification. And no matter how 'nicely' it may be wrapped or sold by some fanciful preacher.

Any divisive and sectarian mindset - which is always based on ego's need to feel superior - *immediately* excludes God's love. The attitude of 'us versus them' or 'we the saved versus the poor souls that need to be saved' exists purely on the ego level and disconnects *anyone* (no matter how 'exalted' we may think we are) - *automatically and instantly*, by default. What remains is just empty talk and gesture, devoid of any sweetness or life.

True love breeds real understanding. Thereby it *broadens* our mind and expands our consciousness. The non-religious or spiritually weary too are able to feel love in many shapes and forms. And ultimately, by divine design every soul will be able to once again attain and feel love of God. It is only a matter of desiring it, or not. As such it is only a matter of time.

Jesus outlines a path of pure spiritual love. He knows that thereafter all else will be given to us, automatically. Seek, find and cherish the love of God, love your self and love each other. By doing so we already live in a heavenly space in the here and now as heaven is the place of eternal love and peace, joy and happiness.

People who live a life of darkness don't see the shining path of love that leads to happiness and heaven. The absence of light is darkness.

Love *is* light. And thereby it dispels all darkness. The only key that is able to unlock the gates of heaven is the universal key of love.

Jesus lives and prescribes pure love. There is therefore no difference between his words and deeds and who he eternally is in his very essence. *He is love and thereby he is the way.* He made love his central commandment and very clearly so. He is the first and only one to make the importance of love so explicit and indeed, paramount. That is what makes him so special.

Love is the way and the truth and the life. No one comes to the Father except through love.

Love is always available and accessible to anyone at any time. No one can stop us from living a life of love. And no one can take it away from us either, no matter how hard they tried. By living a life of love we are helping to extend the reaches of heaven even though we are physically still here in our earthly bodies.

The eternal reality of love in all its shades, shapes and forms is not exclusive to Christians. Love exists since time immemorial, no matter how imperfect it may be at times. The central importance of love has been taught in many ways and in many places throughout history. Every soul inherently recognizes and knows love even though we may temporarily avoid or neglect to feel and live it.

Love of God has been called the 'essence of Judaism'. [112] In the Book of Deuteronomy, the fifth book of the Hebrew Bible and of the Jewish Torah, it is written:

"And you shall love the Lord your God with all your heart and with all your soul and with all your might." (Deuteronomy 6:5)

Love of God is also the highest spiritual attainment in Islam (even though that seems rather doubtful when one considers the current state of affairs in the world. Nevertheless, the highest goal of Islam is love as understood by all enlightened practitioners):

"Yet there are men who take (for worship) others besides God, as equal (with God): They love them as they should love God. But those of Faith are overflowing in their love for God." (Quran 2:165)

"O lovers! The religion of the love of God is not found in Islam alone. In the realm of love, there is neither belief, nor unbelief." Rumi [113]

Once one of the most important of the early Sufi poets and mystics was asked, *"Do you love God?"* She answered *"Yes."* *"Do you hate the devil?"* She answered, *"No, my love of God leaves me no time to hate the devil."* Rabia [114]

For thousands of years some Hindus have been practicing *Bhakti Yoga*[115] to first and foremost cultivate their love of God; "a practice of devotion toward God, solely motivated by the sincere, loving desire to please God, rather than the hope of divine reward or the fear of divine punishment."

And Lao Tzu, the author of the Tao Te Ching and founder of philosophical Taoism, said well over 2'500 years ago that: *"Being deeply loved by someone gives you strength, while loving someone deeply gives you courage."*

Last but not least, here are a few insights by well-known contemporary Buddhists:

"Love and compassion are necessities, not luxuries. Without them humanity cannot survive." Dalai Lama [116]

"The Buddha's teachings on love are clear. It is possible to live twenty-four hours a day in a state of love. Every movement, every glance, every thought, and every word can be infused with love." Thich Nhat Hanh [117]

"If there is love, there is hope that one may have real families, real brotherhood, real equanimity, real peace. If the love within your mind is lost and you see other beings as enemies, then no matter how much knowledge or education or material comfort you have, only suffering and confusion will ensue." Dalai Lama

The Golden Rule that 'one should treat others as one would like others to treat oneself' was already known in the Mohism, Taoism, and Confucianism of Ancient China. It was taught thousands of years ago in Hinduism, Buddhism, Zoroastrianism, and Ancient Greece. [118]

"Never impose on others what you would not choose for yourself." Confucius (551-479 BC)

"Do not do to others what would anger you if done to you by others." Isocrates (436-338 BC)

No matter the various names we assign to the Absolute Truth, or the particular ways we celebrate and worship in our creed and culture, we are all children of God. We are all equal parts and parcels of creation, no matter our individual thoughts, feelings and desires, no matter the color of our bodies' skin, no matter where we were born or how we were raised.

"Did not just one God create us all? Why then does humankind deal treacherously with one another? This betrays the teachings of our ancestors." (Malachi 2:10)

Every child of God can (re)discover divine love within their hearts and minds. We all experienced it while we were still within the womb of our mothers - regardless of the particular part of planet Earth we were destined to be born nine months later. Pure love after all is both eternal and universal.

'Many roads lead to Rome', respectively take us back to God. And of course there is only one God who created it all. It wasn't the Catholic God that created the sun, a Protestant one who fixed the moon, a Jewish one who came up with the idea of creating planet Earth, and so on and so forth.

Some roads are more direct than others, some are smoother than others, some take us there quicker than others. In the end however, we will all reach our destinations once again.

Christianity can show us the easy, quick and happy way - for as long as we concentrate on the essence and avoid arguing over irrelevant details that only cause separation and conflict. Love *is* the essence. Trying to deny it to others by various mental concoctions only means (and reveals) that we ourselves don't actually feel it in the first place.

When we cultivate what is basically a form of 'club consciousness' and feel better than members of other clubs (churches or congregations or assemblies of atheists, etc.) *we* instantly cut *ourselves* off the love of God. Because at the core of who we are we know that we are very wrong and thereby feel a bit guilty and not quite worthy of God's love.

Identifying one's self and others as 'club members' to be either cheered or jeered is a clear sign of living in 'ego-land', or the 'world of labels', rather than being anchored in the spiritual truths of the eternal universe of love.

Disconnection to the divine also happens when we judge and condemn others, are arrogant or condescending, anytime we feel superior or 'above' our fellow brothers and sisters. That is just a simple little spiritual truth that most of us get to experience; some of us occasionally only, others perhaps most of the time. Until we all become aware of this obstacle to love and decide to instead live happily ever after. With lots of love. In peace and harmony. Both within our hearts and minds, and with everyone and everything we meet and encounter.

"Don't condemn others, and God won't condemn you. God will be as hard on you as you are on others! He will treat you exactly as you treat them." (Matthew 7:1-2)

Love is open and available at all times to all of humanity, and indeed, way beyond. Animals of all kinds display great love, affection and care within both their immediate and extended families. We can also witness much love and cooperation between different species, even among the most unlikely kind of animals. [119]

In the end it doesn't really matter whether we call ourselves Christians or not. For anyone who follows the principles laid out by Jesus and reaffirmed within these pages is a Christian - not in name only but in actual reality. And that is all that matters. Because it is what is most pleasing to God, the universe of love.

God is the primal principle at the heart of the universe. And, *God is love* (1 John 4:8). Therefore love is the fundamental force at the core of *All There Is*.

"And now abideth faith, hope, and love, even these three: but the chiefest of these is love." (1 Corinthians 13:13)

The Divine Deal

Why is it that people abandon God and turn themselves into skeptics, cynics, or atheists? Why is it that some feel disappointed, neglected or abandoned? Others are more or less consciously angry with God because of prayers that seemingly went unanswered. Or because they secretly blame him for all their ills and sorrows, their trials and tribulations.

Suffering in the world is often taken as evidence that there can be no God. Or if there is one, he must be quite ruthless or heartless, perhaps even to the point of being sadistic. It is a particularly easy conclusion to make for those who believe in a world of mere luck where everything is just the result of coincidence respectively the chaos theory (which despite its atheist proponents is only a theory, to be assumed or believed in, to be amended and eventually, abandoned).

When they extrapolate their materialistic belief and proceed to discuss the possible existence of the divine, it is only natural for them to conclude at best a capricious, or simply an unjust and unfair God. A deity who dishes out blessings or condemnations at random, or a cruel one who often ends up punishing the good and brave while rewarding the wicked and evil. And of course, it would be a rather silly or not worthwhile endeavor to worship such an arbitrary God.

In the Abrahamic religions (Judaism, Christianity, and Islam) and Hinduism, God is considered and believed to be *omniscient* (Latin for omnis 'all' and sciens 'knowing'), *omnipotent* (omni 'all' and potens 'power'), and *omnibenevolent* (omni 'all' and benevolent 'good'). Some of the very faithful (mis)take this to believe in total predestination, the notion that *all events* have been willed and determined by God.

Yet that would essentially mean that nothing ever happen without God's prior approval. It would also mean that we can't change our destiny. It would therefore mean that God really is the ultimate culprit or villain and fully responsible for everything *we* do because he knows everything, and lets or wills it all to happen. The good, the bad, *and* the ugly. That would not sound very benevolent, to say the least. And it would only promote the erroneous concept of a God to be feared, instead of loved (see also chapters *Love God* and *Feel God's Love*).

Ironically, the belief in predestination leads to the very same conclusions as the ones reached by atheists and cynics. Furthermore, it would also mean that there really are no sinners. And sin itself could not exist, otherwise God would be the one and only sinner (since, according to their logic, he determines all that happens).

Reality is that we have been given free will. The free will to choose and make decisions as we please. We are here to play 'God in a teacup' kind of thing. The desire to be and play God is one reason why some people don't even want to hear about the possibility that a supreme intelligent energy and/or being could exist. Because God's very existence would interfere with our ambition to play-act God.

How could we possibly play 'the big guy' if we were constantly aware that there is a bigger boss 'up there' somewhere? It would kind of ruin the fun, wouldn't it? As kids when we used to play robber and cop and were totally convinced to be the hero who always gets the bad guys and saves the world, well, the last thing we'd want to hear is the elder brother saying that it's all just a game and that we're merely silly little things sitting in a sandbox getting dirty!

How do we know that we have free will and free choice? It is simply self-evident for everyone in every day's life. No one can possible deny this simple fact. It starts with the very little things in life and extends all the way to the very important matters:

I can choose what to eat for breakfast, or to skip it altogether. I can choose to exercise first or watch some TV instead. I can choose to sleep early or stay up late. I can choose to study diligently and keep learning in life. Or to take it easy and go fishing with my friends and drink beer all day long. Be ambitious and pursue a challenging career or to be content with a simple job that just pays the bills. Have a victim's or a victor's attitude. And so on.

Life is full of choices and decisions. This is true for everybody. But obviously, the richer we are, the more possibilities we have to choose from. With more money we have a wider range of cars to buy from. We can elect to fly business or first class instead of having to sit back in 'cattle class'. We can choose to walk, bicycle, take the bus or train, drive, or be driven around in a limousine, while the very poor only have the choice between either walking or running.

God doesn't decide for us, nor does anyone else. Well, not quite so for those who allow their minds to be manipulated by clever advertising campaigns and so on (see also chapter *Mind your Mind*). Regardless, it is us who need to decide which washing powder to buy from a huge array of choices. God won't bother as he has probably better things to do.

The very fact that I can go out and do bad deeds anytime I wanted to is proof that we have free will and free choice. I could take a six pack of beer and visit my neighbor to discuss issues of mutual concerns in a friendly, respectful and fun setting. Or I could decide to go over there and express my displeasure with a baseball bat and hit him over the head a few times to make sure he won't play loud music while I'd like to have my beauty sleep. There are always many ways and choices to deal with problems.

We have accepted *The Divine Deal* even before we were born into this world. For those who doubt that: It's not that we were born as flesh and bones and suddenly become eternal spiritual souls later on; we already existed before and continue to exist upon leaving our bodies. Beliefs to the contrary only show one to have bought into the Machine man consciousness proposed by atheistic believers who worship matter as their ultimate truth (see also chapter *Be your Self*).

So yes, we really do get to choose and decide to a large degree. But we have also agreed to the flip side of the deal: *We are solely responsible for our choices, words and deeds.* And of course, this includes that we have to accept and live through the consequences of our actions.

We simply cannot hold God responsible for any suffering and pain that may result from our freely chosen undertakings. That wouldn't be very fair at all. Parents give their children guidance, yet will have to let them go out and play with the other kids. First in the neighborhood, and later in the big wide world 'out there'. And sometimes they do get hurt. A mother or father can only do so much to help and give comfort, but never eliminate any and all eventual pain.

We are eternal beings temporarily in a physical body of flesh and blood. As such, we have eternal free will and choice, plus the eternal responsibility that comes with it: *"A man reaps what he sows."* (Galatians 6:7)

"The person who sins will die. The son will not bear the punishment for the father's iniquity, nor will the father bear the punishment for the son's iniquity; the righteousness of the righteous will be upon himself, and the wickedness of the wicked will be upon himself." (Ezekiel 18:20).

The above verses make it crystal clear that we all bear the responsibility for what we do. Each and every person is responsible as an individual. When you sow carrots, *you* will reap carrots. Not me nor anybody else. And it's not going to be potatoes or anything else; it will be carrots. If you give love, *you* will receive love. Give respect and you will receive respect. Be appreciative and you will be appreciated. Be generous and you will have plenty. It is very easy and it is very fair.

"Happiness is not a reward - it is a consequence. Suffering is not a punishment - it is a result." Robert Green Ingersoll

Throughout the ages this universal law has been expressed differently by various cultures, yet it always means the very same thing. Like attracts like. Birds of feather flock together. What goes around comes around. The law of attraction. Issac Newton formulated it in his third law of motion as 'actio est reactio', Latin for 'action is reaction'. Every force or action on one object is followed by a reaction on another - of equal magnitude, but opposite direction (back to its origin).

Eastern philosophy refers to this universal law as 'Karma'. Popular but erroneous belief is that karma is somehow like a ledger where plus and minus points are kept; a kind of universal recording or bookkeeping of all good and bad deeds that will (eventually) result in an overall balance. A credit or debt-like situation - just like in a bank account - where at the end of the day, one has either some money left to spend (and enjoy), or some debts to endure (and pay back).

Yet to keep the balance of the universe each action will produce its own corresponding reaction: A good deed done (sowed) will result in (harvesting) an equally good outcome. But likewise with the bad ones. They won't just get canceled out or deleted by a deed done well. Every seed produces its own harvest. Therefore if someone likes to keep track in terms of categories like good and bad, one would really need to keep two separate ledgers. And obviously it's best to keep adding to the plus column while keeping the score on the minus side as closely to zero as possible.

Whatever the ledger may be for each one of us, we really don't need to be worried about our future or be overly concerned about our destiny when we live a life of love, peace and happiness. Because the seeds of love will sprout further love. It will literally lighten up our life in every way and at all times. In the here and now as well as in the hereafter.

"Above all, love each other deeply, because love covers over a multitude of sins." (1 Peter 4:8)

"Repentant tears wash out the stain of guilt." Saint Augustine

Concerns about salvation and the like are solely the product of a fearful disconnected mind that identifies itself as being a physical body only. Feeling love for God and loved by God is the light that dispels all fear and illuminates all darkness.

All of us will leave our bodies behind, sooner or later. There is no cheating or other way out on this. The only question is where will we go? The Bible doesn't actually mention the mythical hell where sinners get supposedly poked and roasted (or worse) for all of eternity. Jesus however makes it clear that there are many different places we can go to:

*"In my Father's house are **many mansions**: if it were not so, I would have told you. I go to prepare a place for you."* (John 14:2)

*"There are also **heavenly bodies and there are earthly bodies**; but the splendor of the heavenly bodies is one kind, and the splendor of the earthly bodies is another. The sun has one kind of splendor, the moon another and the stars another; and star differs from star in splendor."* (1 Corinthians 15:40,41)

*"To the LORD your God belong **the heavens, even the highest heavens**, the earth and everything in it."* (Deuteronomy 10:14)

Where exactly (or which one of the higher or lower heavens, many mansions, or heavenly bodies) we will go to all depends on our consciousness. The way we live while on Planet Earth - what we think, feel and do - also depends on how much or how little we are conscious about the big picture of things. The less we are conscious the more we are only concerned with the needs of our 'little self', the selfish demands of our ego. Or the demands and urges of our immediate physical life.

And as we know, like attracts like. So if we live a rather selfish life we are sowing and will be reaping the according place in another dimension. It will be more or less free and pleasant. It's up to us only. God's universe is very efficient and fair, even if we currently limited souls can't fully perceive its total perfection or infinite scope.

What about suffering in general, why does it exist in the first place? There are two aspects to consider. One is more immediate or microscopic and the other the big picture view of things.

First, when we analyze the different type of suffering in the world we will fairly quickly see that most of it is really man-made: War is a primary reason for premature losses of (physical) life and much of the suffering that preceded or followed it. This is true throughout the history of mankind.

And yes, one could point out the role of organized religion in some of these wars, but that completely neglects the two primary drivers:

Money and power. Religion was often used as an external manufactured reason, but in the end it was really all about the gold and silver, and who gets to rule and control over the lands and its people. Who gets to sit on the throne and live in the palace versus those who do the serving and slaving. That game is as old as humanity itself.

War is always caused by man alone; God has nothing to do with it. Therefore the responsibility of all that suffering and dying fully lies with the instigating men (and some women too). Other suffering is also caused by governments, like the imposition of blockades and economic sanctions that consistently hurt the ruled of a country, but rarely if ever the rulers.

Ironically, another origin of pain and sorrow is quite often our attempt to improve things or 'do good'. Throughout history there are many such examples where we interfered with complex systems that were not yet fully understood. And despite the best of intentions we got more harmful than beneficial results. That may be the price we have to pay to make progress; sooner or later we usually learn from a particular mistake and correct what went wrong. Yet again, the point is that God is not the culprit to be blamed for our suffering.

A great deal of anguish is caused by sheer mistakes, human folly or simply greed. The mistake of men who have built their houses too close to the beach or sea shore only to get flooded or washed away by tidal waves. The building on obvious (and historically proven) flood planes, close to rivers or in the path of potential land slides or avalanches causes eventual suffering. Erecting cities or nuclear power plants on top of known earthquake fault lines or in close proximity of active volcanoes is also very likely to result in pain and sorrow.

Stating the above is not a matter of 'blaming the victims', but simply one of taking responsibility. Sure, there are historical reasons as to why we have erected our houses and cities in obvious danger zones; it's what our ancestors have chosen to do and we now simply stick to the status quo for a variety of reasons. While this is entirely understandable we also need to conclude that God cannot be faulted for the results of our personal or collective decision-making (the exercising of our right to free will and choice).

Yes, one could say that some areas of the world are far more prone to natural disasters than others and it is not always easy to prevent injury and death. This is especially true in highly populated parts of the world. Yet it is also a consequence of the restrictions on free movement and immigration in our modern societies. And those exist mostly for political and economical reasons (that are again, man-made).

In contrast, our ancestors where able to freely roam the face of the Earth and choose the safest and otherwise most suitable spots to live. There was no need for passports or visas or social security numbers and the like.

Another undeniable fact is that quite a few people leave their bodies due to consequences of their own curiosity and complacency, carelessness and miscalculation, thrill-seeking and competing. It is mostly us ourselves who are responsible, no matter how cruel that may sound at first, in particular to the loved ones left behind who may now wish to blame *someone*, trying to alleviate their utter despair and pain. If no obvious culprit can be found then 'poor' God has to take the blame…

We sometimes (or oftentimes) rush through life and otherwise become careless (mindless). As a result we could get injured in accidents of all kinds. We may drink too much alcohol and/or take a host of both legal (many prescription drugs produce severe side-effects that impair concentrated safe driving) and illegal drugs yet choose to drive home anyway…

Texting or otherwise using the phone while walking or driving on the road is not exactly a recipe for a long and happy life either, yet we can witness it every day and everywhere…

Other human mistakes involve eating too much sugary fat that masquerades as food; the ubiquitous junk 'food' quickly fills our bellies yet lacks the essential natural nutrients our bodies need to function properly; instead it burdens our systems with all kinds of toxic (man-made) sludge that needs to be eliminated as well - often though it just gets stored away in fat tissue to be dealt with later, somehow or another...

To not move enough or exercise our bodies is a man-made 'non-activity' too. Sitting too long on the couch and eating potato chips while watching soapy shows (or bad, sad and mad movies and news) is likely to have an unhappy ending as well. And so does the neglecting of personal hygiene or the adoption of other unhealthy habits.

Much hardship is also caused by the action or reaction (and sometimes mistakes) of other people. Often by the very ones we know or live with. It is us alone who (more or less consciously) decide how we treat others, the ways we interact with our friends, family and colleagues. With love and respect and civility, or the very absence of it - with all the corresponding consequences. At any given moment *we* get to choose how we will react to other people's words and deeds (see also chapter *Follow Love*).

All suffering caused by various crime and acts of violence is solely caused by us humans. For all kinds of reasons. But once again, God has nothing to do with any of that. Very much the opposite: It is *a lack of God, the absence of love*, that produces so many dramas and the resulting pain!

None of the items on the following list of prominent causes of deaths in the USA has anything to do with divine intention or sentencing (in descending order): Tobacco use, medical errors, unintentional injuries, alcohol abuse, motor vehicle accidents, unintentional poisoning, drug abuse, unintentional falls, homicides.

In the Western world a great many of prevalent diseases are simply lifestyle related, in other words they are diseases of modern civilization that virtually did not exist among hunter-gatherers or highly cultured ancient civilizations (like Egypt, Greece, Roman, Chinese, Hindu). These diseases of affluence (e.g. hypertension, obesity, coronary heart disease, type 2 diabetes, epithelial cell cancers, autoimmune disease, and osteoporosis) are being increasingly introduced to developing nations as they keep advancing their economies further. [120]

In poor countries, hunger and inadequate nutrition directly results in suffering, respectively is the underlying factor for all kinds of fatal diseases. Yet we are already growing an over-supply of food that could feed a great many more people, if required. No one needs to go hungry, but still many do. The reasons why are distribution or storage issues, but mostly, bad politics, economics, and well, bad manners. Starting with bad manners, about a third of the food produced in the world goes to waste, in some countries up to 50 percent. [121]

One example of bad politics is the fact that a huge percentage of food crops is now 'consumed' by turning them into ethanol for burning in our cars and trucks (instead of using far more suitable crops like industrial hemp). On the bad economics' side, farmers (feel the need to) regularly destroy and therefore waste their own crops, publicly or not, in order to get higher prices for the remaining parts that make it to our tables. All hunger is man-made. God created a world of plenty.

Another major cause of suffering comes from being in a disturbed mental and emotional state that eventually starts to manifest itself in some form of physical ailment. Anxieties, fears, various degrees of depression, loneliness, anger, and sadness are all frequent causes of suffering. As previously mentioned, this harmful Nocebo effect is the very opposite of the *healing* placebo effect and can even lead to a premature death, without any external or observable cause. [58]

Once we have come to know and experience how to stay connected at least most of the time and are thus able to influence the directions and polarity of our thoughts and feelings, we will once again realize that God has *absolutely* nothing to do with our suffering.

Quite the opposite: Ultimately, much suffering are effects of the spiritual loneliness caused by feeling separated from our very source. This spiritual vacuum or emptiness literally leaves the mind open and thereby vulnerable to its own pitiful, dark and depressed delusions, devoid of the gentle and bright guiding light of God within.

A perhaps tough but necessary realization is that we have to attribute a great deal of the suffering we experience on Planet Earth to ourselves only. We simply can't blame God. It would neither be fair nor correct.

Nevertheless, even if we'd become much smarter and more careful (full of care) and caring than we currently are, there are still some forms of suffering that cannot be totally avoided.

For example, we can mitigate but not fully eliminate the suffering caused by too hot or cold weather. Or the anxiety of watching and feeling our bodies become older with age. And to know that the end is getting ever nearer, and that one day, we'll have to say a temporary *Goodbye* to our loved ones. That can be very tough even for a usually merry Christian - not to speak of atheists who are literally on their own, courtesy of their self-chosen beliefs (see also chapter *Love in Separation*).

"Every adversity, every failure, every heartache carries with it the seed on an equal or greater benefit." Napoleon Hill

Death and danger is simply a built-in part of physical life. By default there must be ways for us to leave our bodies behind. Because for us individual souls this world is only temporary. It is not designed to be our eternal abode. The material universe of time and space is built upon physical realities and the laws of nature like physics and so on. And because there is time and space there is also movement and change. Birth, decay and death. By definition the temporary cannot be eternal.

"In the end, it's not the years in your life that count. It's the life in your years." Abraham Lincoln

In a world of duality pain is simply the opposite of pleasure. Without feeling occasional thirst, water may not taste as good. Or we might forget that it does. A little bit of the occasional inconvenience or small discomfort is perhaps a gentle reminder that we are indeed not just our bodies. That this beautiful and lovely planet is not our real eternal home. That we are just visitors here and will go back once our time is up. If we'd get too comfortable here, we might never want to leave…

Yet a body that eventually and inevitably gets old and frail is naturally a good reason for wanting to move on. This is true even for those who are morbidly afraid of death - perhaps to the point of swallowing a couple of hundred supplement pills a day, desperately trying to escape the inescapable. [122]

"Death is a release from the impressions of the senses, and from desires that make us their puppets, and from the vagaries of the mind, and from the hard service of the flesh." Marcus Aurelius

When we feel once again united in divine love we simply *know* that God is all good. Completely benevolent, well-wishing and meaning. God does not prescribe any of his children suffering of any kind. Or sentence us to some. That idea is a completely man-made concept steeped in ignorance and fear. Or worse, the desire of some to manipulate and control people by guilt and fear, or shame and blame, in order to advance their own position of wealth and power.

"The Lord is good! His love is everlasting; and his truth endureth to all generations." (Psalm 100:5)

Sometimes things do happen that don't seem to make sense - with our limited vision and understanding of things. Our minds simply can't know the full picture of it all. While we have free will and choice there may be good reasons why some of us have decided to go through some rather 'tough stuff' during their lives in the here and now.

Such often quiet heroes may have wanted to teach us 'survivors' something - whether it's their family or friends, or society as a whole - and have chosen to take on the role of an example, to teach us something we really need to learn. Or to help us improve things. And yes, at times that could even mean to make the 'ultimate sacrifice', perhaps already at a young age.

Predestination could very well be the explanation for certain very major events or turning points in our lives. However, the reality of free will and choice makes it most unlikely that it was God who has made such a big decision for us before we were born in this world of matter (See also *Be your Self*). It is more likely that it is us ourselves who have made these major arrangements beforehand - in order to experience, learn or impart something in the here and now. Or to do, settle or make up something that needed to happen to keep the balance and harmony of It All.

"I shall tell you a great secret, my friend. Do not wait for the last judgment, it takes place every day." Albert Camus

Nevertheless let's remember that the above and many other questions and discussions are on the mental and analytical level of our being alone. And that many answers will increasingly come to our minds as we experience ever more divine love. Yet some truths may always stay hidden from the inquiring mind and we will only know them once again *after* we have departed planet Earth. Perhaps we will already know on 'our way out'. Until then the absolute and ultimate reality must be felt and experienced within each and every one of us individually as there is no such thing as becoming 'collectively enlightened' (despite some wishful thinking in that direction).

The eternal reality we can come to feel and therefore know is that all of God's children are connected with God in the deepest love imaginable. Yet we tend to ignore this love by focusing solely on the external life we can see, hear, smell, taste and touch. We are always so very busy with work and play, earning a living, or looking after our earthly possessions. 'External' or non-core emotions of fear and anger or blame and shame only 'serve' to further bury and cover up this natural ever-present love that makes and keeps us happy.

Love is one of the true feelings, inherent in every soul. It is a real and central part and characteristic of the spiritual eternal self. And once we have come to realize this reality again and decided to henceforth always live and 'indulge' in the universe of love, the need to learn the 'essence of what we have come to learn' has disappeared. Simply because we did it already; we have graduated!

And now the task is to live accordingly with love in words and deeds, to remember to stay connected, away from the pitfalls of the world of labels and a mistaken identity of self.

Many people are wondering whether God intervenes in the material world in general and on our planet Earth in particular ("general providence"). And if so, when where how and why? My take on the matter is that God's universe is so perfect (conscious) that it is self-organizing and self-sustaining with love being both the fundamental principle, motivation, and direction.

As such there are also divine angels and spirit guides to look after each and every one of us; teaching, protecting and helping us. Plus there are divine assistants and enlightened agents (souls) assigned to maintain the natural order of things. Or to intervene in certain extreme circumstances. Like when certain crazies would attempt to blow up this planet with nuclear weapons. That would very likely bring about an intervention because it would go totally against the heartfelt desires and primary interests of billions of individual souls, besides interrupting the divine order of our universe as a whole.

How would such an intervention look like? Well, somehow or another it would simply not be possible to happen. It could be a malfunction or last minute rebellion. Or it could be a decision maker who listens to his conscience, like a Soviet soldier did in 1983, a time when all nuclear weapons systems were on hair-trigger alert; he had to make the split-second decision to launch nukes or not. And fortunately he listened to his instincts and made the right decision! There were (too) many other very close calls that were averted in the last minute, often by a single and perhaps well-placed person. [123]

(As an aside, it would be really great to be able to get rid off all nuclear weapons; they are a perversion to human intelligence, indeed, life itself. Is that even possible? Yes, it would be; all we need is to find and elevate the loving and thus enlightened leaders with the common sense and intelligence to identify innovative solutions that ensure the safety of all nations and people without such horrific weapons.)

Does God directly look after us children too ("special providence")? The short answer is *Yes*, but we are still free to choose and listen, or not:

God is helping us not just by being there for us at all times but also by putting insights into our minds; we can observe thoughts constantly coming and going just like clouds that are drifting by. Some are black, some are white, and others are in all kinds of shades in between. The origin of perhaps most of our thoughts is worldly while others are divinely-inspired, whether we may consciously realize it or not. The ratio all depends on our consciousness; whether we live mostly in the big picture view of things or not, whether we are mostly connected in love, or not.

By guiding us with directly 'injected' thoughts, or put differently, inspiration (*in spirit*, inside or internal spiritual guidance), God offer us the most intelligent alternatives to the purely materialistic deliberations we have picked up via external sources. If we choose to follow up on divine ideas and suggestions we will experience not just different outcomes but by far the best ones possible. Both in our own lives and subsequently the lives of people we interact with every day; witness the ripple effect of divine love and intelligence in action!

How about favoritism; does God discriminate and dish out favors or winning lotto tickets and more in an arbitrary way, a bit willy-nilly here and there? A chaotic and perhaps at times a bit moody creator who decides important matters on a whim?

The answer is, of course not, as God loves us all and wishes us only the best. But we all have different intentions and requirements to achieve the individual objectives that we have decided to accomplish while in the here and now. Besides, winning a lotto ticket has been a curse for a great many winners who subsequently had to learn some rather tough lessons in life, including ending up destitute and broke.

Regarding direct divine attention, there is another aspect that we can all easily recognize and relate to: Parents pay particular attention to the one child that is always very (or totally) helpless, clumsy, and perhaps a bit awkward too. Yet the same parents also tend to give much more space and seemingly less help to their other child that is from an early age on so very independent, fearless and clever.

This is not a sign of partiality or favoritism, but practicality. And it is the respecting of our freedom of will and choice. Some children do get more help simply because they well and truly want or need more help. And often they ask for it even without asking. Others get clearly less support because they actually don't ask or even feel the need for it, and instead prefer to feel entirely independent, self-sufficient and strong.

After all, hey 'they are the dudes', the winners of the world! So there is simply no point (see also chapter *Surrender*). God always respects us and our choices, even us turning a blind eye to his most amazing benevolent being.

"Draw near unto God, and He will draw near unto you." (James 4:8)

"For prayer is nothing else than being on terms of friendship with God." Saint Teresa of Avila

Those who are always, mostly or very often 'tuned in' know full well that divine interventions occur all the time. Such miracles do happen when we *let them happen*. But of course we also need to recognize them as such and that is not always a given either.

"A man's heart deviseth his way: but the Lord directeth his steps." (Proverbs 16:9)

The inner guidance that comes from divine love within is gentle providence that respects our free will and choice. This non-intrusive yet ever-present God-vibration of love blesses and guides us all quietly yet constantly. However it is only felt and directly experienced by those who have decided to actually 'tune in' to this freely available 'channel'. Those who are not interested or otherwise busy with the 'external playgrounds' only just won't know - by their own choice.

We can all get respectively perceive the 'special attention' by God that is always there simply by staying connected to love all or most of the time.

In the end it is up to each one of us to make the happy choice that will keep us merry:

Love and feel loved!

Merry Money

Like love, much has and can be said about money. The mere subject can cause many of us real anxiety, worries and stress. Even outright fear to the point of panic. After all money is seemingly ever-present and certainly always needed so we tend to associate it with our very survival. And for many it continues to be a matter of life and death even though they have already accumulated a lot more money than they could ever spend in several lifetimes.

'Money makes the world go round', or so we like to say. Indeed it is likely to be more important in our modern societies than in olden days when most people still grew their own food or engaged in barter trading of all kinds.

The subject of money is certainly a topic that needs to be covered in the context of this book. Money can and does affect our happiness. This is true for everyone including Christians who oftentimes have a bit of an ambivalent attitude or mixed feelings about money. To say the least. After all Jesus said that *"It is easier for a camel to enter the eye of a needle than for a rich man to enter the Kingdom of God."* (Mark 10:25)

So quite a few Christians somewhat associate money with something bad or dirty. And surprise surprise, as a result of such negative connotations they are likely to not have much of it, even to the point of actually struggling to pay their bills. That is most unfortunate and certainly not the intent of our loving Father who wishes us all to thrive and be well.

The old Romans had a very true saying: "Pecunia non olet" - money does not stink". We need to realize that money is neutral. It is a form of energy, a bit like a tool. Like a hammer, it can be used for both good and evil. Let's just think about all the good things we can do with money. Bill and Melinda Gates (and others) are shining examples of how surplus wealth can and is being used in the service of mankind.

Yes of course, money can and does corrupt some people, yet the emphasis is on the word 'some'. It's not going to be all people, and it doesn't have to be you or me. We don't need to be concerned with what others do or don't do when we solely focus on us doing the right things. As a Christian you have the opportunity to use the energy of money to make the world an even better place, helping to alleviate suffering and spreading ever more love, peace and happiness.

Money buys comfort and sometimes, better health. Or it makes something unpleasant less so. It is certainly nicer (and healthier) to travel in a Business or First Class seat than to get perched in like cattle in the back cabin and eat rather questionable food. Money may not prevent problems in life but it will help to solve them quicker and easier.

For a merry Christian with the heart and mind in the right spot it is certainly desirable to strive for at least a modicum of wealth. Of course, wealth is a very relative term and we all need to decide for ourselves how much is plenty to live comfortably and free. After all, being super rich is often accompanied by a lot of responsibilities and quite a bit of stress. It simply comes with its own array of anxieties and worries. And funnily, many of the world's billionaires still struggle to 'keep up with the Joneses', albeit of the fellow billionaire kind!

To know when 'enough is enough', and long before it turns into greed, is a form of the art of life; the ability to keep our priorities straight; a mental clarity that always keeps the big picture in mind. After all, no one has ever laid on their death bed and wished to have worked harder and accumulated just a little bit more money. Or to have spent some extra time in front of the computer doing this or that!

The definition of wealth changes as we grow older in our bodies, when things like good health and spending quality time with friends and family become far more important than colored pieces of paper (or plastic notes like here in Australia).

Of course, the rich have generally more options to choose from in life. Why only 'in general'? Because it all depends on one's state of physical and mental health. Many of the world's regular folks enjoy a healthy and happy balance while quite a few of the wealthy don't. They are prone to become too caught up in a very narrow mental cage of self-limiting beliefs, or feel obliged to follow other rather restrictive norms exclusively practiced by the world's elite, e.g. cultivating certain acquired tastes or living in places and ways that actually excludes *real* freedom and joy.

Furthermore those who have it all and have nothing really to strive for anymore are quite often a bit resigned to life, depressed rather than enthusiastic, tired instead of being truly well and alive. And perhaps more often than not they have become addicted to alcohol and drugs of many kinds.

Money by itself will not make us happy. Some claim that it is better to be rich and unhappy than to be poor and unhappy. That is probably true. And likewise, that it's better to be poor yet happy and healthy, than being unhappy and sick but with lots of money in the bank. Best of course is to be happy, healthy, wealthy and wise. All in unison.

Jesus said to his disciples, *"Truly I say to you, it is hard for a rich man to enter the kingdom of heaven."* (Matthew 19:23) Why did he say so? What makes it is so hard?

Well, people who choose to first and foremost pursue the accumulation of ever more money tend to be rather disinterested in God - even if they think or claim otherwise. Essentially they have 'bought into' the materialistic concept of life that we are all just competing smart animals. 'Winner takes all' or 'big fish eats small fish'. There is no (or not much) room for a God or other 'silly superstitions'.

Leading an overly materialistic life is usually the result of a spiritual vacuum where we try to fill an empty life with goodies to make up for the lack of real love within the core of our very being. The more we are disconnected from God's love the emptier we feel. And the more we need to stuff our bodies and lives full of the things we think will make us happier.

Of course, it doesn't really work that way: It's a bit like painting the exterior of a house and now expect the inside to look nice too. Or like putting on some Band-Aids to fix a broken bone. In other words it tries to solve a problem with a solution that is impossible to work simply because it is applied in the wrong place respectively dimension (see also chapter *Be your Self*).

Besides, the satisfaction we get from material stuff wears off rather quickly, just like the flavors of chewing gum. That's why we have to keep adding more and more, perhaps hoping that it will satisfy us one day. Which reminds me of the definition of insanity (widely attributed to Albert Einstein) about doing the same thing over and over again yet expecting different results.

And yes, besides emptiness and greed another motive for always wanting more and more is the age-old competition of egos trying to win the essentially unwinnable - as there is always going to be someone who is prettier, richer, smarter, stronger, you name it!

What are other obstacles to the rich living in the kingdom of heavenly love, even while alive in the here and now?

One big stumbling block is that quite often the very well off do feel superior to others. It kind of comes with the territory. The arrogance of the 'elite' (in various fields) can be truly mind-blowing. I have witnessed this in every culture and society around the world while selling them stuff they don't really need (Swiss luxury watches). And as we have discussed already, arrogance and the like is always both the origin and recipe for further separation and loneliness, depression and fear.

Surrounded by material comfort and luxury the wealthy often have less room for God even if they do believe. For a billionaire it is simply a lot harder to feel meek and humble or equal to one's poorer cousins, not to speak of all their spiritual brothers and sisters. And likewise it is more difficult to not take a certain level of things for granted respectively having rather extreme expectations. Living 'on top of the world' is so often accompanied by a sense of entitlement that easily excludes any concern for the well-being of others.

Usually as countries and societies become wealthier, economists observe a corresponding diminishing importance of religion. With lots of money, who needs God? Quite a few of us have the tendency to turn to God in desperate times yet kind of 'forget about it' while having a good time.

Fact however is that no amount of money can buy life. Or good health. Yes, the well off can buy superior medical treatments but that is often in vain, past a certain point of age or deterioration. No matter the size of our bank accounts, good health and indeed our very life in all its dimensions and complexities, depends on the unlimited life-giving and sustaining energies of God. We all depend on God, the very source of it all, even if we choose to believe otherwise.

So is there hope for the wealthy? Of course, there is and here is how:

Jesus replied, *"What is impossible for people is possible with God."* (Luke 18:27)

It is great to have plenty of everything, including money, as long as we *always stay connected* to who we truly are and what really matters. To always live in the spheres of eternal love, no matter what, means to have our priorities right. With God's love in our hearts everything becomes possible. Even being super rich *and* going to the higher heavens. Or better, already 'feeling heavenly' while still living on planet Earth, in love and harmony with everybody and everything else.

"Delight yourself in the Lord, and he will give you the desires of your heart." (Psalm 37:4)

Amazingly there are some 'modern-day Christians' who believe that wealth is a form of Grace of God. And so they kind of worship the wealthy, perhaps hoping to thereby get a few crumbs off their tables. Their idea is that one should not be harsh with those who have 'obviously' received the 'visible grace' of God in the form of a Ferrari or big mansions or whatever. Because hey, they must be some kind of very special and 'super holy' type of people otherwise they would not be so rich (blessed).

Economic and financial success however comes to all kinds of folks, including mafia bosses, drug kingpins, brutal dictators, slave masters, corrupt politicians or bureaucrats, and so on. There is not much grace to be seen in such circles or so it seems. And yes, there are those who well and truly deserve all they have thanks to their great contributions to both our individual lifestyles and collective well-being.

(By the way, the convictions of the above-mentioned 'modern-day Christians' would also imply that the poor are somehow wicked and destitute only because they don't have (or worse, deserve) grace and wealth…Wow, now that is wicked!)

Much has been said about the growing numbers of super-wealthy people around the world, the 0.1 percent who benefited immensely from the central bank policies implemented since 2008, the start of the global financial crisis. At the same time the very same erroneous measures have helped to further reduce the middle classes that are most important to the harmonious functioning of our economies and societies. And indeed to the continued existence of democracy itself.

As a whole these are all man-made problems, issues of economics, politics and their underlying philosophies. Or put differently, a result of how we currently manage our world. The global economic, financial and political systems are certainly in need of a major overhaul and reorganization, yet obviously it's not something that we can solve within these pages.

What we can do however is to improve our own personal situation. And the more of us do so individually and have thus the capacity to contribute to the greater good of all mankind, the better the world will be. Hopefully every well situated person comes to the understanding that there won't be lasting peace (or personal security!) without overall justice and fairness.

When we speak about money and those who have lots of it, we need to also address the very issue that prevents us first and foremost from having plenty of it ourselves: The worst emotion we can possibly feel about money is jealousy and envy. Such sentiments are a form of complaining about experiencing lack and scarcity that will only ensure that we will experience more of just that!

As we have discussed elsewhere, complaining is the opposite of appreciation. It's a focusing on the negative that keeps us in exactly that very space. We simply can't experience God's treasures while complaining about not having anything of value. Or worse, to feel jealous and envious of those who do already experience material success.

In short, envy or jealousy is a mindset that only ensures that we won't get what we really desire. It comes from the ego-based world of fear, separation, and insecurity.

Some people perceive some kind of 'divine discrimination' or a plethora of worldly conspiracies when they look at those who seem to 'have it all', those who live a life of ease and comfort, compared with the 'unlucky' ones who don't. Yet things are rarely the way they look like from an observer's point of view; we are simply not in the position to know it all unless or until we could somehow walk in another person's shoes. And not only in a seemingly happy moment but for quite some time…

After all, external luxuries quite often hide internal desolation and devastation. For some folks their (often inherited) wealth is a bit like a curse while for others it really is a blessing to be able to lead a more modest life full of love, leisure and laughter.

Furthermore, the very fact that there are people living a prosperous and fulfilling life is proof positive that this is indeed possible for all of us. If that's what we really want… The world is full of self-made billionaires that came from very poor backgrounds and still 'made it'. Just look at the country that was so impoverished not all that long ago but is now sporting the most billionaires: China (with about 600 of them in 2015). And in the USA there is at least one billionaire who was actually homeless before! [124]

It is far better to feel motivated by such stories and feel confident in one's own abilities and goodness than to feel envious, hopeless and angry. The choice is always ours. What our most loving God wants us to choose is quite obvious, isn't it?!

And that brings us to another obstacle to having always enough money in our lives: Guilt, the perception that we don't deserve it. That for our past wrong-doings we somehow don't merit to live well and prosperous. This is of course a most unfortunate way to go through life. And especially so since it is entirely unnecessary as every soul living in the spheres of love will know.

"Ask and it will be given to you; seek and you will find; knock and the door will be opened to you." (Matthew 7:7)

"The Lord is my shepherd; I shall not want." (Psalm 23:1)

Let's make a quick detour and look at a few non-philosophical points about money. Things that are not financial advice per se but more common sense stuff that may not be all that common anymore these days:

A dollar saved is a dollar earned. Actually, it's even better than that! For most people, before a dollar can be spent, we have already paid income taxes on it. So an after-tax dollar is worth quite a bit more than a dollar earned minus the tax paid. So every dollar not spent on useless stuff is like earning say a dollar and thirty cents (presuming the tax rate is about 23 percent).

Always go for quality and durability. Saving a dollar does not mean to buy shoddily manufactured stuff that kind of falls apart already in the shop still in its packaging, respectively cheap imitations that are built to last only a very short time. Whenever possible it is always better to wait and save up for a while and then buy a really well made item that lasts seemingly 'forever'. And then of course, take good care of those belongings, using them with gratitude and pride.

Having and surrounding yourself with only a few but great quality items - often hand made by a master crafts(wo)man - is a source of delight; it saves money and nerves; and it protects the environment. It's a smart philosophy that has served me well over decades.

Buy only what you really want or need. And that essentially translates into: Stop buying things just because someone tells you that you need them (to be in or hip or hop, whatever). And don't get caught by the 'perennial sale scam': These days every shop displays *constant* Sale signs to seduce us to buy a 'bargain'. Which nowadays mostly means buying at full retail price despite the seemingly generous discount.

Use your own money and stay free. Fact is that we don't own any of the things we have purchased with a credit card; they own us and our peace of mind. In other words, it's the old adage: Never borrow money you don't have to buy things you can't afford to impress people you don't even know (or hang out with).

"And the borrower becomes the lender's slave." (Proverbs 22:7)

Sometimes there are circumstances where it may make sense to borrow money from a bank. Like buying real estate at certain times in the economic cycle. But only if that is easily paid for by our income. Buying or building something small but nice always beats having the mega mansion with an equally big and heavy mortgage that will keep us up at night. Going into debt for cars and consumer goods is most certainly a bad idea giving only little joy in the beginning but lots of headaches for a long time to come.

Take a vocation vacation and be happy. Since the beginning of modern times most if not all successful people keep saying that to do what we love doing is the best recipe for achieving both wealth and happiness. What is your vocation, the things you would love to do if money were not an object? How would you create a better life for yourself, your loved ones and the world as a whole?

What are your unique talents, or what is your calling? It is certainly worth the time to find out! And yes, initially our ideas, hopes and dreams may sound a bit far-fetched or crazy. So it's as always good to ask, *What does love say?*

"Often people attempt to live their lives backwards; they try to make more things, or more money, in order to do more of what they want, so they will be happier. The way it actually works is in reverse. You must first be who you really are, then do what you need to do, in order to have what you want." Margaret Young

"Success is not the key to happiness. Happiness is the key to success. If you love what you are doing, you will be successful." Albert Schweitzer [125]

Let me also share some words of wisdom I luckily learned from my father at an early age. It goes something like this:

"House yourself above your means. Dress yourself according to your means. Eat and drink below your means." Hans Ulrich Klingenberg

To live in a place that costs a bit more than what we could actually comfortably afford increases our happiness because we spend a lot of time in our home (especially nowadays as many of us work at home). To dress oneself in clothes that we can comfortably afford means to represent ourselves honestly in society. To eat and drink below our means is a recipe for a healthy life by not overindulging in too much food or wine (that will only make us sick in the long run).

These days there is plenty of money in the world. And there is an abundance of other forms of 'stored wealth' too, like gold and silver, real estate, shares and so on. For macro-economic reasons it is likely that for a long time to come ever more money is going to be printed pretty much on a daily basis (more precisely, it is digitally created on the computer screens of central banks and subsequently loaned into existence by commercial bankers).

The realization that the world is awash with wealth may not appear to be an overly helpful insight, particularly if there is a lack of money in our own bank accounts. And yet, knowing that there is a glut of money 'out there' is a first step to having more of it yourself. The issue is not a lack of money in the same way as there is plenty of food and everything else in the world.

"So do not worry, saying, 'What shall we eat?' or 'What shall we drink?' or 'What shall we wear?

... seek first his kingdom and his righteousness, and all these things will be given to you as well." (Matthews 6:31, 6:33)

God created a world of plenty. We can see and feel this when we observe the beauty and abundance of nature in its original pristine state. To come to know and cherish God's bounty also means to appreciate wealth in its many forms which includes the man-made medium of exchange we call money. That is not a call to love money by and of itself, something that we are rightfully told (in *1 Timothy 6:10*) to be the root of much evil and suffering (together with the lust for power respectively the urge to control others).

Recognize, experience and enjoy abundance in all its many forms and you will increasingly live a life of plenty. It will increase your joy and happiness. And it will enable you to share the bounties you receive with love and appreciation.

"And why do you worry about clothes? See how the flowers of the field grow. They do not labor or spin." (Matthew 6:28)

The key to having plenty of money is not to love money (or to struggle to get some). It is the appreciation of the money we actually have! Even if it's 'just a little bit'. *To just be grateful for what we do have already right now rather than feeling sorry for ourselves for the money we don't have* (or worse, to be jealous of the ones who have more).

As a kid we are likely to feel very rich with only a few bucks in our pockets while there are elderly billionaires who actually (in their own words) feel rather insecure just because they have lost ten or twenty billions and are now 'worth' only a few billion dollars. [126]

Young children are often still unspoilt in so many if not most aspects of life. And that includes their early relationship with the energy form we call money. But sooner or later their innocence will get blemished by the assorted indoctrination and manipulation of adults. See (again) for yourself the joy of a young child upon receiving and having just a dollar or two. Later on as an adult, the same child is likely to scoff at receiving far bigger amounts, deeming it to be not good enough, always wanting more and more…

Being happy with what we have and make do with it is a great foundation of great wealth. If that is our goal. Being grateful for receiving some, even if it's just stumbling upon a humble coin on the side of the road, is the second part of the secret to always having plenty of merry money.

And yes, taking some inspired action is the third and final part.

"Heaven never helps the man who will not act." Sophocles [127]

"Pray as though everything depended on God. Work as though everything depended on you." Saint Augustine

With lots of love in our hearts money can and will further increase happiness - our own plus whomever we like to help and support.

Money buys us the freedom to do what we want or need to experience in life.

It helps us to help making the world a better place.

And it buys us more time as we can delegate things and focus on what really matters for us.

But of course it won't buy us even one minute longer when our time has come...

"Let us more and more insist on raising funds of love, of kindness, of understanding, of peace. Money will come if we seek first the Kingdom of God - the rest will be given." Mother Teresa

"Therefore I tell you, whatever you ask for in prayer, believe that you have received it, and it will be yours." Mark 11:24

REALIZATIONS:

I love to have money

I love to receive money

I love to use money for good

Love in Separation

"To lose a loved one is certainly the toughest experience one can go through in life, and by default, sooner or later this happens to all of us. The loss of a beloved husband/wife/partner is particularly hard to fathom, and so is the premature death of one's child.

Missing a loved one is a good thing that should be welcomed, rather than something we need to overcome as if it were a disease. That may sound strange at first, but while we miss someone dearly we are actually closest together - spirit to spirit, soul to soul.

We can experience this while the beloved is still with us in the here and now. Sometimes we get only briefly separated and at other times for a whole day, week or even longer, yet regardless of time, all we can think of is our dear darling. What is s/he doing right now? Is s/he alright? And so on. We miss the person during the day, at night and while waking up in the morning, deeply thinking, missing and loving him/her.

And when we're honest with ourselves, these are often the moments we enjoy our partner more than when we're right next to each other, perhaps watching TV or getting otherwise occupied with our chores or little daily routines, when we take the other somewhat (and unintentionally) for granted to the point of hardly looking or smiling at each other, even noticing as s/he is such a normal presence we simply 'got used' to having around…

So in a way we love and treasure each other more intensely when we are not together, when we miss each other. There is no real separation in love. Love is us and it transcends time and space.

So don't try to gradually forget a loved one and 'move on'. It is not possible anyway. Yes, you can (learn to once again) move from one happy and joy-filled moment to the next in life, and yet those will and should always include the moments you feel deeply connected in love, missing each other, talking with each other, asking questions, remembering the joyful moments experienced together, and even sharing a laugh or smile.

That last bit may sound a bit strange, and yet it is what I've experienced when I had a vision of a dearly loved one actually smiling at me, and making a funny comment about the sad music currently playing at her own funeral. Even though I was so sad I had a happy moment when we mentally connected and laughed together, somewhere and somehow in a dimension we shared.

To feel anger at a loved departed one is very normal and should not be suppressed either; after all it is a sign of love. Allow the anger and connect again in love and you will come to understand ever deeper why and how something has happened, gain increasingly deeper insights into your life and his/her. Because when we love we easily and naturally understand. We can't blame or feel guilty when we love. Love truly understands.

And love is the ultimate connection. It is faster than the speed of light, even the speed of mind. It is the most direct and intimate embrace there is. And yes, we will always miss hearing the voice and feeling the physical presence of the beloved, for as long as we inhabit our physical body. But remember, we *are* the soul or spirit, as opposed to those who mistake themselves to *be* their body but having a soul somehow and somewhere…

When we communicate with someone and refer to the other purely as being a body, it would be just the same as when we talked to his/her clothes… imagine that!

When we are united in love we are feeling joy, even if there is a lingering pain that we are physically separated. But in those moments when all we feel is pure love for our partner and feel loved by him/her, we feel joy and happiness, heart to heart, soul to soul. Welcome, treasure and enjoy these moments to the fullest.

Sometimes we may even experience physical sensations while being immersed in love, feelings of relief, sensations of light, the quickening of energy flows, a tingling of nerves in our brain or body, pulsating muscles, flashes of pictures or other mental insights, and so on. It will be healing and helping you to cope, feeling ever better to the point of being able to enjoy life once again, as much as possible, more and more. Every day.

Do remember him/her every day. For me it's an everyday moment, before breakfast, to light an incense in front of a particularly nice picture with a beautiful fresh flower next to it. I remember and reflect, miss and love, have a word, and by now usually end up with a loving smile.

Keep a few favorite pictures in a couple of places only (not in every room as you need to have some space for your current 'solo' life and that includes a bit of 'privacy' too) and treasure them. Dust and change them from time to time. Remember all anniversaries and special days/dates you had together by cooking a nice meal, or going out to a special place. Raise your glass and make a toast.

Celebrate the life of your loved one, admire the achievements made, talk about him/her with love and appreciation for the good times you spent in this wonderful and heroic adventure we call life.

Cry whenever you feel like it. Don't force yourself to be all cheerful and chirpy all the time. It must be real, and it will be so again. Let the tears wash away your pain, but hang onto your love and fully let yourself go in its gentle embrace. And increasingly, you will cry tears of love in separation and actually feel good, instead of crying out of self-pity that only feels bad and separates you from enjoying the fruits of your mutual love in the current here and now.

And finally, remember that love is never possessionary or exclusionary. It is self-sufficient and radiating, being its own reward. So love leaves room for loving others as well. The more the merrier. There are many types or flavors of love. They all come in the active and passive form. And none have to come at the exclusion of others. After some time has passed, it is even possible to find another love in the here and now, to spend time and do pleasant things together. Of course, that will

neither replace our loved one nor negate or diminish our mutual love. Real love is eternal. It is always well-wishing, only wanting the best for each other…

Feeling depressed upon losing a loved one is normal for a while, sometimes for a very long while. Researchers have found that people who were suffering grief had higher blood pressure and an increased heart rate. It can weaken our immune system. And our heart pains can lead to a real heart attack. This would be completely uncalled for, certainly by our beloved who wishes nothing more than us to be healthy and happy during our remaining days in our bodies - while already looking forward to welcoming and seeing us again when it is our time to leave this dimension.

For meeting again we will, for sure. Because like attract like. Those who love each other will always attract each other, no matter the obstacles, no matter the dimensions. Love is the instant and infallible guiding light that brings and keeps us together. Love transcends time and space as it pervades all dimensions throughout the Universe.

The loss of a loved one is not the end. It is the beginning of a deepening of our relationship.

It is also helping us to remember who *we really are*. To grow beyond the mirage of this particular dimension, preparing us to make the transition ourselves, for we all have to do that one day. In a way it is even making it easier for us as we look so much forward to seeing each other again. Our love literally opens the door to the eternal spiritual worlds."

The above text of this chapter has a bit of a story of its own: An article I wrote sixteen years ago to promote my first book was kindly published on a leading self help website, and republished in August 2013. One reader asked in the comments section about how it is possible to be happy again after her dear husband had passed away. The editor asked for my input and I wrote the above as my contribution to help alleviate Pam's pain. Thereafter it got published as a separate feature article. [128]

I'm sharing this background as an example of how God truly works in mysterious ways: Two days after posting my reply, on 8.8.2013, my dear father, Hans Ulrich Klingenberg, passed away suddenly, and I found myself in an airplane flying from Australia to Switzerland to attend his funeral.

"Seize the moments of happiness, love and be loved! That is the only reality in the world, all else is folly. It is the one thing we are interested in here." Leo Tolstoy[129]

"The art of living well and the art of dying well are one." Epicurus[130]

Merry Realizations

Last but not least let's review the full list of Merry Realizations we have made together; they are the distilled essence of all the previous chapters and may hopefully serve you as an easy reference, reminder and reinforcement in times of troubles or doubts.

Meditating, contemplating and praying upon these individual insights will make them ever more forceful and steady; the more the merrier!

But if you do feel a bit uneasy about one or the other realization, it may be a good idea to revisit and address this particular issue by re-reading the associated chapter and asking for divine guidance.

Quite often such stumbling blocks reveal an especially important lesson that we really have to understand and incorporate into our lives. Such doubts may also identify an erroneous belief that simply needs to be discarded as it serves no further purpose, or worse, may hinder our continued progress.

So here we go with all the *54 Merry Realizations*:

I love to love God

I love to feel God's love

I love to feel Your love

I love to love

I love to feel loved

I love to appreciate

I love to feel appreciated

I love to be grateful

I love to feel blessed

I love to smile

I love to be joyful

I love to laugh

The world is good and getting even better

I accept people as they are

Everything happens at the right time

I love to surrender in love

I love to feel hopeful

I love to hope for the best

I like to love, hope, and surrender

I love to breathe calmly

I love to breathe deeply

I love to be kind

I love to learn

I love to grow

I love to feel calm

I love my silent mind

May love enlighten my mind

I love to feel fine

I love to be healthy and strong

May love heal my body

I love to know the truth

I love to truly know my self

I love to be my original self

God wants me to the best I can be

I love to follow love

I love to let love guide me

I love to give respect

I love to feel respected

I respect myself as I am

I love to admire beauty in all its forms

I love to admire all that is good

I love to admire all that is God

I love to wish well

I wish myself all the best

I wish everybody all the best

I love to give help

I love to get help

I love to do it with care

I love to act with love

I love to rest and relax

I love to feel relaxed and well

I love to have money

I love to receive money

I love to use money for good

In conclusion, Christianity is a most beautiful philosophy and way of life when it is felt and lived in all its sublime simplicity, true to the very core of what God and Jesus and the Saints desire for us and life on Planet Earth - unity in love, peace and happiness!

"But the fruit of the Spirit is love, joy, peace, patience, kindness, goodness, faithfulness," (Galatians 5:22)

Indeed, we can come to realize that Christianity as outlined in these pages is actually the perennial philosophy of the ancients. Its wisdom is well and truly timeless. Because eternal truth knows no time or boundaries. And as such it will continue to shine well into the future. Provided we learn to live a life of love as we are both intended and instructed to live.

"The same thing which is now called Christian religion existed among the ancients. They have begun to call 'Christian' the true religion which existed before." Saint Augustine

"The thing that hath been, it is that which shall be; and that which is done is that which shall be done: and there is no new thing under the sun." (Ecclesiastes 1:9)

Merry Christians: *How to be a happy Christian and co-create Heaven on Earth* does not aim or claim to reinvent the wheel or anything the like. All it intends to do is to fully focus on the very real beauty and the totally amazing happiness inherent in Christianity - once it is stripped of the unnecessary squabbles we humans tend to introduce when our minds are focused on the small picture view of competing and fighting when in reality we have been provided a world of amazing beauty and sheer abundance. To share in a free, fair and happy way.

In the previous chapters we have discussed that every single aspect of life will greatly benefit from simply following the first and second foremost commandments that Jesus has asked and implored us to follow, on behalf of God the Father. We have seen how divine love is able to transform our life in its entirety, helping us to realize our fullest potential in the here and now.

Love (God) is the strongest force in the universe (omnipotent); it is everpresent and accessible (omnipresent); it is all-knowing and understanding (omniscient). So much good is happening because of love. And so much bad is happening because of a lack of love.

We all just want to be happy, no matter whether we are aware of it or not, and regardless of how we may go about it in our daily lives. God knows that because wanting to be happy is inherent in every soul; it's a natural attribute of spirit just like water is wet in its liquid state. Indeed, our heartfelt desire to be happy is proof of the love and goodness of God who wants us to be the best we can be.

He knows that when we do love a lot, we will naturally also smile and laugh a lot, we will be kind and caring, we will love to admire and appreciate all that is good, we will have less or little worries, and will simply feel relaxed and well, living in peace and at ease. In other words we will feel mostly fine, full of energy and very happy, as these are the byproducts of leading a life of love. God knows this and therefore prescribes it!

But if we do the very opposite of it all, are hateful and tense, criticize and ridicule a lot, are mostly jealous and spiteful, highly competitive yet a lousy loser, with always much to worry and frown upon, we will simply feel bad and unhappy all the time. Again, by default. The choice is always ours to make. But the recipe for a happy and successful live is clearly outlined in all of God's prescriptions, and made so explicit by his son, Jesus Christ. It is in our own best interest to listen and choose to follow the prescribed road to happiness, tuning in to the universe of love that is God.

Much if not most of what we do is for love. We just want to love and feel loved. We compete and strive to be a winner for love. We chase and accumulate riches for love. We want to look beautiful to attract love. We yearn for power and fame for love. A nice house, a great car and much much more, all for love. The hunger for love is also behind our desire to feel accepted and respected, to get attention and admiration.

Since love is what we all want and need we might as well give it to ourselves and each other freely and happily without the need for detours and distractions. Let's love and feel loved. First and foremost. All good will happen. Love is. Everywhere and all the time. Tune in! And stay tuned in.

God is love. And Christ is love. Christianity at its best is very simple yet most profound. At its core it is so easy and uncomplicated. It is a most practical philosophy and real-happy-life experience that will elevate and enrich everyone - regardless of their current culture or creed.

We could actually summarize the essence of The Merry Way with the first four of its twenty tenets:

Love God. Feel God's Love. Love your Self. Love All.

Because once we do so *everything* else outlined will follow automatically. Such is the beauty of the foremost commandments Jesus Christ came to teach. If most if not all Christians will well and truly heed and follow his call for living a life of love, it will not only make and keep them merry as individuals, but ultimately also unite all Christian denominations in peace and harmony.

Imagine if our churches - regardless of their history or particular style - would become meeting places not just to worship but also places to be merry and have fun. Where we could also be a bit light-hearted and even dance to some beautiful music. Have a glass of ale or wine and earnestly but happily talk about things together. And perhaps even help each other to solve personal problems or participate in divinely inspired projects; churches serving as incubators and accelerators for mutually beneficial start-ups and more.

Or being places where single people of any age could meet among other like-minded people. Where the old teach the young new tricks, and vice versa. Where both Christians (of all denominations or none) and non-Christians alike - indeed anyone who is lonely, sad and depressed, or empty, bored and curious - could simply and easily stop by. And be a warmly welcomed part of a caring and compassionate, devout yet merry congregation of lovely and loving equals.

"Spread love everywhere you go. Let no one ever come to you without leaving happier."

Mother Teresa

Love makes it all possible. And a lot more. That is its power and promise. Jesus Christ told us so. And he insists that we make it so. And once we do he will be here with us. All the time.

The combined force of *such divine love will shine an irresistible light to all of mankind* and be the clarion call that will bring about *Heaven on Earth*.

Imagine the day when all people in the world - regardless of their external labels - will be living a life of pure love. And all the good that comes with it. That will be the day when we all have become Christians. Even if we don't choose to call it like that.

"May the grace of the Lord Jesus Christ and the love of God and the fellowship of the Holy Spirit be with you all." (2 Corinthians 13:14)

I hope that you have thoroughly enjoyed this book and that it will help you to always be a very merry Christian!

With my love and respect,

Post Scriptum

You are very welcome to send me your comments and reviews by email (arneklingenberg@gmail.com) or visit ArneKlingenberg.com for further information, including updates about upcoming new books.

You are also cordially invited to connect or follow me on social media:

https://twitter.com/arneklingenberg

www.facebook.com/arne.klingenberg

www.linkedin.com/in/ArneKlingenberg

www.google.com/+ArneKlingenberg

www.amazon.com/author/arneklingenberg

About the Author

Arne Klingenberg is a Swiss-Australian philosopher, economist and entrepreneur; he writes books, advises both corporate and private clients (in four languages), and runs various online ventures.

For more information please visit ArneKlingenberg.com.

Notes Merry Christians

Please note: To save time and effort, print books readers are cordially invited to visit ArneKlingenberg.com for a linked version of *Notes Merry Christians* (Ebook versions feature internally linked URLs that can easily be clicked to visit any of the following 320 web pages).

[1] Yes I Am Happy Now! by Arne Klingenberg
Beam Publishing, October 1, 1999.
www.amazon.com/exec/obidos/ASIN/1876538007/beampublishing/002-3757616-4304834

[2] Teresa of Ávila, also called Saint Teresa of Jesus, baptized as Teresa Sánchez de Cepeda y Ahumada (28 March 1515 - 4 October 1582), was a prominent Spanish mystic, Roman Catholic saint, Carmelite nun, an author of the Counter Reformation and theologian of contemplative life through mental prayer.
http://en.wikipedia.org/wiki/Saint_Teresa_of_Avila

[3] Saint Francis of Assisi, 1181/1182 - October 3, 1226) was an Italian Catholic friar and preacher. He founded the men's Order of Friars Minor, the women's Order of St. Clare, and the Third Order of Saint Francis. He is known as the patron saint of animals, the environment, and is one of the two patron saints of Italy (with Catherine of Siena).
http://en.wikipedia.org/wiki/Francis_of_Assisi

[4] A timeline of the global persecution of Christians:
http://en.wikipedia.org/wiki/Persecution_of_Christians

See also :
http://en.wikipedia.org/wiki/Anti-Christian_sentiment

And:
http://en.wikipedia.org/wiki/Open_Doors

[5] Blaise Pascal (19 June 1623 - 19 August 1662) was a French mathematician, physicist, inventor, writer and Catholic philosopher.
http://en.wikipedia.org/wiki/Blaise_Pascal

[6] http://en.wikipedia.org/wiki/Beatitudes

[7] www.multnomah.edu/about/office-of-the-president/presidents/dr-joseph-c-aldrich/
www.rapidnet.com/~jbeard/bdm/BookReviews/lifestyl.htm

[8] http://en.wikipedia.org/wiki/Christianity

[9] Augustine of Hippo (13 November 354 - 28 August 430), also known as Saint Augustine or Saint Austin, was an early Christian theologian and philosopher whose writings were very influential in the development of Western Christianity and Western philosophy.
http://en.wikipedia.org/wiki/Saint_Augustine

[10] http://en.wikipedia.org/wiki/Keith_Green

[11] http://en.wikipedia.org/wiki/Friedrich_Nietzsche

[12] George MacDonald (10 December 1824 - 18 September 1905) was a Scottish author, poet, and Christian minister.
http://en.wikipedia.org/wiki/George_MacDonald

[13] 'And The Happy Rabbit Says…' is a daily email series of 365 inspiring and uplifting sayings and suggestions by Arne Klingenberg, sent millions of times for free to subscribers from around the world (2005 - 2015). For more information please visit ArneKlingenberg.com

[14] http://myhero.com/directory/
http://heroicstories.org/

[15] Johann Christoph Friedrich von Schiller (10 November 1759 - 9 May 1805) was a German poet, philosopher, historian, and playwright.
http://en.wikipedia.org/wiki/Friedrich_Schiller

[16] Thomas Merton, O.C.S.O. (January 31, 1915 - December 10, 1968) was an American Catholic writer and mystic. A Trappist monk of the Abbey of Gethsemani, Kentucky, he was a poet, social activist, and student of comparative religion. In 1949, he was ordained to the priesthood and given the name Father Louis.
http://en.wikipedia.org/wiki/Thomas_Merton

[17] Blessed Teresa of Calcutta, M.C., commonly known as Mother Teresa (26 August 1910 - 5 September 1997), was a Roman Catholic

Religious Sister and missionary of Albanian origin who lived for most of her life in India. Mother Teresa was the recipient of numerous honours including the 1979 Nobel Peace Prize.
http://en.wikipedia.org/wiki/Mother_Teresa

[18] Thomas Sprat (1635 - 20 May 1713), English divine, was born at Beaminster, Dorset, and educated at Wadham College, Oxford, where he held a fellowship from 1657 to 1670. In 1669 he became canon of Westminster Abbey, and in 1670 rector of Uffington, Lincolnshire. He was chaplain to Charles II in 1676, curate and lecturer at St. Margaret's, Westminster, in 1679, canon of Chapel Royal, Windsor in 1681, Dean of Westminster in 1683 and Bishop of Rochester in 1684.
http://en.wikipedia.org/wiki/Thomas_Sprat

[19] http://en.wikipedia.org/wiki/Toleration

[20] Khalil Gibran (January 6, 1883 - April 10, 1931) was a Lebanese artist, poet, and writer. Gibran is the third best-selling poet of all time, behind Shakespeare and Laozi.
http://en.wikipedia.org/wiki/Kahlil_Gibran

[21] Epictetus (AD c. 55 - 135) was a Greek sage and Stoic philosopher.
http://en.wikipedia.org/wiki/Epictetus

[22] Antoine de Saint-Exupéry, officially Antoine Marie Jean-Baptiste Roger, comte de Saint Exupéry,(29 June 1900 - 31 July 1944) was a French aristocrat, writer, poet, and pioneering aviator. He became a laureate of several of France's highest literary awards and also won the U.S. National Book Award.
http://en.wikipedia.org/wiki/Antoine_de_Saint-Exup%C3%A9ry

[23] Barclay James Harvest are an English progressive rock band. They were founded in Saddleworth, Yorkshire, United Kingdom, in September 1966 by John Lees, Les Holroyd, Stuart "Woolly" Wolstenholme (1947-2010), and Mel Pritchard (1948-2004).
http://en.wikipedia.org/wiki/Barclay_James_Harvest

"Fantasy: Loving Is Easy" was written by John Lees.
www.youtube.com/watch?v=gigzqA-nUwA

[24] Ralph Waldo Emerson (May 25, 1803 - April 27, 1882) was an American essayist, lecturer, and poet, who led the Transcendentalist movement of the mid-19th century. He was seen as a champion of individualism and a prescient critic of the countervailing pressures of society, and he disseminated his thoughts through dozens of published essays and more than 1,500 public lectures across the United States.
http://en.wikipedia.org/wiki/Ralph_Waldo_Emerson

[25] Changing borders in Europe:
www.youtube.com/watch?v=l53bmKYXliA
www.youtube.com/watch?v=nq0KNfS_M44

It's a changing world:
www.youtube.com/watch?v=e8OEuj6-pVg

[26] Benjamin Franklin FRS (January 17, 1706 - April 17, 1790) was one of the Founding Fathers of the United States and in many ways was "the First American". A world-renowned polymath, Franklin was a leading author, printer, political theorist, politician, postmaster, scientist, inventor, civic activist, statesman, and diplomat.
http://en.wikipedia.org/wiki/Benjamin_Franklin

[27] Mark Paul "Corky" Siegel (born October 24, 1943) is an American musician, singer-songwriter, and composer.
http://en.wikipedia.org/wiki/Corky_Siegel

[28] Phyllis Ada Driver (July 17, 1917 - August 20, 2012), better known as Phyllis Diller, was an American stand-up comedienne, actress, singer, dancer, and voice artist, best known for her eccentric stage persona, her wild hair and clothes, and her exaggerated, cackling laugh.
http://en.wikipedia.org/wiki/Phyllis_Diller

[29] http://en.wikipedia.org/wiki/Smile

[30] The Tower of Babel forms the focus of a story told in the Book of Genesis of the Bible. According to the story, a united humanity of the generations following the Great Flood, speaking a single language and migrating from the east, came to the land of Shinar.
http://en.wikipedia.org/wiki/Tower_of_Babel

[31] The parable of the Good Samaritan is a parable told by Jesus and is mentioned in only one of the Canonical gospels of the New Testament. According to the Gospel of Luke (10:29-37) a traveller is beaten, robbed, and left half dead along the road. First a priest and then a Levite come by, but both avoid the man. Finally, a Samaritan comes by. Samaritans and Jews generally despised each other, but the Samaritan helps the injured man.
http://en.wikipedia.org/wiki/Good_Samaritan

[32] Johann Wolfgang von Goethe (28 August 1749 - 22 March 1832) was a German writer and statesman. His body of work includes epic and lyric poetry written in a variety of metres and styles; prose and verse dramas; memoirs; an autobiography; literary and aesthetic criticism; treatises on botany, anatomy, and colour; and four novels. In addition, numerous literary and scientific fragments, more than 10,000 letters, and nearly 3,000 drawings by him are extant.
http://en.wikipedia.org/wiki/Johann_Wolfgang_von_Goethe

[33] John Emerich Edward Dalberg-Acton, 1st Baron Acton, KCVO, DL (10 January 1834 - 19 June 1902)—known as Sir John Dalberg-Acton and usually referred to simply as Lord Acton—was an English Catholic historian, politician, and writer.
http://en.wikipedia.org/wiki/John_Dalberg-Acton,_1st_Baron_Acton

[34] Aesop (c. 620-564 BCE) was an Ancient Greek fabulist or story teller credited with a number of fables now collectively known as Aesop's Fables.
http://en.wikipedia.org/wiki/Aesop

[35] Albert Einstein (14 March 1879 - 18 April 1955) was a German-born theoretical physicist and philosopher of science. He developed the general theory of relativity, one of the two pillars of modern physics (alongside quantum mechanics). He received the 1921 Nobel Prize in Physics "for his services to theoretical physics, and especially for his discovery of the law of the photoelectric effect". The latter was pivotal in establishing quantum theory.
http://en.wikipedia.org/wiki/Albert_Einstein

[36] Desmond Mpilo Tutu (born 7 October 1931) is a South African social rights activist and retired Anglican bishop who rose to worldwide fame during the 1980s as an opponent of apartheid.
http://en.wikipedia.org/wiki/Desmond_Tutu

[37] Twitter is an online social networking service that enables users to send and read short 140-character messages called "tweets".
http://en.wikipedia.org/wiki/Twitter

[38] Thomas à Kempis, C.R.S.A. (Thomas van Kempen or Thomas Hemerken or Haemerken, litt. "small hammer"; c. 1380 - 25 July 1471) was a German canon regular of the late medieval period and the author of *The Imitation of Christ*, which is one of the best known Christian books on devotion.

Homo proponit, sed Deus disponit. "For the resolutions of the just depend rather on the grace of God than on their own wisdom; and in Him they always put their trust, whatever they take in hand. For man proposes, but God disposes; neither is the way of man in his own hands."
https://en.wikipedia.org/wiki/Thomas_%C3%A0_Kempis

[39] Samuel Smiles (23 December 1812 - 16 April 1904), was a Scottish author and government reformer. He is most known for writing Self-Help, which "elevated [Smiles] to celebrity status: almost overnight, he became a leading pundit and much-consulted guru".
http://en.wikipedia.org/wiki/Samuel_Smiles

[40] Emily Elizabeth Dickinson (December 10, 1830 - May 15, 1886) was one of the most important American poets. Throughout her life, Dickinson wrote poems reflecting a preoccupation with the teachings of Jesus Christ and, indeed, many are addressed to him.
http://en.wikipedia.org/wiki/Emily_Dickinson

[41] https://en.wikipedia.org/wiki/Emotional_contagion
http://en.wikipedia.org/wiki/Empathy
http://greatergood.berkeley.edu/article/item/six_habits_of_highly_empathic_people1

⁴² "There's a sucker born every minute" is a phrase most likely spoken by David Hannum, in criticism of both P. T. Barnum, an American showman of the mid 1800s, and his customers. The phrase is often credited to Barnum himself. It means "Many people are gullible, and we can expect this to continue."
https://en.wikipedia.org/wiki/There%27s_a_sucker_born_every_minute

⁴³ Hanns-Joachim Gottlob Scharff (December 16, 1907 - September 10, 1992) was a German Luftwaffe interrogator during the Second World War. He has been called the "Master Interrogator" of the Luftwaffe. He has been highly praised for the success of his techniques, in particular because he never used physical means to obtain the required information.
https://en.wikipedia.org/wiki/Hanns_Scharff

⁴⁴ William Makepeace Thackeray (18 July 1811 - 24 December 1863) was an English novelist of the 19th century. He was famous for his satirical works, particularly Vanity Fair, a panoramic portrait of English society.
http://en.wikipedia.org/wiki/William_Makepeace_Thackeray

⁴⁵ Bertrand Arthur William Russell, 3rd Earl Russell, OM, FRS (18 May 1872 - 2 February 1970) was a British philosopher, logician, mathematician, historian, social critic and political activist.
http://en.wikipedia.org/wiki/Bertrand_Russell

⁴⁶ Garbage in, garbage out (GIGO) in the field of computer science or information and communications technology refers to the fact that computers, since they operate by logical processes, will unquestioningly process unintended, even nonsensical, input data ("garbage in") and produce undesired, often nonsensical, output ("garbage out").
http://en.wikipedia.org/wiki/Garbage_in,_garbage_out

⁴⁷ Marcus Aurelius (Marcus Aurelius Antoninus Augustus; 26 April 121 - 17 March 180 AD) was Roman Emperor from 161 to 180. He ruled with Lucius Verus as co-emperor from 161 until Verus' death in 169. He was the last of the Five Good Emperors, and is also considered

one of the most important Stoic philosophers.
http://en.wikipedia.org/wiki/Marcus_Aurelius

[48] Laozi (also Lao-Tzu or Lao-Tze) was a philosopher and poet of ancient China. He is known as the reputed author of the Tao Te Ching and the founder of philosophical Taoism, and as a deity in religious Taoism and traditional Chinese religions.
https://en.wikipedia.org/wiki/Laozi

[49] François VI, Duc de La Rochefoucauld, Prince de Marcillac (15 September 1613 - 17 March 1680) was a noted French author of maxims and memoirs.
https://en.wikipedia.org/wiki/Fran%C3%A7ois_de_La_Rochefoucauld_(writer)

[50] Confucius (September 28, 551 - 479 BC) was a Chinese teacher, editor, politician, and philosopher of the Spring and Autumn period of Chinese history.
https://en.wikipedia.org/wiki/Confucius

[51] Robert Green "Bob" Ingersoll (August 11, 1833 - July 21, 1899) was an American lawyer, a Civil War veteran, political leader, and orator of United States during the Golden Age of Free Thought.
https://en.wikipedia.org/wiki/Robert_G._Ingersoll

[52] Ralph Washington Sockman (October 1, 1889 - August 29, 1970) was the senior pastor of Christ Church (United Methodist) in New York City, United States. He gained considerable prominence in the U.S. as the featured speaker on the weekly NBC radio program, National Radio Pulpit, which aired from 1928 to 1962, and as a writer of several best-selling books on the Christian life.
https://en.wikipedia.org/wiki/Ralph_Washington_Sockman

53a]

A shocking admission by the editor of the world's most respected medical journal, The Lancet, has been virtually ignored by the mainstream media. Dr. Richard Horton, Editor-in-chief of the Lancet recently published a statement declaring that a shocking amount of published research is unreliable at best, if not completely false, as in,

fraudulent.
http://journal-neo.org/2015/06/18/shocking-report-from-medical-insiders
www.thelancet.com/pdfs/journals/lancet/PIIS0140-6736%2815%2960696-1.pdf
http://nsnbc.me/wp-content/uploads/2013/05/BSEM-2011.pdf

53b]

Your body's many Cries for Water by F. Batmanghelidj, M.D

This book explains a new discovery that lack of water in the body-chronic dehydration-is the root cause of many painful degenerative diseases, asthma, allergies, hypertension, excess body weight, and some emotional problems, including depression.
www.amazon.com/Your-Bodys-Many-Cries-Water/dp/1452656975/beampublishing
http://bebrainfit.com/human-brain-facts/
www.ncbi.nlm.nih.gov/pubmed/22855911
http://fluoridealert.org/

According to H.H. Mitchell, Journal of Biological Chemistry 158, the brain and heart are composed of 73% water, and the lungs are about 83% water. The skin contains 64% water, muscles and kidneys are 79%, and even the bones are watery: 31%.
http://water.usgs.gov/edu/propertyyou.html

[54] Princeton University researchers find that high-fructose corn syrup prompts considerable weight gain. Rats with access to high-fructose corn syrup gained significantly more weight than those consuming table sugar, even when their overall caloric intake was the same. In addition to causing significant weight gain in lab animals, long-term consumption of high-fructose corn syrup also led to abnormal increases in body fat, especially in the abdomen (e.g. non-alcoholic fatty liver disease), and a rise in circulating blood fats called triglycerides. Researchers have found an association between consumption of high fructose corn syrup and the prevalence of Type 2 diabetes, according to a new study published in the journal Global Public Health.

www.princeton.edu/main/news/archive/S26/91/22K07/
www.huffingtonpost.com/2012/11/27/high-fructose-corn-syrup-diabetes-hfcs-type-2_n_2194173.html
www.huffingtonpost.com/dr-mark-hyman/high-fructose-corn-syrup_b_4256220.html
http://naturalsociety.com/newly-discovered-side-effect-of-high-fructose-corn-syrup-is-alarming/
www.theguardian.com/society/2015/jul/21/sugary-drinks-may-cause-type-2-diabetes-regardless-of-size-research-says
https://en.wikipedia.org/wiki/Lifestyle_disease
www.dovepress.com/the-western-diet-and-lifestyle-and-diseases-of-civilization-peer-reviewed-article-RRCC

Social diseases, civilization diseases or lifestyle diseases?
www.ncbi.nlm.nih.gov/pubmed/18350729

Processed snack foods aren't really food at all.

They are "food-like" concoctions developed by scientists aiming for the "bliss factor" — the perfect balance of fat, sugar, and salt that make these foods intentionally addictive.
http://bebrainfit.com/best-brain-food-snacks/
www.nytimes.com/2013/03/18/books/salt-sugar-fat-by-michael-moss.html

McDonalds fast food: toxic ingredients include putty and cosmetic petrochemicals
www.examiner.com/article/mcdonalds-fast-food-toxic-ingredients-include-putty-and-cosmetic-petrochemicals
http://theantimedia.org/happens-leave-chicken-mcnuggets-happy-meal-6-years/

MSG
http://foodmatters.tv/articles-1/the-dangers-of-msg
http://articles.mercola.com/sites/articles/archive/2007/08/28/dangers-of-msg.aspx

New study finds significant differences between organic and non-organic food

In the largest study of its kind, an international team of experts led by Newcastle University, UK, has shown that organic crops and crop-based foods are up to 69% higher in a number of key antioxidants than conventionally-grown crops.

Analysing 343 studies into the compositional differences between organic and conventional crops, the team found that a switch to eating organic fruit, vegetable and cereals - and food made from them - would provide additional antioxidants equivalent to eating between 1-2 extra portions of fruit and vegetables a day.

The study, published today in the prestigious British Journal of Nutrition, also shows significantly lower levels of toxic heavy metals in organic crops. Cadmium, which is one of only three metal contaminants along with lead and mercury for which the European Commission has set maximum permitted contamination levels in food, was found to be almost 50% lower in organic crops than conventionally-grown ones.
http://blog.journals.cambridge.org/2014/07/13/new-study-finds-significant-differences-between-organic-and-non-organic-food/
http://journals.cambridge.org/bjn/organic

Acetylsalicylic acid is made from petrochemicals, and it is the active ingredient in many well-known over-the-counter medicines such as aspirin. Synthetic vitamins are also made from petrochemicals— this is especially bad for fat-soluble vitamins such as A, D, E and K, because they accumulate in the body's fat deposits and liver, as opposed to water-soluble vitamins that flush out of the body.

Petrochemicals are found in food additives, which are in many canned foods to increase their shelf life. Many food colorings are added to food to make them more attractive (making a green apple greener), and many of those food colorings are made from petroleum.
www.huffingtonpost.com.au/entry/9-shocking-things-made-fr_n_570796.html?section=australia

[55] Good gut health has a positive impact on mental function and overall health. Probiotics and prebiotics help restore the balance of good and bad bacteria.

Prebiotics are non-digestible, fiber compounds that pass undigested through the upper part of the gastrointestinal tract and stimulate the growth or activity of advantageous bacteria that colonize the large bowel by acting as substrate for them.

Your intestinal tract contains hundreds of kinds of bacteria that are essential to your health.

The brain in your head isn't your only brain. There's a "second brain" in your intestines that contains 100,000 neurons that's been called the "backup brain".

Your gut bacteria are responsible for making over 30 neurotransmitters including the "happy" molecule serotonin.
http://bebrainfit.com/benefits-probiotics-brain/

18 Ways Gut Dysbiosis (Bad Bacteria) Ruins Health
https://youtu.be/cbJuVvT6ALQ

[56] Oscar Fingal O'Flahertie Wills Wilde (16 October 1854 - 30 November 1900) was an Irish playwright, novelist, essayist, and poet
https://en.wikipedia.org/wiki/Oscar_Wilde

[57] François-Marie Arouet (21 November 1694 - 30 May 1778), known by his nom de plume Voltaire, was a French Enlightenment writer, historian, and philosopher famous for his wit, and his advocacy of freedom of religion, freedom of expression, and separation of church and state.
https://en.wikipedia.org/wiki/Voltaire

[58] A placebo can be a sugar pill, saline infusion, fake surgery, and other methods; they work even when we know that we are taking a placebo:

'If your pain is eased after taking a fake pill, that's occurring through exactly that same biological mechanism as you would get if you take a drug. You haven't just imagined it, it's really there.'

'In Parkinson's disease, for example, patients who respond to placebos get a flood of dopamine in the brain—this is the neurotransmitter they are lacking that is causing their symptoms.

'With altitude sickness, researchers have found that you can give people fake oxygen and then you will see a reduction in [the] chemicals that are behind many of the symptoms of altitude sickness.'

'if you respond to a fake painkiller there is a genuine release of endorphins in your brain.
www.abc.net.au/radionational/programs/allinthemind/science-of-mind-over-body-jo-marchant/7267100

The Nocebo Effect: Negative Thoughts Can Harm Your Health

In another study, patients about to undergo surgery who were "convinced" of their impending death were compared to another group of patients who were merely "unusually apprehensive" about death. While the apprehensive bunch fared pretty well, those who were convinced they were going to die usually did.
www.psychologytoday.com/blog/owning-pink/201308/the-nocebo-effect-negative-thoughts-can-harm-your-health

The Strange Powers of the Placebo Effect
https://youtu.be/yfRVCaA5o18

Is there scientific proof we can heal ourselves?
http://youtu.be/LWQfe__fNbs

Spontaneous Remission Bibliography Project
http://noetic.org/research/projects/spontaneous-remission

Among those conditions that have proven responsive to placebo treatment are angina pectoris, cancer, rheumatoid arthritis, warts, asthma, ulcers, migraine headaches, allergies, multiple sclerosis, diabetes, and psychiatric disorders.
http://noetic.org/research/projects/spontaneous-remission/faqs
http://science.howstuffworks.com/life/inside-the-mind/human-brain/placebo-effect.htm
www.psychologytoday.com/blog/brain-sense/201201/the-placebo-effect-how-it-works

You Are the Placebo: Making Your Mind Matter Paperback by Dr. Joe Dispenza www.amazon.com/You-Are-Placebo-Making-Matter/dp/1401944590/beampublishing

[59] William Aloysius Keane (October 5, 1922 - November 8, 2011), better known as Bil Keane, was an American cartoonist most notable for his work on the long-running newspaper comic The Family Circus. https://en.wikipedia.org/wiki/Bil_Keane

[60] A study by the prestigious Mayo Clinic and Olmsted Medical Center found that nearly 70 percent of all Americans are on at least one prescription drug, and more than half take two; twenty percent of all Americans are on five or more prescription drugs.

"Antibiotics, antidepressants and painkilling opioids are most commonly prescribed, their study found."
www.mayoclinic.org/news2013-rst/7543.html

Americans account for approximately five percent of the global population yet buy over 50 percent of pharmaceutical drugs.
www.technologyreview.com/featuredstory/520441/a-tale-of-two-drugs/

The New York Times says that more than 30 million Americans are currently taking antidepressants.
http://well.blogs.nytimes.com/2013/08/12/a-glut-of-antidepressants/?_php=true&_type=blogs&_r=0

Americans also consume a whopping 80 percent of all prescription painkillers.
www.cnn.com/2014/08/29/health/gupta-unintended-consequences/
www.scientificamerican.com/article/the-medicated-americans/
www.zerohedge.com/news/2014-02-15/drugging-america-summarized-19-mind-altering-facts

"In a paper last year in the Lancet Psychiatry journal, Professor Gotzsche argued our use of antidepressants is causing more harm than good.

He said as the evidence against drugs such as Valium and Xanax emerged, they have been replaced with anti-depressants that are equally as addictive and their side-effects just as dangerous.

Furthermore, he says research that showed small benefits over placebos was biased, as it did not properly hide whether patients were in the active or placebo group."

"Professor Gotzsche's list of medicine to avoid:

Anti-depressants for all, as they very likely don't even work for severe cases of depression

All brain-active drugs in children

Anti-psychotics and other brain-active drugs for the elderly. Psychotropic drugs should be used as little as possible and mostly in very acute situations, as they are very harmful when used long term Anti-dementia drugs, as they very likely don't work

Non-steroidal anti-inflammatory drugs used for arthritis, muscle pain and headaches, including over-the-counter, low-dose ibuprofen. These drugs should be used as little as possible.

Mammography screening, as it doesn't prolong life whereas it makes many healthy women ill through overdiagnosis and leads to the premature death for some because radiotherapy and chemotherapy increases mortality when used for harmless cancers detected at screening

Drugs for urinary incontinence, as they very likely don't work"
www.smh.com.au/national/health/peter-gotzsche-founder-of-the-cochrane-collaboration-visits-australia-to-talk-about-dangers-of-prescription-drugs-20150207-136nqc.html
www.thelancet.com/journals/lanpsy/article/PIIS2215-0366(14)70280-9/abstract
www.ncbi.nlm.nih.gov/pubmed/21810886?dopt=Abstract

Marketing the myth of serotonin, the 'happy chemical' by ADRIANA BARTON

The Globe and Mail

Published Sunday, May. 17 2015

If serotonin is the "happy chemical," then boosting our serotonin levels should keep depression at bay. After all, low serotonin brings on the blues, right?

But the truth is, depression is not a serotonin deficiency. The idea that depression is caused by low serotonin levels is based on flimsy evidence dating to the 1950s. Pharmaceutical companies promoted the low serotonin story to sell Prozac and related antidepressants. They marketed a myth.
www.theglobeandmail.com/life/health-and-fitness/health/marketing-the-myth-of-serotonin-the-happy-chemical/article24457686/
www.theguardian.com/society/2008/feb/27/mentalhealth.health1

American Psycho - Has The United States Lost Its Collective Mind? by Roberts Bridges

"The top-selling drug in America is an antipsychotic, happily named Abilify. Aside from the fact that Americans are buying antipsychotic medication by the truckload, there's another disturbing thing about Abilify: Nobody, not even the Food and Drug Administration (FDA), has any idea what makes it effective. According to the USPI label that accompanies each bottle: "The mechanism of action of aripiprazole… is unknown. However, the efficacy of aripiprazole could be mediated through a combination of partial agonist activity at D2 and 5-HT1A receptors and… etc, etc."

In other words, millions of Americans are ingesting an antipsychotic drug that not even the scientific community can say exactly what makes it work. Is that not in itself the very definition of insanity?"
www.zerohedge.com/news/2015-10-16/guest-post-american-psycho-has-united-states-lost-its-collective-mind

A short excerpt from the list of possible side-effects as per the manufacturer's website:

"Uncontrollable movements of face, tongue, or other parts of body, as these may be signs of a serious condition called tardive dyskinesia (TD). TD may not go away, even if you stop taking ABILIFY. TD may also start after you stop taking ABILIFY."

"High fever, stiff muscles, confusion, sweating, changes in pulse, heart rate and blood pressure may be signs of a condition called neuroleptic malignant syndrome (NMS), a rare and serious condition that can lead to death."

"Antidepressants may increase suicidal thoughts or behaviors in some children, teenagers, and young adults, especially within the first few months of treatment or when the dose is changed."
www.abilify.com/

"To be a top seller, a drug has to be expensive and also widely used," Steven Reidbord M.D. wrote in Psychology Today. "Abilify is both. It's the 14th most prescribed brand-name medication, and it retails for about $30 a pill. Annual sales are over $7 billion, nearly a billion more than the next runner-up."
www.psychologytoday.com/blog/sacramento-street-psychiatry/201503/americas-top-selling-drug

According to the Centers for Disease Controls, every day in America, 44 people die from overdose of prescription painkillers. The CDC blames the overdose surge on a "dramatic increase in the acceptance and use of prescription opioids for the treatment of chronic, non-cancer pain, such as back pain or osteoarthritis (The most common drugs involved in prescription overdose deaths include: Hydrocodone (e.g., Vicodin), Oxycodone (e.g., OxyContin), Oxymorphone (e.g., Opana) and Methadone (especially when prescribed for pain).

In 2013, nearly two million Americans abused prescription painkillers. Each day, almost 7,000 people are treated in emergency rooms for abusing the medication.
www.cdc.gov/drugoverdose/epidemic/index.html

CDC: Antidepressants most prescribed drugs in U.S.
http://edition.cnn.com/2007/HEALTH/07/09/antidepressants/index.html?eref=rss_topstories#cnnSTCVideo

A Brief History of Psychotropic Drugs Prescribed to Mass Murderers

By Daren Savage
www.ladailypost.com/content/brief-history-psychotropic-drugs-prescribed-mass-murderers

Xanax, Anti-Depressants Linked to Mass Shootings - Again

By Christina Sarich
http://naturalsociety.com/xanax-elliot-roger-linked-mass-shootings/

Prescription drug spending in the US exploded in 2014 to nearly $374 billion, a whopping 13.1 percent increase in growth, according to a new report from IMS Institute for Healthcare Informatics.
http://blogs.wsj.com/pharmalot/2015/04/14/why-did-prescription-drug-spending-hit-374b-in-the-us-last-year-read-this/

Suicide Rates Rise Sharply in U.S.

By Tara Parker-Pope

"Another factor may be the widespread availability of opioid drugs like OxyContin and oxycodone, which can be particularly deadly in large doses."
www.nytimes.com/2013/05/03/health/suicide-rate-rises-sharply-in-us.html?_r=3&

30 Million Americans On Antidepressants And 21 Other Facts About America's Endless Pharmaceutical Nightmare By Michael Snyder
www.zerohedge.com/news/2014-09-03/30-million-americans-antidepressants-and-21-other-facts-about-americas-endless-pharm

Young people on antidepressants more prone to violence, study finds

Prozac and Seroxat may also make 15-24 year olds more likely to be involved in non-violent crime and to have alcohol problems
www.theguardian.com/world/2015/sep/16/study-finds-young-people-on-antidepressants-more-prone-to-violence
http://journals.plos.org/plosmedicine/article?id=10.1371/journal.pmed.1001875

Anti-depressant paroxetine linked to youth suicide and no more effective than a placebo, researchers find

The World Today By Nick Grimm

"An Australian-led review of a popular anti-depressant drug has found it can tip young people into suicide and is no more effective than a placebo.

The study, published in the British Medical Journal, reviewed data used by pharmaceutical companies to help market the drug, which is sold in Australia under the names

Aropax and Paxil. It is also known as paroxetine."
www.abc.net.au/news/2015-09-17/anti-depressant-linked-to-youth-suicide-in-damning-review/6783332

Antidepressant Nightmares

SSRI Stories is a collection of over 6,000 stories that have appeared in the media (newspapers, TV, scientific journals) in which prescription drugs were mentioned and in which the drugs may be linked to a variety of adverse outcomes including violence.
http://ssristories.org/?sort=date

'St John's Wort plant as effective as Prozac for treating depression', say scientists By Daniel Martin

The study's lead author, Dr Klaus Linde, from the Centre for Complementary Medicine in Munich, pooled data from 29 studies involving 5,489 patients with mild to moderately severe depression.

'Overall, the St John's Wort extracts tested in the trials were superior to placebo, similarly effective as standard anti-depressants, and had fewer side effects than standard anti-depressants,' he said.
www.dailymail.co.uk/health/article-1072414/St-Johns-Wort-plant-effective-Prozac-treating-depression-say-scientists.html

Lawmaker Calls For Study On Links Between Pharmaceuticals And Mass Killers
www.zerohedge.com/news/2015-10-07/lawmaker-calls-study-links-between-pharmaceuticals-and-mass-killers

Patients are being deceived into taking drugs they do not need, that do not work and even put lives at risk, according to a scathing review of the influence big drug companies have on healthcare.

Drug companies "masterfully influenced" medicine, a review by Australian, British and US researchers has found.

The researchers described how the enormous profit involved in making and selling drugs gave the industry power to influence every stage of the health system.

"The benefits of drugs and other products are often exaggerated and their potential harms are downplayed," the research, published in the European Journal of Clinical Investigation, said.

A co-author of the paper, Emmanuel Stamatakis, of the University of Sydney's school of public health, said it was "entirely illogical" to rely on the pharmaceutical industry to fund medical research.

"The profits involved are just too large and the temptation to manipulate the evidence is difficult to resist, even when this may lead to the loss of lives," Dr Stamatakis said.

He cited anti-diabetic drugs, which he said increased the risk of heart problems and were prescribed despite interventions such as exercise being more effective.

Undue industry influences that distort healthcare research, strategy, expenditure and practice: a review

Emmanuel Stamatakis, Richard Weiler and John P.A. Ioannidis

European Journal of Clinical Investigation

Volume 43, Issue 5, pages 469-475, May 2013
http://onlinelibrary.wiley.com/doi/10.1111/eci.12074/abstract
http://onlinelibrary.wiley.com/doi/10.1111/eci.12074/pdf

[61] An Orthopedic Doctor's Near Death Experience - Dr Mary Neal (To Heaven and Back)

Dr. Mary Neal is a board-certified orthopaedic spine surgeon who drowned while kayaking on a South American river. She experienced life after death. She went to heaven and back, conversed with Jesus and experienced God's encompassing love. She was returned to Earth with some specific instructions for work she still needed to do. Her life has been one filled with the miracles and intervention of God. Her

story gives reason to live by faith and is a story of hope.
https://youtu.be/9-QjMRF1gkI

Dr. Jeffrey Long - Near Death Experiences

Near Death Experience testimony from six people who tell their stories of the afterlife. Excellent short documentary.
http://youtu.be/LwyVFW9kT8k

"Beyond Our Sight" is an independant documentary that talks about near-death experiences, human consciousness, and the possibility of communication with other dimensions. Includes interviews with Dr. Alan Hugenot, Karen Hanning, Terry Yoder, Lewis Griggs, Dr. Dean Radin and Savonn Champelle.
www.youtube.com/watch?v=xpSuO8DtiMM

Pam Reynold's Near Death Experience

This case comes the closest to hard evidence that consciousness survives physical death. During her brain operation, blood was drained from the brain and the heart stopped. She was incapable of hallucinating, yet she was out of the body and her observations come close to proving it. Debunkers have worked extra hard to try to disprove this case. But cardiologist Michael Sabom who studied this case and others says that Pam Reynolds was really out of the body and having a spiritual experience.
www.youtube.com/watch?v=Bu1ErDeQ0Zw
www.near-death.com/science/evidence/people-have-ndes-while-brain-dead.html
https://vimeo.com/25629985

Kim Clark Finds the Tennis Shoe and Proves Near Death Experiences Are Real
www.youtube.com/watch?v=WPXK2Ls-xzQ

Reverend George Rodonaia (died October 12, 2004) underwent one of the most extended cases of a near-death experience ever recorded. Pronounced dead immediately after he was hit by a car in 1976, he was left for three days in the morgue. He did not "return to life" until a doctor began to make an incision in his abdomen as part of an autopsy

procedure. Prior to his NDE he worked as a neuropathologist. He was also an avowed atheist. Yet after the experience, he devoted himself exclusively to the study of spirituality, taking a second doctorate in the psychology of religion. He then became an ordained priest in the Eastern Orthodox Church. He served as a pastor at St. Paul United Methodist Church in Baytown, Texas.
www.near-death.com/science/evidence/some-people-were-dead-for-several-days.html
https://youtu.be/S8j2g-IsBPQ

The International Association for Near Death Studies (IANDS)

As an educational nonprofit 501(c)(3) organization, the International Association for Near-Death Studies (IANDS) focuses most of its resources into providing the highest quality information available about NDE-related subjects.
http://iands.org/home.html

A Lawyer Presents the Evidence for the Afterlife Paperback - May 14, 2013

by Victor Zammit & Wendy Zammit
www.amazon.com/Lawyer-Presents-Evidence-Afterlife/dp/1908733225/beampublishing
www.victorzammit.com/evidence/Outofbody.htm
www.victorzammit.com/evidence/nde.htm

Evidence of the Afterlife: The Science of Near-Death Experiences Paperback by Jeffrey Long
www.amazon.com/Evidence-Afterlife-Science-Near-Death-Experiences/dp/0061452572/beampublishing

Dr. Pim van Lommel of the Netherlands, world-renowned cardiologist, author, and university lecturer, has empirically investigated the near-death experiences (NDE) of his patients who survived cardiac arrest. His research suggests that our waking awareness does not always coincide with the functioning of the brain; moreover, it is possible to experience consciousness separate from the body.
www.pimvanlommel.nl/?home_eng

Consciousness Beyond Life: The Science of the Near-Death Experience Paperback by Pim van Lommel
www.amazon.com/Consciousness-Beyond-Life-Near-Death-Experience/dp/0061777269/beampublishing

Dr. Alan Ross Hugenot tells us about his near-death experience, explains the nature and capabilities of our consciousness, and why science has to change its viewpoint to really understand it.
https://youtu.be/Xug3tii0WaQ
www.afterlife.pro
http://afterlife.pro/video-audio/

Dr. Stanislav Grof, M.D., is a psychiatrist and one of the leading researchers into non-ordinary states of consciousness. In Tom Harpur's NDE documentary, Life After Death, Dr. Grof explains a theory of consciousness based on these non-ordinary states. Dr. Grof theorizes consciousness to be nonlocalized and that the brain may instead function as a "reducing valve" minimizing the cosmic energy input bombarding our body. Consciousness then arises as a product of this reducing function of the brain.
www.near-death.com/experiences/triggers.html
www.near-death.com/experiences/out-of-body.html

NDE Stories

Every day, all over the world, an increasing number of people, from all walks of life, are reporting near-death experiences (and related phenomena). This website has been created to gather, study, and share the most compelling of these experiences.
http://ndestories.org

International Academy of Consciousness trainer Luis Minero talks to the South Bay Chapter of IANDS about the out-of-body experience and the near-death experience.
https://youtu.be/Ey8b9YnEzqk

Luis Minero (part two) OBEs and NDEs
https://youtu.be/ZgVlDh8q53k

Luis Minero (part three) OBEs and NDEs
https://youtu.be/zDWFVM5hRZ4

Demystifying the Out-of-Body Experience: A Practical Manual for Exploration and Personal Evolution by Luis Minero
www.amazon.com/Demystifying-Out-Body-Experience-Exploration/dp/0738730793/beampublishing

[62] William Ellery Channing (April 7, 1780 - October 2, 1842) was the foremost Unitarian preacher in the United States in the early nineteenth century and along with Andrews Norton, (1786-1853), one of Unitarianism's leading theologians. He was known for his articulate and impassioned sermons and public speeches, and as a prominent thinker in the liberal theology of the day.
https://en.wikipedia.org/wiki/William_Ellery_Channing

[63] The tall poppy syndrome is a pejorative term primarily used in the United Kingdom, Australia, New Zealand, and other Anglosphere nations to describe a social phenomenon in which people of genuine merit are resented, attacked, cut down, or criticised because their talents or achievements elevate them above or distinguish them from their peers. This is similar to begrudgery, the resentment or envy of the success of a peer.
https://en.wikipedia.org/wiki/Tall_poppy_syndrome

[64] Thales of Miletus (c. 624 - c. 546 BC) was a pre-Socratic Greek philosopher, mathematician and astronomer from Miletus in Asia Minor, current day Milet in Turkey, and one of the Seven Sages of Greece. Many, most notably Aristotle, regard him as the first philosopher in the Greek tradition.
https://en.wikipedia.org/wiki/Thales

[65] The Top Five Regrets of the Dying: A Life Transformed by the Dearly Departing by Bronnie Ware
www.amazon.com/Top-Five-Regrets-Dying-Transformed/dp/140194065X/beampublishing

[66] William Ellery Channing (April 7, 1780 - October 2, 1842) was the foremost Unitarian preacher in the United States in the early nineteenth century and along with Andrews Norton, (1786-1853), one

of Unitarianism's leading theologians.
https://en.wikipedia.org/wiki/William_Ellery_Channing

[67] Napoleon Hill (October 26, 1883 - November 8, 1970) was an American author and impresario who cribbed freely from the new thought tradition of the previous century to become an early producer of personal-success literature. At the time of Hill's death in 1970, his best-known work, Think and Grow Rich (1937) had sold 20 million copies.
https://en.wikipedia.org/wiki/Napoleon_Hill

[68] Sir Arthur Charles Clarke, CBE, FRAS (16 December 1917 - 19 March 2008) was a British science fiction writer, science writer and futurist, inventor, undersea explorer, and television series host.
https://en.wikipedia.org/wiki/Arthur_C._Clarke

[69] Paramahansa Yogananda (5 January 1893 - 7 March 1952), born Mukunda Lal Ghosh, was an Indian yogi and guru who introduced millions of westerners to the teachings of meditation and Kriya Yoga through his book, Autobiography of a Yogi.
https://en.wikipedia.org/wiki/Paramahansa_Yogananda

[70] François-Marie Arouet (21 November 1694 - 30 May 1778), known by his nom de plume Voltaire was a French Enlightenment writer, historian, and philosopher famous for his wit, his attacks on the established Catholic Church, and his advocacy of freedom of religion, freedom of expression, and separation of church and state.
https://en.wikipedia.org/wiki/Voltaire

[71] The Evolution of Atheism: The Politics of a Modern Movement by Stephen LeDrew
www.amazon.com/exec/obidos/ASIN/0190225173/beampublishing
www.counterpunch.org/2016/01/29/new-atheism-worse-than-you-think/
www.theguardian.com/science/occams-corner/2013/mar/04/myth-scientists-religion-hating-atheists
https://en.wikipedia.org/wiki/List_of_Christians_in_science_and_technology

www.famousscientists.org/25-famous-scientists-who-believed-in-god/
www.adherents.com/people/100_Nobel.html

[72] Werner Karl Heisenberg (5 December 1901 - 1 February 1976) was a German theoretical physicist and one of the key pioneers of quantum mechanics.
https://en.wikipedia.org/wiki/Werner_Heisenberg

[73] Francis Bacon, 1st Viscount St Alban (22 January 1561 - 9 April 1626) was an English philosopher, statesman, scientist, jurist, orator, and author. He served both as Attorney General and as Lord Chancellor of England.
https://en.wikipedia.org/wiki/Francis_Bacon

[74] Upton Beall Sinclair, Jr. (September 20, 1878 - November 25, 1968) was an American author who wrote nearly 100 books and other works across a number of genres. Sinclair's work was well-known and popular in the first half of the twentieth century, and he won the Pulitzer Prize for Fiction in 1943.
https://en.wikipedia.org/wiki/Upton_Sinclair

[75] Mohandas Karamchand Gandhi (2 October 1869 - 30 January 1948) was the preeminent leader of the Indian independence movement in British-ruled India. Employing nonviolent civil disobedience, Gandhi led India to independence and inspired movements for civil rights and freedom across the world.
https://en.wikipedia.org/wiki/Mahatma_Gandhi

[76] Gautama Buddha, also known as Siddhartha Gautama, Shakyamuni Buddha, or simply the Buddha, was an ascetic and sage, on whose teachings Buddhism was founded. He is believed to have lived and taught mostly in the eastern part of the Indian subcontinent sometime between the sixth and fourth centuries BCE.

He is recognized by Buddhists as an enlightened or divine teacher who attained full Buddhahood, and shared his insights to help sentient beings end rebirth and suffering.
https://en.wikipedia.org/wiki/Gautama_Buddha

⁷⁷ Materialism is a form of philosophical monism which holds that matter is the fundamental substance in nature, and that all phenomena, including mental phenomena and consciousness, are results of material interactions.
https://en.wikipedia.org/wiki/Materialism

⁷⁸ Soren Aabye Kierkegaard (5 May 1813 - 11 November 1855) was a Danish philosopher, theologian, poet, social critic and religious author who is widely considered to be the first existentialist philosopher.
https://en.wikipedia.org/wiki/S%C3%B8ren_Kierkegaard

⁷⁹ Friedrich Wilhelm Nietzsche (15 October 1844 - 25 August 1900) was a German philosopher, cultural critic, poet, and Latin and Greek scholar whose work has exerted a profound influence on Western philosophy and modern intellectual history.
https://en.wikipedia.org/wiki/Friedrich_Nietzsche

⁸⁰ Swami Vivekananda (12 January 1863 - 4 July 1902), born Narendranath Datta, was an Indian Hindu monk, a chief disciple of the 19th-century Indian mystic Ramakrishna. He was a key figure in the introduction of the Indian philosophies of Vedanta and Yoga to the Western world.
https://en.wikipedia.org/wiki/Swami_Vivekananda

⁸¹ William Shakespeare (26 April 1564 - 23 April 1616) was an English poet, playwright, and actor, widely regarded as the greatest writer in the English language and the world's pre-eminent dramatist.
https://en.wikipedia.org/wiki/William_Shakespeare

⁸² Victor Marie Hugo (26 February 1802 - 22 May 1885) was a French poet, novelist, and dramatist of the Romantic movement. He is considered one of the greatest and best-known French writers.
https://en.wikipedia.org/wiki/Victor_Hugo

⁸³ Socrates (470/469 - 399 BC) was a classical Greek (Athenian) philosopher credited as one of the founders of Western philosophy. He is an enigmatic figure known chiefly through the accounts of classical writers, especially the writings of his students Plato and Xenophon and the plays of his contemporary Aristophanes.
https://en.wikipedia.org/wiki/Socrates

[84] Carl Gustav Jung (26 July 1875 - 6 June 1961), often referred to as C. G. Jung, was a Swiss psychiatrist and psychotherapist who founded analytical psychology. His work has been influential not only in psychiatry but also in philosophy, anthropology, archaeology, literature, and religious studies. He was a prolific writer, though many of his works were not published until after his death.
https://en.wikipedia.org/wiki/Carl_Jung

[85] Kurt Donald Cobain (February 20, 1967 - c. April 5, 1994) was an American musician who was best known as the lead singer, guitarist, and primary songwriter of the rock band Nirvana.
https://en.wikipedia.org/wiki/Kurt_Cobain

[86] Pierre Teilhard de Chardin SJ (1 May 1881 - 10 April 1955) was a French idealist philosopher and Jesuit priest who trained as a paleontologist and geologist and took part in the discovery of Peking Man. He conceived the idea of the Omega Point (a maximum level of complexity and consciousness towards which he believed the universe was evolving) and developed Vladimir Vernadsky's concept of noosphere.
https://en.wikipedia.org/wiki/Pierre_Teilhard_de_Chardin

[87] Vatican City, Mar 17, 2016 / 11:50 am (CNA/EWTN News).- In a recently published interview on issues of justification and faith, Benedict XVI has addressed issues of mercy and our need for forgiveness, salvation through the cross, the necessity of baptism, and the importance of sharing in Christ's redeeming love.

The discussion with Fr. Jacques Servais, SJ, took place ahead of an October, 2015 conference in Rome studying the doctrine of justification by faith.

Benedict's answers, originally in German, were read aloud as a text at the conference by the Prefect of the Pontifical Household, Archbishop Georg Gänswein.

They were later published as the introduction to a book in Italian on the conference texts and conclusions, titled "Through Faith: Doctrine of Justification and Experience of God in the Preaching of the Church and the Spiritual Exercises," by Fr. Daniel Libanori, SJ.

The discussion then turned to the missionary impulse, which was once informed by the conviction that all who died unbaptized would certainly go to hell.

Benedict noted, "there is no doubt that on this point we are faced with a profound evolution of dogma" and that since the 1950s "the understanding that God cannot let go to perdition all the unbaptized… has been fully affirmed."

He noted that the great missionaries of the 1500s were compelled by their belief in the absolute necessity of baptism for salvation, and that the changing understanding of this necessity led to "a deep double crisis": a loss of motivation for missionary work, and a loss of motivation for the faith itself.

"If it is true that the great missionaries of the 16th century were still convinced that those who are not baptized are forever lost - and this explains their missionary commitment - in the Catholic Church after the Second Vatican Council that conviction was finally abandoned. From this came a deep double crisis. On the one hand this seems to remove any motivation for a future missionary commitment. Why should one try to convince the people to accept the Christian faith when they can be saved even without it? But also for Christians an issue emerged: the obligatory nature of the faith and its way of life began to seem uncertain and problematic. If there are those who can save themselves in other ways, it is not clear, in the final analysis, why the Christian himself is bound by the requirements of the Christian faith and its morals. If faith and salvation are no longer interdependent, faith itself becomes unmotivated."

"… the well-known thesis of the anonymous Christians of Karl Rahner. He sustains that the basic, essential act at the basis of Christian existence, decisive for salvation, in the transcendental structure of our consciousness, consists in the opening to the entirely Other, toward unity with God. The Christian faith would in this view cause to rise to consciousness what is structural in man as such. So when a man accepts himself in his essential being, he fulfills the essence of being a Christian without knowing what it is in a conceptual way. The Christian, therefore, coincides with the human and, in this sense, every man who accepts himself is a Christian even if he does not know it. It is true that this theory is fascinating, but it reduces Christianity itself to a pure conscious presentation of what a human being is in himself and therefore overlooks the drama of change and renewal that is central to Christianity. " www.catholicnewsagency.com/news/full-text-of-benedict-xvis-recent-rare-and-lengthy-interview-26142/

[88] Dag Hjalmar Agne Carl Hammarskjöld (29 July 1905 - 18 September 1961) was a Swedish diplomat, economist, and author. The second Secretary-General of the United Nations, he served from April 1953 until his death in a plane crash in September 1961. At the age of 47 years, 255 days, Hammarskjöld is the youngest to have held the post. He is one of only four people to be awarded a posthumous Nobel Prize.
https://en.wikipedia.org/wiki/Dag_Hammarskj%C3%B6ld

[89] Marianne Deborah Williamson (born July 8, 1952) is an American spiritual teacher, author and lecturer. She has published eleven books, including four New York Times number one bestsellers.
https://en.wikipedia.org/wiki/Marianne_Williamson

[90] William Ashley "Billy" Sunday (November 19, 1862 - November 6, 1935) was an American athlete who, after being a popular outfielder in baseball's National League during the 1880s, became the most celebrated and influential American evangelist during the first two decades of the 20th century.
https://en.wikipedia.org/wiki/Billy_Sunday

[91] https://en.wikipedia.org/wiki/Psychopathy
www.huffingtonpost.com/david-freeman/are-politicians-psychopaths_b_1818648.html

[92] John Ruskin (8 February 1819 - 20 January 1900) was the leading English art critic of the Victorian era, also an art patron, draughtsman, watercolourist, a prominent social thinker and philanthropist. He wrote on subjects as varied as geology, architecture, myth, ornithology,

literature, education, botany and political economy.
https://en.wikipedia.org/wiki/John_Ruskin

[93] https://en.wikipedia.org/wiki/Uncertainty_principle
https://en.wikipedia.org/wiki/Observer_effect_%28physics%29
https://en.wikipedia.org/wiki/EPR_paradox
https://en.wikipedia.org/wiki/Quantum_entanglement

One of the biggest problems with quantum experiments is the seemingly unavoidable tendency of humans to influence the situation and velocity of small particles. This happens just by our observing the particles, and it has quantum physicists frustrated.
http://science.howstuffworks.com/innovation/science-questions/quantum-suicide2.htm

The so-called EPR paradox, named for Albert Einstein, Boris Podolsky and Nathan Rosen, supplies an even stranger example of quantum weirdness, in which two subatomic particles thousands of light-years apart can instantaneously respond to each other's motions. Scientists have observed this phenomenon, called entanglement, at the particle level, and in 2009, managed to produce the effect with linked superconductors.
http://science.howstuffworks.com/science-vs-myth/everyday-myths/quantum-weirdness.htm
www.wired.com/2009/09/quantum-entanglement/

Quantum Entanglement is a mysterious aspect of quantum mechanics: This phenomenon is so weird that even Einstein - who gave us black holes and warped space-time - couldn't believe it, disparagingly calling it "spooky action at a distance", because quantum entanglement allows distant particles to remain instantaneously connected.
www.abc.net.au/news/2016-02-08/mcfadden-it-seems-life-really-does-have-a-vital-spark/7148448

[94] Abraham Harold Maslow (1 April 1908 - 8 June 1970) was an American psychologist who was best known for creating Maslow's hierarchy of needs, a theory of psychological health predicated on fulfilling innate human needs in priority, culminating in self-actualization. Maslow was a psychology professor at Alliant

International University, Brandeis University, Brooklyn College, New School for Social Research, and Columbia University. He stressed the importance of focusing on the positive qualities in people, as opposed to treating them as a "bag of symptoms."
https://en.wikipedia.org/wiki/Abraham_Maslow

[95] The World Is Not Falling Apart. Never mind the headlines. We've never lived in such peaceful times.

The kinds of violence to which most people are vulnerable—homicide, rape, battering, child abuse—have been in steady decline in most of the world. Autocracy is giving way to democracy. Wars between states—by far the most destructive of all conflicts—are all but obsolete.

How can we get a less hyperbolic assessment of the state of the world? Certainly not from daily journalism. News is about things that happen, not things that don't happen. We never see a reporter saying to the camera, "Here we are, live from a country where a war has not broken out"—or a city that has not been bombed, or a school that has not been shot up. As long as violence has not vanished from the world, there will always be enough incidents to fill the evening news. And since the human mind estimates probability by the ease with which it can recall examples, newsreaders will always perceive that they live in dangerous times. All the more so when billions of smartphones turn a fifth of the world's population into crime reporters and war correspondents.
www.slate.com/articles/news_and_politics/foreigners/2014/12/the_world_is_not_falling_apart_the_trend_lines_reveal_an_increasingly_peaceful.html

War and Peace after 1945; the very long-term perspective and wars since 1945.
https://ourworldindata.org/war-and-peace-after-1945/

"The most peaceful time in our species' existence"

The Visual History of the Rise of Political Freedom and the Decrease in Violence
https://ourworldindata.org/VisualHistoryOf/Violence.html#/title-

slide
https://ourworldindata.org/homicides/
https://ourworldindata.org/child-labor/

It's a cold, hard fact: our world is becoming a better place

Max Roser, a James Martin Fellow researching income inequality and inclusive growth at the Institute for New Economic Thinking, Oxford Martin School, explains the ethos behind online resource OurWorldInData.org
www.oxfordmartin.ox.ac.uk/opinion/view/274
http://stevenpinker.com/files/pinker/files/has_the_decline_of_violence_reversed_since_the_better_angels_of_our_nature_was_written.pdf
www.worldhunger.org/2015-world-hunger-and-poverty-facts-and-statistics/

2015 marks the end of the monitoring period for the two internationally agreed targets for hunger reduction. The target for the Millennium Development Goals for developing countries as a whole was to halve the proportion of hungry people by 2015 from the base year(s) of 1990-2, or from 23.2% to 11.6%. As the proportion in 2014-16 is 12.9%, the goal has almost been met.
www.worldhunger.org/2015-world-hunger-and-poverty-facts-and-statistics/#hunger-number

According to the most recent estimates, in 2012, 12.7 percent of the world's population lived at or below $1.90 a day. That's down from 37 percent in 1990 and 44 percent in 1981. There has been marked progress on reducing poverty over the past decades. The world attained the first Millennium Development Goal target—to cut the 1990 poverty rate in half by 2015—five years ahead of schedule, in 2010. In October 2015, the World Bank projected for the first-time, that the number of people living in extreme poverty was expected to have fallen below ten percent.
www.worldbank.org/en/topic/poverty/overview

Female Victims of Sexual Violence, 1994-2010
www.bjs.gov/content/pub/pdf/fvsv9410.pdf

[96] Historians and sociologists have remarked on the occurrence, in science, of "multiple independent discovery". Robert K. Merton defined such "multiples" as instances in which similar discoveries are made by scientists working independently of each other. Merton believed that it is multiple discoveries, rather than unique ones, that represent the common pattern in science.

Commonly cited examples of multiple independent discovery are the 17th-century independent formulation of calculus by Isaac Newton, Gottfried Wilhelm Leibniz and others, described by A. Rupert Hall; the 18th-century discovery of oxygen by Carl Wilhelm Scheele, Joseph Priestley, Antoine Lavoisier and others; and the theory of evolution of species, independently advanced in the 19th century by Charles Darwin and Alfred Russel Wallace.

Electromagnetic induction was discovered by Michael Faraday in England in 1831, and independently about the same time by Joseph Henry in the U.S

Electrical telegraph - Charles Wheatstone (England), 1837, Samuel F.B. Morse (United States), 1837.

Helium - Pierre Jansen, Norman Lockyer (both in 1868).

In 1876, Elisha Gray and Alexander Graham Bell filed a patent on discovery of the telephone on the same day.

The Hall-Héroult process for inexpensively producing aluminum was independently discovered in 1886 by the American engineer-inventor Charles Martin Hall and the French scientist Paul Héroult.

Discovery of radioactivity (1896) independently by Henri Becquerel and Silvanus Thompson.

In computer science, the concept of the "universal computing machine" (now generally called the "Turing Machine") was proposed by Alan Turing, but also independently by Emil Post, both in 1936. Similar approaches, also aiming to cover the concept of universal computing, were introduced by S.C. Kleene and by Alonzo Church that same year. Also in 1936, Konrad Zuse tried to build a binary electrically-driven mechanical calculator with limited programability; however, Zuse's machine was never fully functional.

The atom bomb was independently thought of by Leó Szilárd, József Rotblat and others.
https://en.wikipedia.org/wiki/List_of_multiple_discoveries
https://en.wikipedia.org/wiki/Multiple_discovery

[97] Max Karl Ernst Ludwig Planck, FRS (23 April 1858 - 4 October 1947) was a German theoretical physicist whose work on quantum theory won him the Nobel Prize in Physics in 1918.
https://en.wikipedia.org/wiki/Max_Planck

[98] A radical breakthrough in tackling climate change has been made after scientists found a rapid way to turn heat-trapping carbon-dioxide into rock.

The exclusive two year project, called CarbFix, pumped a carbon dioxide and water mix 540m underground into basalt rock at the Hellisheidi geothermal power plant in Iceland. The acidic mixture dissolved the rocks' calcium magnesium and formed limestone, permanently and naturally trapping the gas, according to Juerg Matter of the University of Southampton and the lead author of a study detailing the experiment.
www.independent.co.uk/news/world/europe/climate-change-breakthrough-as-iceland-turns-carbon-dioxide-into-snow-a7073691.html

A newly discovered plastic-eating bacterium may hold the key to safely degrading millions of tonnes of polyethylene terephthalate (PET) plastics dumped each year.

PET plastic is a global pollution problem. A team of Japanese researchers, led by Dr Shosuke Yoshida from the Kyoto Institute of Technology, have discovered a new species of bacteria that produces a never-before-seen plastic-eating enzyme.

The environmentally benign breakdown products, ethylene glycol and terephthalic acid, are then used by the bacteria as an energy source.

www.abc.net.au/news/2016-03-11/plastic-eating-bacterium-can-break-down-pet/7238614

It turns out glucose, the naturally-occurring sugar compound that provides energy to living things (including us humans), can be harnessed to power electronic devices, according to new research out of Joseph Fourier University in France. The breakthrough could have far-reaching implications for makers of medical devices ranging from pacemakers to artificial organs.

According to MIT's Technology Review, this is the first time scientists have proved that electrical energy can be derived from organic body fluids.
http://venturebeat.com/2010/05/18/glucose-biofuel-cell-could-revolutionize-medical-technology/
www.technologyreview.com/s/418970/power-from-glucose/

The biofuel of the future could well be gasoline. That's the hope of one biotech startup that described for the first time how it is coaxing bacteria into producing hydrocarbons that could be processed into fuels like those made from petroleum. LS9 has genetically engineered various bacteria, including E. coli, to custom-produce hydrocarbon chains.
www.technologyreview.com/s/408334/making-gasoline-from-bacteria/

A professor in Texas A&M University's chemical engineering department envisions the bacteria as a future source of energy, helping to power our cars, homes and more.

By genetically modifying the bacteria, Thomas Wood, a professor in the Artie McFerrin Department of Chemical Engineering, has "tweaked" a strain of E. coli so that it produces substantial amounts of hydrogen.
www.sciencedaily.com/releases/2008/01/080129170709.htm

Nylon-eating bacteria are a strain of Flavobacterium that is capable of digesting certain byproducts of nylon 6 manufacture. This strain of Flavobacterium sp. KI72, became popularly known as nylon-eating bacteria, and the enzymes used to digest the man-made molecules

became collectively known as nylonase.
https://en.wikipedia.org/wiki/Nylon-eating_bacteria

From plastic to asbestos, cardboard to jet fuel, fungi will eat just about anything. Now researchers have found another dish in the fungal diet: radiation. Not radioactive compounds, which have long been known to be on the menu — radiation itself. Ekaterina Dadachova and her colleagues at the Albert Einstein College of Medicine in New York have discovered that some fungi can use a molecule called melanin, a pigment also found in human skin, to harvest the energy from radiation and use it for growth. Some fungi can decompose radioactive material such as the hot graphite in the remains of the Chernobyl reactor.
www.nature.com/news/2007/070521/full/news070521-5.html

"The fungal kingdom comprises more species than any other plant or animal kingdom, so finding that they're making food in addition to breaking it down
www.einstein.yu.edu/news/archive/356/einstein-researchers-discovery-of-radiation-eating-fungi-could-trigger-recalculation-of-earths-energy-balance-and-help-feed-astronauts/
www.plosone.org/doi/pone.0000457

The Gulf of Mexico Microbe That Eats Oil Slicks

A newly discovered species of microbe is breaking down oil from the BP spill in the Gulf of Mexico much faster than scientists thought possible.
www.telegraph.co.uk/finance/newsbysector/energy/oilandgas/7964175/Microbe-eating-spilled-oil-in-Gulf-of-Mexico.html

The Heavy Metal Superworms That Feast on Poisonous Metals

The Berkeley Pit Bacteria, a protozoan called Euglena mutabilis that can not only survive the toxic metals and acid, but is thriving. It works by way of photosynthesis, the same process plants use to make oxygen. Only, Euglena mutabilis uses it to oxidize the metals in the water by increasing the general oxygen level of the pit. This, in turn, causes the metals to harmlessly precipitate away. And what does it crap? A potential cure for cancer.

A Bacteria That Eats Poison and Makes Electricity
www.cracked.com/article_19133_6-ways-nature-cleans-up-our-messes-better-than-we-do.html
http://news.softpedia.com/news/Metal-Eating-Worms-Could-Help-Reduce-Pollution-95135.shtml
http://news.nationalgeographic.com/news/2008/10/081007-super-worms.html
www.wired.com/2007/08/ff-lagoon/?currentPage=all
www.ncbi.nlm.nih.gov/pubmed/17031638

[99] Annie Besant (1 October 1847 - 20 September 1933) was a prominent British theosophist, women's rights activist, writer and orator and supporter of Irish and Indian self-rule.
https://en.wikipedia.org/wiki/Annie_Besant

[100] https://en.wikipedia.org/wiki/Universe

An extremely young galaxy cluster has been found to weigh as much as 500 trillion suns, NASA has announced. The cluster, called IDCS J1426.5+3508 (IDCS 1426), is located 10 billion light years from Earth.
www.abc.net.au/news/2016-01-08/nasa-finds-galaxy-cluster-weighs-500-trillion-suns/7076622
www.geek.com/geek-cetera/trillions-of-earths-300-sextillion-stars-say-scientists-1356479/

At the atomic scale, the numbers get even more inconceivable. At this level, it is estimated that the there are between 10(78) to 10(82) atoms in the known, observable universe. In layman's terms, that works out to between ten quadrillion vigintillion and one-hundred thousand quadrillion vigintillion atoms.
www.universetoday.com/36302/atoms-in-the-universe/

Nobel Prize-winner Frank Wilczek talks to SPIEGEL about the universe's extraordinary symmetry, the overlap between beauty and physics and why we may be on the verge of a bigger discovery than the Higgs particle.

SPIEGEL: What is "beautiful" about physics?

Wilczek: Don't you find it compelling, for example, that the equations that have been developed to describe musical instruments are very nearly the same as the equations that govern how atoms work? In a violin or a piano, sounds are produced by the vibrations of sounding boards or strings. In atoms, the things that vibrate are more abstract: They are associated with the colors of light that a particular kind of atom likes to emit or absorb. And this, by the way, is very much the same idea that Pythagoras was groping towards when he associated the movement of the planets with music of the spheres. Electrons do in fact go around the atomic nucleus much the same as planets go around the sun. We can think of atoms as musical instruments that produce a very real and very perfect music of the spheres.
www.spiegel.de/international/physicist-frank-wilczek-interview-about-beauty-in-physics-a-1048669.html

[101] An adult is made up of around 7,000,000,000,000,000,000,000,000,000 (7 octillion) atoms.

The atoms that make up your body are mostly empty space, so despite there being so many of them, without that space you would compress into a tiny volume. The nucleus that makes up the vast bulk of the matter in an atom is so much smaller than the whole structure that it is comparable to the size of a fly in a cathedral. If you lost all your empty atomic space, your body would fit into a cube less than 1/500th of a centimetre on each side.

On sheer count of cells, there is more bacterial life inside you than human. There are around 10 trillion of your own cells, but 10 times more bacteria. Many of the bacteria that call you home are friendly in the sense that they don't do any harm. Some are beneficial.
www.theguardian.com/science/2013/jan/27/20-human-body-facts-science
http://bebrainfit.com/benefits-probiotics-brain/
http://bebrainfit.com/human-brain-facts/

A microbiota is "the ecological community of commensal, symbiotic and pathogenic microorganisms that literally share our body space".

The human microbiome consists of about 100 trillion microbial cells, outnumbering human cells 10 to 1. It accounts for about for 1-3% total body mass and can significantly affect human physiology.
https://en.wikipedia.org/wiki/Microbiota

The human microbiota is the aggregate of microorganisms, a microbiome that resides on the surface and in deep layers of skin (including in mammary glands), in the saliva and oral mucosa, in the conjunctiva, and in the gastrointestinal tracts. They include bacteria, fungi, and archaea.
https://en.wikipedia.org/wiki/Human_microbiota

Neurotransmitters, also known as chemical messengers, are endogenous chemicals that enable neurotransmission. They transmit signals across a chemical synapse, such as a neuromuscular junction, from one neuron (nerve cell) to another "target" neuron, muscle cell, or gland cell.
https://en.wikipedia.org/wiki/Neurotransmitter

The human brain is far more advanced and efficient, and possesses more raw computational power than the most impressive supercomputers that have ever been built.

At the time of this writing, the fastest supercomputer in the world is the Tianhe-2 in Guangzhou, China, and has a maximum processing speed of 54.902 petaFLOPS. A petaFLOP is a quadrillion (one thousand trillion) floating point calculations per second. That's a huge amount of calculations, and yet, that doesn't even come close to the processing speed of the human brain.

In contrast, our miraculous brains operate on the next order higher. Although it is impossible to precisely calculate, it is postulated that the human brain operates at 1 exaFLOP, which is equivalent to a billion billion calculations per second.
www.scienceabc.com/humans/the-human-brain-vs-supercomputers-which-one-wins.html
http://gizmodo.com/an-83-000-processor-supercomputer-only-matched-one-perc-1045026757

[102] How Many Species Are There on Earth and in the Ocean?
http://journals.plos.org/plosbiology/article?id=10.1371/journal.pbio.1001127

Species count put at 8.7 million
www.bbc.co.uk/news/science-environment-14616161

Number of species on Earth tagged at 8.7 million. Most precise estimate yet suggests more than 80% of species still undiscovered.
www.nature.com/news/2011/110823/full/news.2011.498.html

[103] http://en.wikipedia.org/wiki/Unintended_consequences

[104] "The media is too concentrated, too few people own too much. There's really five companies that control 90 percent of what we read, see and hear. It's not healthy."

Ted Turner (founder of CNN)
www.businessinsider.com.au/these-6-corporations-control-90-of-the-media-in-america-2012-6
https://en.wikipedia.org/wiki/Concentration_of_media_ownership
www.safehaven.com/article/31677/10-corporations-control-nearly-everything-you-buy-6-media-corporations-control-nearly-everything-you-read-or-watch
www.freepress.net/ownership/chart

Just 6 percent of people say they have a lot of confidence in the media, putting the news industry about equal to Congress and well below the public's view of other institutions.
http://bigstory.ap.org/article/35c595900e0a4ffd99fbdc48a336a6d8/poll-vast-majority-americans-dont-trust-news-media

[105] State of the American Workplace
www.gallup.com/topic/employee_engagement.aspx
www.gallup.com/poll/181289/majority-employees-not-engaged-despite-gains-2014.aspx
http://blogs.wsj.com/atwork/2013/06/11/the-state-of-the-american-workplace-is-meh/
www.cbsnews.com/news/study-most-americans-unhappy-at-work/

[106] My first job at age six was all about squeezing warranty cards into plastic envelopes to earn some pocket money. Later I cleaned in a big supermarket, e.g. all toilets (both male and female) every two hours, occasionally interrupted when a customer vomited on the floor or dropped something else like a jar of jam or a bottle of OJ. Another job was working in a machinery sweatshop, sitting at the same machine, doing exactly the same procedure for 9 hours a day.

I also had jobs as a gardener and landscaper. Or as a forest worker. I worked on various construction jobs at small and large building sites. Or in a sawmill plus at a window manufacturing and installing company. This was a particularly tough one: Shoveling cement powder in a cement factory in dimly lit underground tunnels and shafts, next to very hot furnaces, wearing plastic boots, a protective suit, face mask and helmet during 9,5 hour shifts. Sugar jobs were: Doing telephone interviews and door-to-door surveys for chocolate companies, cigarette manufacturers and government agencies. A job with perks was selling ice creams and soda in a cinema, before cleaning up after the movies ended (my girlfriends were granted free entry). Bicycling around town as a corporate mail delivery & pack-room boy was rather nice too as I got to be out in fresh air.

After graduation with tertiary degrees in macro and microeconomics (among others), I became an Assistant Sales Manager for a Swiss luxury watch manufacturer. Later I held various positions as a Sales Manager, Sales Director, Vice President Marketing & Sales, COO, and CEO/executive Chairman of the Board of subsidiaries in Hong Kong and Japan. In 1995, at age 32, I decided to retire from my well-paid corporate career to focus on doing what I really love doing: Helping people by writing practical philosophy books (etc.) and advising both personal and corporate clients from around the world.

[107] "Sleep has a fundamental function but we do not know what that function is," he says. "We do not know why people sleep. We know what happens when they don't sleep in terms of things like cognitive deterioration but we don't understand the fundamental function of sleep."

Harvard Medical School professor David White, one of the world's foremost experts on disorders like obstructive sleep apnoea, says the science backs up what many instinctively know is true: our brain functions very differently in a sleep-deprived state.
www.theguardian.com/philips-healthier-brighter-future/2015/nov/23/the-sleep-factor-setting-the-clock-for-performance

Sleep deprivation reduces perceived emotional intelligence and constructive thinking skills.
www.ncbi.nlm.nih.gov/pubmed/17765011
www.researchgate.net/publication/6075439_Sleep_deprivation_reduces_perceived_emotional_intelligence_and_constructive_thinking_skills
http://greatergood.berkeley.edu/article/item/does_sleeping_well_make_us_more_socially_adept

The Effects of 53 Hours of Sleep Deprivation on Moral Judgment
www.journalsleep.org/Articles/300314.pdf

Here's A Horrifying Picture Of What Sleep Loss Will Do To You
www.huffingtonpost.com/2014/01/08/sleep-deprivation_n_4557142.html
www.cdc.gov/mmwr/volumes/65/wr/mm6506a1.htm?s_cid=mm6506a1_e
www.telegraph.co.uk/news/health/11765723/Sleep-deprivation-as-bad-as-smoking.html
https://en.wikipedia.org/wiki/Sleep_deprivation

Lack of sleep makes us more likely to own up to things we HAVEN'T done: Tiredness impairs our judgement and causes us to make false confessions; the study was carried out by Elizabeth Loftus and her team at the University of California, Irvine.
www.dailymail.co.uk/sciencetech/article-3437464/Lack-sleep-makes-likely-things-HAVEN-T-Tiredness-impairs-judgement-causes-make-false-confessions.html

[108] Some research shows that higher pay does not lead workers to do more. Rather, they may work less. A famous study by Colin Camerer and colleagues, which looked at taxi drivers, reached a controversial

conclusion. The authors suggested that taxi drivers had a daily income "target", and that:

When wages are high, drivers will reach their target more quickly and quit early; on low-wage days they will drive longer hours to reach the target.

Alternatively, the graph above might suggest that people who work fewer hours are more productive. This idea is not new. Adam Smith reckoned that the man who works so moderately as to be able to work constantly, not only preserves his health the longest, but in the course of the year, executes the greatest quantity of works.
http://people.hss.caltech.edu/~camerer/web_material/cabscvfbook.pdf

A paper released yesterday by the New Zealand Productivity Commission showed that even if you work more hours, you do not necessarily work better.
http://img.scoop.co.nz/media/pdfs/1309/Cut_to_the_Chase__Research_Paper_Productivity_by_the_numbers_September_2013_final.pdf
www.computerworld.com/article/2485967/emerging-technology/gartner-s-dark-vision-for-tech—jobs.html

In Praise of Idleness by Bertrand Russell
www.zpub.com/notes/idle.html

John Maynard Keynes, 1st Baron Keynes, (5 June 1883 - 21 April 1946), was an English economist whose ideas fundamentally changed the theory and practice of modern macroeconomics and the economic policies of governments. He built on and greatly refined earlier work on the causes of business cycles, and is widely considered to be one of the most influential economists of the 20th century and the founder of modern macroeconomics. His ideas are the basis for the school of thought known as Keynesian economics and its various offshoots.
https://en.wikipedia.org/wiki/John_Maynard_Keynes
www.econ.yale.edu/smith/econ116a/keynes1.pdf

Originally, Parkinson's law is the adage that "work expands so as to fill the time available for its completion", and the title of a book which made it well-known. However, in current understanding, Parkinson's

law is a reference to the self-satisfying uncontrolled growth of the bureaucratic apparatus in an organization.
https://en.wikipedia.org/wiki/Parkinson's_law

[109] Irving Berlin (born Israel Isidore Baline; May 11, 1888 - September 22, 1989) was an American composer and lyricist, widely considered one of the greatest songwriters in American history.
http://en.wikipedia.org/wiki/Irving_Berlin

[110] www.theguardian.com/technology/2015/aug/09/who-killed-the-video-gamers-simon-parkin-taiwan
www.newscientist.com/article/mg22730350-700-death-by-video-game-a-power-like-no-other/
www.ranker.com/list/8-people-who-died-playing-video-games/autumn-spragg

[111] Addicted to being busy…

In his 2012 book by the same name, German neuroscientist Manfred Spitzer coined the term "digital dementia" to describe the deterioration of cognitive ability that comes from overuse of digital technology.
www.smh.com.au/national/health/generation-overstimulation-generation-ys-addiction-to-being-busy-20150628-ghxsde

In his 2014 book, The Organised Mind: Thinking Straight in the Age of Information Overload, American neuroscientist Daniel Levitin describes the cognitive cost of this "21st-century mania for cramming everything we do into every single spare moment of downtime".

"Make no mistake: email-, Facebook- and Twitter-checking constitute a neural addiction," Levitin writes.
www.theguardian.com/science/2015/jan/18/modern-world-bad-for-brain-daniel-j-levitin-organized-mind-information-overload

The Truth About Adrenal Fatigue (It's Not What You Think)
https://youtu.be/ac0npV7dA70

Adrenaline is a substance that is released in the body of a person who is feeling a strong feeling, such as excitement, fear or anger. The adrenaline rush usually occurs when the body senses danger, the "Fight or Flight" moment. Some people, known as sensation-seekers,

are adrenaline junkies.
www.psychologytoday.com/blog/science-choice/201508/can-you-be-addicted-adrenaline
http://stress.about.com/od/situationalstress/a/adrenaline0528.htm
http://mentalhealthdaily.com/2013/03/02/how-to-overcome-adrenaline-addiction-tips-from-a-former-addict/
www.drnorthrup.com/adrenal-exhaustion/
www.custommedicine.com.au/adrenal/
https://en.wikipedia.org/wiki/Fight-or-flight_response

Epinephrine is normally produced by both the adrenal glands and certain neurons. It plays an important role in the fight-or-flight response by increasing blood flow to muscles, output of the heart, pupil dilation, and blood sugar.
https://en.wikipedia.org/wiki/Epinephrine

[112] The love of God has been called the "essence of Judaism". "And you shall love the Lord your God with all your heart and with all your soul and with all your might." (Deut 6:5)
https://en.wikipedia.org/wiki/Love_of_God

[113] Rumi (1207 - 17 December 1273), was a 13th-century Persian poet, jurist, Islamic scholar, theologian, and Sufi mystic.
http://en.wikipedia.org/wiki/Rumi

[114] Rabia al-Basri (717-801 C.E.) was a female Muslim saint and Sufi mystic.
https://en.wikipedia.org/wiki/Rabia_Basri

[115] Bhakti yoga is a spiritual path or spiritual practice within Hinduism focused on the cultivation of love and devotion toward God. It has been defined as a practice of devotion toward God, solely motivated by the sincere, loving desire to please God, rather than the hope of divine reward or the fear of divine punishment.
https://en.wikipedia.org/wiki/Bhakti_yoga

[116] The 14th Dalai Lama (Born 6 July 1935) is the current Dalai Lama and received the Nobel Peace Prize in 1989.
https://en.wikipedia.org/wiki/14th_Dalai_Lama

[117] Thich Nhat Hanh (born as Nguyen Xuan Bao on October 11, 1926) is a Vietnamese Buddhist monk, teacher, author, poet and peace activist. He has published more than 100 books, including more than 40 in English.
https://en.wikipedia.org/wiki/Th%C3%ADch_Nh%E1%BA%A5t_H%E1%BA%A1nh

[118] The Golden Rule or law of reciprocity is a moral maxim or principle of altruism found in many human cultures and religions, suggesting it may be related to a fundamental human nature.
http://en.wikipedia.org/wiki/Golden_Rule

[119] Unlikely Animal Friends
http://channel.nationalgeographic.com/wild/unlikely-animal-friends/

Unbelievable Unlikely Animal Friendships Compilation
www.youtube.com/watch?v=mrudR-kIB1k

Unlikely Animal Friendships
www.huffingtonpost.com/news/unlikely-animal-friendships/
www.boredpanda.com/unusual-animal-friendships-interspecies/

Black panther and a rabbit

Cutest Animal Odd-Couples
www.youtube.com/watch?v=eeB2vVBOLOw

Lioness Adopts a Baby Antelope
www.youtube.com/watch?v=mZw-1BfHFKM
www.youtube.com/watch?v=Q7BJeTKrcvo

A lion called Christian - The whole Documentary (Full length)
www.youtube.com/watch?v=4enNZqNrwYc

[120] Leading Causes of Death
www.cdc.gov/nchs/fastats/leading-causes-of-death.htm

List of causes of death by rate
http://en.wikipedia.org/wiki/List_of_causes_of_death_by_rate
http://en.wikipedia.org/wiki/Lifestyle_disease

Compare 10 big "killers" in the U.S.
http://jpfo.org/alerts2013/alert20130101.htm

[121] Half of all US food produce is thrown away, new research suggests

The demand for 'perfect' fruit and veg means much is discarded, damaging the climate and leaving people hungry
www.theguardian.com/environment/2016/jul/13/us-food-waste-ugly-fruit-vegetables-perfect

A new study has found that a staggering 50 per cent of the world's food goes to waste.
www.guardian.co.uk/environment/2013/jan/10/half-world-food-waste
www.abc.net.au/news/2013-01-11/half-of-worlds-food-going-to-waste/4460322?WT.svl=news5

Roughly one third of the food produced in the world for human consumption every year — approximately 1.3 billion tonnes — gets lost or wasted…
www.fao.org/news/story/en/item/74192/icode/
www.lovefoodhatewaste.com/
www.wastedfood.com/

Approx 1/3 from producers/ supply chain, 1/3 from retail and 1/3 from households

[122] Kurzweil does not believe in half measures. He takes 180 to 210 vitamin and mineral supplements a day, so many that he doesn't have time to organize them all himself. So he's hired a pill wrangler, who takes them out of their bottles and sorts them into daily doses, which he carries everywhere in plastic bags. Kurzweil also spends one day a week at a medical clinic, receiving intravenous longevity treatments. The reason for his focus on optimal health should be obvious: If the singularity is going to render humans immortal by the middle of this century, it would be a shame to die in the interim.
www.wired.com/2008/03/ff-kurzweil/
www.quora.com/Of-the-250-supplements-that-Ray-Kurzweil-takes-daily-which-are-the-most-important-and-have-the-most-significant-evidence-to-support-their-usage

[123] On 26 September 1983, the nuclear early warning system of the Soviet Union twice reported the launch of American Minuteman

intercontinental ballistic missiles from bases in the United States. These missile attack warnings were correctly identified as a false alarm by Stanislav Yevgrafovich Petrov, an officer of the Soviet Air Defence Forces. This decision is seen as having prevented a retaliatory nuclear attack based on erroneous data on the United States and its NATO allies, which would have likely resulted in nuclear war and the deaths of hundreds of millions of people. Investigation of the satellite warning system later confirmed that the system had malfunctioned. https://en.wikipedia.org/wiki/1983_Soviet_nuclear_false_alarm_incident

Accidental Nuclear War: a Timeline of Close Calls
http://futureoflife.org/background/nuclear-close-calls-a-timeline/

Secrets of the Dead: The Man Who Saved the World.
www.youtube.com/watch?v=4VPY2SgyG5w
www.pbs.org/wnet/secrets/episodes/the-man-who-saved-the-world-watch-the-full-episode/905/

[124] 16 Billionaires Who Were Once Dirt Poor
www.businessinsider.com.au/billionaires-who-were-once-poor-2014-12?op=1?r=US&IR=T#kenny-troutt-the-founder-of-excel-communications-paid-his-way-through-college-by-selling-life-insurance-1

The Once-Homeless Billionaire: My Keys to Success

John Paul Dejoria, co-founder of John Paul Mitchell Systems and Patron Tequila, is living the American Dream on steroids. He tells Bloomberg the business ethos that fueled his meteoric rise to the top.
www.youtube.com/watch?v=biG6NFbM0Yk

[125] Albert Schweitzer (14 January 1875 - 4 September 1965) was a French-German theologian, organist, philosopher, and physician.
https://en.wikipedia.org/wiki/Albert_Schweitzer

[126] "To drop out of that league, that was hard to do," Turner said. "I've had the experience of being on top and riding the roller coaster down again, nearly to the bottom. You know, if you economize and don't buy new airplanes or long-range jets, or that sort of thing, you can get

by on a billion or two." Ted Turner
http://piersmorgan.blogs.cnn.com/2012/05/03/ted-turner-i-lost-jane-i-lost-my-job-here-i-lost-my-fortune-most-of-it/

I lost my fortune, most of it. I have a billion or two left, you can get by on that if you economize," jokes Turner. "But I was worth seven or eight billion at one point. But I - you carry on. And I found other things to do."
http://money.cnn.com/magazines/fortune/fortune_archive/2003/05/26/343113/index.htm

He gets that feeling when he's thinking, which he often is, about his fortune. Or what's left of it. As AOL Time Warner stock tumbled 81% from its high in 2000 to $13, Turner's holdings declined from $10.7 billion to $1.4 billion, in shares he owns directly or controls. That's a drop of over $9 billion.

[127] Sophocles (497/6 - winter 406/5 BC) is one of three ancient Greek tragedians whose plays have survived.
https://en.wikipedia.org/wiki/Sophocles

[128] Be Happy Now! by Arne Klingenberg (2000)
www.soulfulliving.com/behappynow.htm

Guest Article Be Happy Now! (August 5, 2013)
http://soulfulliving.com/dailysoulretreat/guest-article-be-happy-now/

Uniting with Love and Joy with a Departed One by Arne Klingenberg
http://soulfulliving.com/dailysoulretreat/uniting-in-love-and-joy-with-a-departed-one/

[129] Count Lev Nikolayevich Tolstoy (9 September [O.S. 28 August] 1828 - 20 November [O.S. 7 November] 1910), usually referred to in English as Leo Tolstoy, was a Russian writer who is regarded as one of the greatest authors of all time.

His literal interpretation of the ethical teachings of Jesus, centering on the Sermon on the Mount, caused him to become a fervent Christian anarchist and pacifist. Tolstoy's ideas on nonviolent resistance, expressed in such works as The Kingdom of God Is Within You, were to have a profound impact on such pivotal 20th-century figures as

Mohandas Gandhi, Martin Luther King, Jr., and James Bevel. https://en.wikipedia.org/wiki/Leo_Tolstoy

[130] Epicurus (341-270 BC) was an ancient Greek philosopher as well as the founder of the school of philosophy called Epicureanism. https://en.wikipedia.org/wiki/Epicurus

www.ingramcontent.com/pod-product-compliance
Lightning Source LLC
Chambersburg PA
CBHW071220080526
44587CB00013BA/1445